TRAVEL DIARIES
OF A NATURALIST

Peter Scott

TRAVEL DIARIES
OF A NATURALIST

I

AUSTRALIA   NEW ZEALAND
NEW GUINEA   AFRICA   THE GALAPAGOS ISLANDS
ANTARCTICA AND THE FALKLAND ISLANDS

Edited by Miranda Weston-Smith
Photographs by Philippa Scott

COLLINS
HARVILL
Grafton Street, London

*To all those who have worked
to protect the beauty and wonder of nature,
and to those who have made it possible for me
to travel and to enjoy that beauty and wonder
in so many different parts of the world.*

WILLIAM COLLINS SONS & CO LTD,
LONDON · GLASGOW · SYDNEY · AUCKLAND
TORONTO · JOHANNESBURG

First published 1983
© Peter Scott 1983
ISBN 0 00 219554 2
Filmset by Ace Filmsetting Ltd, Frome
Colour and black and white reproduction by
Alpha Reprographics Ltd, Harefield
Made and printed in Great Britain by
William Collins Sons and Co Ltd, Glasgow

Contents

Editor's Preface

It is the wish of Sir Peter that his published travel diaries should retain as much as possible of their original character: therefore irregularities in his abbreviations and style have been left unchanged. On the other hand I felt it was necessary to give a few words of explanation about many of the people mentioned in these diaries, and to include maps showing the places that Sir Peter and Lady Scott visited.
The reader may also like to know the following:

1 There are a few passages in this book which do not originate from Sir Peter's travel diaries; these are indented in the text.

2 Phrases or words enclosed in square brackets have been inserted by me.

3 Only the species names of animals, birds and fishes begin with capital letters, other more general names do not.
   For example: a Santa Cruz Marine Iguana, but an iguana; a Golden-breasted Glossy Starling is the name of a species of bird, a chestnut brown pigeon is not. Italics are used to distinguish scientific from vernacular names as well as for their normal purposes.

4 The illustrations have been reproduced from Sir Peter's diaries most of which are 15.5×22 cm. It has been necessary to reduce some of the pictures and magnify others.

M W-S

Foreword by HRH The Prince of Wales, KG, KT

On the whole I find diaries make 'a good read', and few people can generate more interest in the record of their doings than Sir Peter Scott. Through the pages of his journals we can feel his excitement at new sights, sounds and places, and meet many of the people with whom he has come into contact during his wide and distant travels.

Whether we are knowledgeable naturalists or not, we can enjoy his excellent drawings and sketches of the plants and animals he has encountered – the record of an artist who understands science; of a scientist with an exceptional ability to record what he sees.

As a boy I remember a visit to his house, where his wife Philippa was successfully breeding chamaeleons from Africa. A fly was put on my finger and a Jackson's Chamaeleon took it, shooting its tongue out at lightning speed more than the length of its body. It is pleasant to read that this chamaeleon was taken back to Africa and released in the Nairobi National Park, the release being watched by Sir Julian Huxley, one of the author's mentors in his early youth.

I remember once, when staying with the Scotts at the Wildfowl Trust at Slimbridge, watching from my bedroom window the wild Bewick's Swans flighting in to the lake in front of the house. This is Sir Peter's base, where he returns at the end of each of his journeys of adventure and discovery. It is a home built not only for himself and his family, but also for the birds for whose care and protection the site was chosen and the house designed. It stands within a complex which he has laid out for the enjoyment of visitors, young and old, and I am glad to say, disabled as well as fit, who come to discover the fascination of these wildest of wild birds.

Peter Scott's care for wildlife is international. All over the world he has represented the animals round which his life has centered and advocated their protection and the conservation of their environment. He has managed to convey his enthusiasm through painting, writing, television and radio and his message has reached the younger generation in many countries.

His deep understanding of wildlife and ecology has often influenced and persuaded individuals and governments to take a more respectful and enlightened attitude to the management of this priceless natural heritage.

I welcome most warmly the chance to share, in these pages, some of the experiences of a very full life and at the same time to wish the book every success.

Charles.

Introduction

All my life I have been passionately interested in wild nature. I have delighted in animals and plants – especially birds, butterflies and moths, lizards, frogs, fish and whales. Having been trained as a zoologist and a general naturalist, I have eagerly drawn and painted animals ever since I can remember. It has also been my great good fortune to be able to travel extensively, especially during the 37 years since the second world war. My wife, Philippa, who is a professional photographer, shares my interests and we have almost always travelled together.

Although I have not been a life-long diarist, I have compiled a number of notebooks which record the animals and the people we meet on our various expeditions. Each is a log-book, a sketch-book, an address-book, an engagement book and a scrap-book all rolled into one. If I call them diaries, it is because they are laid out by days and dates, and because it is a shorter word than any of the others. But only rarely are they a daily record of human encounters, emotions and relations. They are not in any way the kind of diary referred to by Algernon Moncrieff in *The Importance of Being Ernest*, when he was proposing to Cecily: 'Do you really keep a diary. I'd give anything to look at it. May I?' 'Oh, no. You see it is simply a very young girl's record of her own thoughts and impressions, and consequently meant for publication. When it appears in volume form, I hope you will order a copy.'

Travel Diaries of a Naturalist consists of extracts and drawings from fifteen of the fifty notebooks covering our travels since 1956. The only records I had kept before that had been of specific activities such as wildfowling, dinghy racing, flying, and the diaries of two expeditions, one to Arctic Canada, and one to Iceland. The last two were the subject of two books: *Wild Geese and Eskimos*, which appeared in 1951, and *A Thousand Geese*, with James Fisher as co-author, which came out in 1953. To a certain extent, this present book continues my story from *The Eye of the Wind* – an autobiography that was published in 1961, and adds a more specific travel dimension to my *Observations of Wildlife*, a retrospective book of my paintings and drawings, published in 1980.

Chapter 1 (of the book you now have in your hands) contains material from Diary No 1, but the order thereafter is not strictly chronological. This allows, for example, six visits to the Galápagos Islands which were spread over a number of years, to follow one another. It also applies to some of the journeys in Africa when we re-visited the same countries and often the very same places after an interval of some months or years.

In the early diaries I tended to write of our adventures in all too great detail, and spent little time drawing, but later it seemed that the drawings were of more interest, so I found myself devoting more time to them, and consequently less to writing.

The greatest of all good fortune has been to have my wife with me on so many of the journeys, and I am especially happy that she is contributing some of her photographs in order to convey the magnificent scenery which has so often been a backdrop and sometimes the stage for our zoological adventures. Her help, encouragement and enthusiasm have been an essential element of all our journeys.

That it has been possible to travel so widely we owe principally to five organisations – first the British Broadcasting Corporation which filmed our tour to Australia, New Guinea and New Zealand, and another to the West Indies, Panama and the Galápagos Islands, all for television transmission under the title *Faraway Look* (part of my *Look* series). Second is Lindblad Travel, who invited me, accompanied by my wife, to join the MV *Lindblad Explorer* as a lecturer – an arrangement which has continued to this day. Third is Survival Anglia Ltd for whom I made film commentaries for many years and ended up as one of the company's directors. Fourth is the World Wildlife Fund of which I was one of the founders, and for whom I have undertaken a number of missions, including four to China. Finally, I shall always be grateful to the United States Navy for flying me to the South Pole with a BBC film team back in 1966. This was my first visit to Antarctica – the first of five so far, the others all being under the auspices of Lindblad Travel.

It is difficult to pick out individual people who have been responsible for all this, but to us one name stands out – Lars Eric Lindblad who originally invited us to go in the 'little red ship' (not so little, for she is 2,200 tons and carries up to 100 passengers). Since she was launched nearly 13 years ago we have been on 24 expeditions in her, sometimes two or even three in a row, and had so many unforgettable experiences that for all our lives we shall be grateful to the man who invented her and has thereby given so much pleasure to us and to so many others.

In compiling my diaries in the first place and in providing recent data to make my earlier findings more meaningful a large number of people have helped me, and I thank them all most cordially, but I hesitate to mention them by name for fear of offending any I may accidentally leave out.

I am enormously indebted to my editor – Miranda Weston-Smith – who has ploughed through the masses of insignificant detail in the notebooks to find passages that may be of interest to those who are not intricately involved in my enthusiasms and their more abstruse technicalities. I believe she has been very successful in the process of selection, and I wish to express my thanks to her for her patient and meticulous work in a very exacting task. She has grappled with the problems of trying to be consistent in presenting scientific and vernacular names. From time to time we have broken our own rules about italics and capital letters, and can only excuse ourselves with the old dictum that 'consistency is the hobgoblin of little minds'. We hope that our rationalisation will not drive our readers mad – it has almost done so to us.

Slimbridge
May, 1983

Nettapus pulchellus

CHAPTER 1

Australia: Northern Territory and Western Australia

DIARY 1   1956

In 1956 the Olympic Games were to be held in Melbourne and, as President of the International Yacht Racing Union, I was invited to be Chairman of the International Jury for the yachting events. We had decided to combine this mission with some travelling to make wildlife films for my *Look* programmes on BBC television, and especially for one which we were planning to call *Faraway Look*.

SUNDAY 4 NOVEMBER

We left the New Grounds [Slimbridge], Phil and I, at a quarter past eight in the morning. It was a horrid wrench leaving the children, but they were both very good. So was Phil. At the airport we met Charles Lagus, our chief camera-man, whose wife had come to see him off. I am to be No 2 camera-man using my own 16 mm film camera, and Phil is to take the stills.

And so we flew ordinarily in a Convair to Amsterdam. I spent 10 minutes in the cockpit during the climb and emergence from the clouds into the brilliant sunshine – always a thrilling moment. The Captain said it was one of the nicest features of his job in winter – that so much of his time was spent in the sunshine.

At Schipol Airport we changed into a Super Constellation, had dinner at Rome and a short night to Basrah. They woke us 2 hours before Basrah to give a huge breakfast after only 5 hours' sleep time. This 'hospital' treatment by the airlines is quite inexplicable and rather unimaginative.

The last news before we left home was that the British and French landings were about to take place at Suez and that there would be a news blackout.

MONDAY 5 NOVEMBER

Arrived Basrah – Saw pelicans flying in the marshes as we came in – also possibly flamingoes. In the airport garden there were Painted Ladies, a skipper which sat on my hand and tasted it, a large blue (sp) and a beautiful small Nymphalid with blue and black pattern and red spots – grey wingtips. Also a dragonfly and a bulbul in the tree above, like a large clumsy Great Tit. Basrah in the early morning was quite cold. Not so Karachi. We had four hours there and went to the KLM Rest House. Here we were given a room with a shower looking out onto a pretty garden. There were frangipanis in bloom with a strong almost too sweet scent, and the more delicate orange blossom smell of the papaya (paw-paw) flowers. In a small tree in the middle of the garden a crow – with off-white body, like a pale rather lanky Hoodie – had a nest and sat tamely beside it about 20 feet from us.

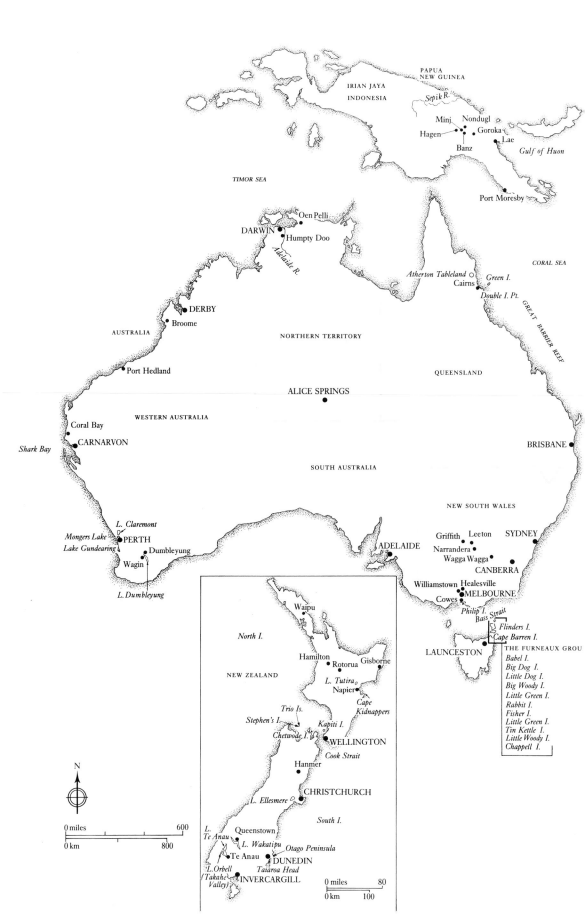

PAPUA
NEW GUINEA

IRIAN JAYA

INDONESIA

Sepik R.

Minj • Nondugl
Hagen • • Goroka
Banz • • Lae

Gulf of Huon

TIMOR SEA

Oen Pelli •

DARWIN •
• Humpty Doo

Adelaide R.

Port Moresby •

CORAL SEA

Atherton Tableland ○ *Green I.*
Cairns •
Double I. Pt.

• DERBY
Broome •

AUSTRALIA

NORTHERN TERRITORY

QUEENSLAND

Port Hedland •

ALICE SPRINGS •

GREAT BARRIER REEF

Coral Bay •
CARNARVON •

WESTERN AUSTRALIA

Shark Bay

SOUTH AUSTRALIA

BRISBANE •

NEW SOUTH WALES

L. Claremont
Mongers Lake • PERTH
Lake Gundearing • Dumbleyung
Wagin •

ADELAIDE •

Griffith • Leeton
Narrandera • • SYDNEY
Wagga Wagga •
CANBERRA •

L. Dumbleyung

Williamstown Healesville
Cowes • MELBOURNE
Philip I.
Bass Strait
Flinders I.
Cape Barren I.

Waipu •

North I.

Hamilton •
• Rotorua • Gisborne
L. Tutira ○
Napier •
Cape Kidnappers

NEW ZEALAND

Trio Is.
Stephen's I.
Chetwode I.
Kapiti I.
WELLINGTON •

Cook Strait

Hanmer •

CHRISTCHURCH •
L. Ellesmere ○

South I.

LAUNCESTON •

THE FURNEAUX GROU
Babel I.
Big Dog I.
Little Dog I.
Big Woody I.
Little Green I.
Rabbit I.
Fisher I.
Little Green I.
Tin Kettle I.
Little Woody I.
Chappell I.

N

0 miles 600
0 km 800

L. Te Anau
Queenstown •
• *L. Wakatipu* *Otago Peninsula*
Te Anau •
DUNEDIN •
'L. Orbell *Taiaroa Head*
(Takahe Valley)
INVERCARGILL •

0 miles 80
0 km 100

A family of mynahs was walking lankily and tamely about in the garden, blackish with a yellow patch behind the eye and a conspicuous white spot on the forewing. Overhead and circling in a thermal were kites (some darker than others) and two kinds of vultures – one white with black wingtips, and the other very dark.

There was a fine black swallowtail with red on the underside of the lower wing and a red abdomen. We saw several of them, flying in a bold smooth flight which could present little difficulty to a bird, so they must be distasteful although the warning colours are not very bright.

We took off at about 7.30, and hours later had dinner in the plane. We particularly asked to be allowed to sleep as long as possible and we were left in the plane at Rangoon. The 'slumberette' seats were excellently flat and with a sleeping pill I had a good night's rest and so did Phil.

TUESDAY 6 NOVEMBER

Both at Rangoon and later on arrival at Bangkok the ventilators blew in thick steam, so much cooler was the cabin of the Super Constellation. At Bangkok, although it was still early morning it felt like stepping out into a hot wet greenhouse – Bangkok has a magnificent airport building where we had breakfast to the accompaniment of parachute dropping which seemed to be part of some manoeuvres.

Swallows were flying through the halls and out on the terrace was a fork-tailed black bird – a drongo. There were also House Sparrows.

Later in the morning we arrived in Singapore where it was raining. As we approached we saw the waters of the various channels and bays dotted with elaborate fish traps.

WEDNESDAY 7 NOVEMBER

We slept late and Phil and I went on our own to the Van Kleef Aquarium. This is very good indeed. It is not terribly large, but its great strength is the salt water collection. The show of three species of anemone fish, all strikingly different, all exquisitely beautiful and all nestling and burrowing in their anemones must be as good an exhibit as can be seen in any aquarium anywhere. Perhaps the most remarkable thing to me was that so few of the fish were even remotely familiar. The marine versions of angel fish (no doubt quite unrelated) in many bright colours were especially exciting and there was a fascinating little shoal of catfish (marine) with a poisonous sting which swim tightly clustered together all touching each other, almost like one fish (*Plotosus anguillaris*). The combinations of colour achieved by selecting the fish and by showing them against various coloured backgrounds were admirably successful, archer fish, groupers, yellow sea horses, shrimp fish (razor fish) which swim vertically with their heads down. Yes, a memorable aquarium. Charles Lagus came out to lunch with Bill and Catherine Bailey. Bill runs the race course and Catherine worked with Phil at Bletchley during the war. Also at lunch was Michael Tweedie from the Raffles Museum [Singapore] – an excellent naturalist. Charles reported that his camera and equipment had not yet arrived. This begins to look serious.

Next morning we flew away to Darwin, joining a plane with lots of Olympic athletes and James McGruer [International Yacht Measurer at many Olympic Yachting Regattas]. We flew down the islands and over the Timor Sea with a sunset of *Cumulus castellatus*.

Plotosus anguillaris.

13

We arrived before dinner and had a tedious and fantastically in-efficient welcome for our first visit to Australia. This ended with all our luggage being opened and a customs man digging in Phil's underclothes and stirring up all her carefully packed clothes, which in this hot damp climate was fairly disastrous. But we were rescued by Harry Frith from the Commonwealth Scientific and Industrial Research Organisation (CSIRO) in Canberra who had come to meet us, with a tall young man – Stephen Davies, who had been at Cambridge, and twice to Slim-bridge.

The next day our adventures began.

FRIDAY 9 NOVEMBER

After various chores – changing travellers cheques etc. in Darwin – we drove out to Humpty Doo which is a rice station and will be our head-quarters.

It is a 40-mile drive south towards Alice Springs and then 20 miles to the flood plain of the Adelaide River. We drove through mile upon mile of sparse *Eucalyptus* forest, with occasional kites visible above the trees. At last, over a corrugated road, we came to the original homestead of Humpty Doo, the farm. Just beyond was the Government Rice Project and a mile or two beyond it again the private enterprise project Territory Rice Ltd. But we forked off after the homestead in order to go down by a track which would show us our first Magpie Geese. The *Eucalyptus* woods gradually gave way to *Pandanus* palms and then we were at the edge of a great open plain with black cultivated earth in the foreground and lush grass beyond. A couple of miles away was a low hill with scrub and trees on and around it, and various groups of trees were dotted about the plain. Just beyond the 'sea-wall' which encom-passed the rice fields was a line of black and white birds nearly half a mile away – our first *Anseranas* (Magpie Geese) – and in the tree where we stopped the Land Rover (long wheelbase, truck type) was a bunch of a dozen white cockatoos – Little Corellas. Hanging on stakes round a small rice paddy were dead birds – a Magpie Goose and half a dozen cockatoos – which the crows were busily eating. Geese and cockatoos and finches are all pests to the rice grower.

At the Territory Rice Headquarters we were given a cabin with wc and shower and its own gecko, and then we went to lunch at a central canteen. By this time of day it was very hot indeed. After lunch we went again to the rice fields. Here Harry and Stephen had put down bait for the geese, but the cockatoos were the only birds to have found it. We walked across the black crumbly earth behind the flood bank in order to get close to a group of 200 geese which were close outside it, and we took some film and some stills. Among the geese I could hear the fami-liar chatter of Radjah Shelducks – always here called Burdikin Ducks. There were 3 of them, two females and a male, and we managed to get pictures of the closest one. The geese were not very wild but would fly at about 100 yards. Further on the bank turned at right angles and here opposite a point which had been baited Harry had built a small hide of sacking (locally called a 'humpy'). Phil and I crept forward to this, but there were no geese on the bait, only a couple of white egrets under the bank on a small stretch of open water. Finally, we all came to this spot and stayed there for an hour or more.

Magpie Goose.

There was a spectacular profusion of water birds in sight. The geese were mostly a few hundred yards away. There was quite a large flock – known in Australia as a mob – which we later estimated at about 1,000 and counted as 1,002! Beyond the geese were half a dozen even larger black and white birds, the huge Jabiru – a very large stork.

We had been there for an hour or so, enjoying so many new birds, when suddenly the whole mob of geese rose and swirled in the air. Some of them came in over us. There were astonishing aerobatics. Whether an eagle was the cause we do not know, but it was a most exciting moment when they came over us in a tight mass. I made some slow motion pictures of them with the 6″ lens. (My camera was a small Kodak 16 mm taking 50 ft magazines). We drove round to another part of the plain.

As we went down a track among the gum trees I suddenly saw what I took to be some sort of a partridge running through the bush. This was a Frilled Lizard (or Frilly Lizard). It ran with a curious upright gait and bolted up a tree. It was very large – perhaps $2\frac{1}{2}$ feet long with a disproportionately large head. We stopped the truck and surrounded the tree. The beast was only about 5 feet up it and we planned to catch it. Creeping up behind the tree with a sack I dislodged it and it jumped down and ran towards Harry who caught it between his feet and enveloped it with the sack. Once we had got hold of it by the back of its rather thin scrawny neck it could do no more harm except to scratch my wrists with its powerful hind claws and its rather spiny tail. We put it in the sack planning to film it later.

Humpty Doo –
flood plains of the
Adelaide River
with Magpie Geese.

Frilly Lizard,
Chlamydosaurus kingi.

Magpie Goose.

Harry took us to another part of the river plain, which was unspoiled by the new rice growing projects – so far. Here again was a great mob of Magpie Geese, perhaps 1,500. Most of them were feeding in a black swamp close to the *Pandanus* jungle across a sort of bay in the open plain. Hitherto we had been very much inclined to believe that these birds were in fact geese. So much of their behaviour seemed characteristically gooselike – their flock reactions, the way they 'decoyed' in and settled just like Pinkfeet, the v-formations in flight, the alarm notes in their language – everything seemed to indicate that *Anseranas* was a goose – not a screamer, not a crane nor a stork, but a goose. But now here was a new feature of their behaviour. They were still arriving at the feeding swamp, flighting in parties from a temporary roost, from the tops of the *Eucalyptus* trees. Several hundred were still perched there on the topmost branches. We wondered particularly about this behaviour when, a few minutes later, we saw a Dingo coming along the edge of the forest. Here was a reason for the tree roosting, but then the Dingo was introduced by humans, or so it is believed, no doubt thousands of years ago. But could the tree habit be of such recent origin we wondered. And then I remembered the newly hatched gosling which had gripped my finger with its long prehensile toes two months ago at Slimbridge. The tree habit is evidently of very long standing. But I still think that *Anseranas* is more of a goose than anything else, albeit an extremely aberrant one.

Further out in this part of the plain were many more geese at the edge of a lagoon near a prominent dead tree. Here, Harry told us, was where he made his record catch of geese with his boom trap – 350 odd. Out there on the plain there were buffaloes, huge grey beasts with back sloping horns, and scrub cattle – both introduced. But the buffalo is well adapted to the country which suits it apparently perfectly. It seems that the buffalo would be more rewarding to farm than the cattle. There were half a dozen great grey birds out on the plain too – Brolgas or Native Companion Cranes.

The Dingo edged along the forest towards the feeding geese, sniffing the wind, obviously interested, but he seemed to think there was no future in it because he went off among the trees and we saw him no more.

As we returned in the evening – which was by no means cool, but on the other hand was not so desperately hot as it had been earlier in the day, we passed through a group of bushes shrill with the twittering and squealing of parakeet. These were the common Banded Lorrikeet which we had first seen in the garden of the Sea Breeze at Darwin. This must be one of the most brilliant of all the parrots, with a complex pattern of red and orange and blue and green – a perfectly glorious little creature. There must have been a hundred or more feeding in the low trees, but they were surprisingly wild and unwilling to be photographed at close range. On the way back to camp there were wallabies beside the road – the Nail-tailed Wallaby. They emerge to feed in the evening, and allow a car to pass within 30 yards without hopping away.

The darkness fell with tropical swiftness when we had returned, but it remained very hot. The windows of the cookhouse where we had supper were lined with mosquito gauze, outside which were a number of 6″ geckos.

We also had in our cabin a very beautiful moth – perhaps a tiger moth – with blue underwings, orange thorax and crimson tip to the abdomen. Inside on the mosquito gauze was the tiniest lizard I have ever seen. It was, I believe, the young of a small brisk skink with a coppery coloured head which was universal outside the cabin and in the forest. Underneath a light which floodlit a part of the camp from a high pole we found two dark brown tree frogs about $2\frac{1}{2}''$ long. We took them back to our cabin, but they 'plopped' during the night and I had to release them.

SATURDAY 10 NOVEMBER

Too hot at night for very much sleep. In the early morning we set out to go to another arm of the river plain where the geese were said to be rather tamer because they had not been shot. They were sitting fairly close in to the *Pandanus* edge just at the end of the road. We crept through the edge of the wood and to within about 70 yards and took some films with the 6" lens. On the way back to breakfast I had a splendid view of the Crimson-winged Parakeet which we had seen flying over on the previous day.

Phil had stayed behind for this early trip, but after breakfast we set off with a packed lunch on an excursion to a special creek on which Harry promised we should find the Green Pygmy Goose. It was a longish drive across a part of the plain which becomes impassable after a rain storm, over a low hill called Beatrice Hill, past a Government rice project, and so down to the creek. For me this drive was enhanced by frequent views of a fine monitor which is known as a Goanna (clearly a corrupted form of iguana). They were astonishingly swift over quite long distances to the nearest cover. As we reached the creek there on the first patch of open water was a trio of Green Pygmy Geese – *Nettapus pulchellus* [see page 10]. They sat alert and motionless watching our clattering approach in the Land Rover. The male looked exactly like a minute Richardson's Goose. The white face pattern is rather variable in individuals and possibly with age.

We worked our way along the creek which was in most parts about 20 yards wide. There were a few geese (Magpies) at various points and three groups of 9 pygmy geese. In one part sitting in trees were Cattle Egrets in full breeding plumage with dark buff heads and backs. Four Spoonbills with black bills were feeding in the creek (*Platalea leucorodia regia?*). After about $\frac{3}{4}$ of a mile the creek gradually dried up. In the last major pool were 50–60 geese, 9 pygmy geese and a pair of Australian Black Ducks. This was the first positive identification of Blacks. They were rather stained and looked very dark among the green floating weeds. The birds finally left this pool and we decided to build a hide at the foot of a bamboo bush by the water's edge. When it was complete Phil and I climbed into it. Harry waded out in the black mud (in spite of alleged crocodile risks) to see how well we were hidden from the water.

Then began a tremendously exciting hour. The geese came back but failed to settle and went away on up the creek. Some of the pygmy geese settled short about 60 yards from us, but some spread on to us, and even past us and then swam back to our pool. At first they were nervous of us but gradually they got used to the camera noise and settled down.

They were in pairs mostly, some trios. They displayed continuously – the females 'tipping' their heads like tufted ducks, the males less intensively doing the same. Males made little rushes at approaching pairs and were counter attacked. There was a short display flight of about 6 feet performed by the male only. The females' chin lifting was done while following the drake and is clearly analagous to the sideways 'sicking' of Mallard and Goldeneye. The little birds spent more than half an hour within 50 ft which meant that one or two filled the screen with the 6″ lens. Finally Harry came up and put them up, perhaps a little sooner than we should have liked, and they flew off up the creek, turned and came back past us again. In flight they have a very prominent white patch on the secondaries. They are very reminiscent of Goldeneyes. As they fly there is a delightful little high whistle which sounds most attractive as the flock goes by. We had a chance to observe the individual variations in bill colour and plumage. The bill is black with a pink nail, but some if not all had pink lower mandibles and in one male the pink spread up half the length of the upper mandible. The top of the head is dark brownish black and it is only the neck and back and wings which are bottle green. The grey breast and flanks are disclosed at close range as superbly marked in bold vermiculations making an almost marbled pattern. The flank feathers rise surprisingly high over the back, in one case a detached tongue of feathers above the speculum. The white of the belly encroaches up the breast and flanks in some individuals of both sexes.

One curious feature is the prominence of the wing tips when folded. They cross to an extreme degree and give a most characteristic appearance. The face pattern of the males was variable some having an entire white cheek to the bill, others (more common) having a dark line downward and slightly forward from the eye and one having nothing but a small lozenge of white on the cheek just like the Canada Geese. They were as beautiful as their scientific name suggests. We had (we hope) made some excellent films of these birds. As we emerged from the hide a fine big Agama lizard with a yellow chin was climbing in the bamboo a few feet above our heads. We moved back along the creek to where an acacia had fallen, but was still growing in a prone position. This gave good shade for the truck and for us as we made our picnic. Harry and Stephen lit a fire and brewed strong black tea and we had an excellent lunch, ending with glorious thirst quenching oranges. It was very hot indeed but after our filming success and our first sight of the pygmy geese there was a great contentment, and the picnic was superbly memorable.

We built another hide after lunch near the picnic tree so that we should have two when we came back with Charles's cameras and his 12″ lens.

We had just finished building it when along the far shore of the creek strolled a Dingo. Harry said it was large. I thought it was very thin. He went into the water and stood shoulder deep drinking. Then he came out again and along the far shore again towards us. The others were right out in the open and about 30 yards from the animal but he didn't

Agama lizard.

notice them at all. Eventually he reached a point which was down wind of us and more or less opposite. At the first whiff he stopped and at the next he was off directly away from us. But I had some film of him.

As we drove home we stopped to film Little Corella Cockatoos feeding on the grass. On Beatrice Hill Harry showed us a stone wall built by a settler in the 1880's who was finally driven out by disease and the natives. On the grassy slopes below the hill were lots of wallabies – looking different from the ones we had seen in the gum forest at Humpty Doo. These, Harry thought, were whiptails, of which there are several species.

At the crest of the hill near a fine banyan tree was a striking black and white bird the size of a thrush. This is known as the Pee-wee or Magpie Lark, but it is not a lark, nor a magpie nor even a Peewit, it is *Grallina tenebrosa*. Such are the confusions of Australian vernacular nomenclature. No more indication of relationship is achieved by the Wood Swallow, the Willie Wagtail, the Swamp Pheasant or indeed the Pygmy Goose!

We decided on the way back to go down to the plain at Tommy Policeman where the geese had been in the morning. The plan was to build another humpy at the edge of the *Pandanus*. But a car was there before us and a dead buffalo lay out on the plain at the end of the road, probably shot from the car. Out to the left was a party of three or four men shooting geese. This was especially sad as the manager of Territory Rice, John Beam, whom we had met in the morning (an ex 1-man submarine type) had promised to keep everyone away from that particular place. When Harry walked out he found that Beam was there himself and had brought an American financier with him. This was a certain Mr Chase, to whom Harry was introduced but to whom he did not trust himself to speak. Feeling was running pretty high at this stage – about going back on his promise to keep the geese quiet and the dead buffalo left where it fell to rot.

We went again down to the rice area where we had first seen the Magpie Geese, to see whether they had found the bait. It was nearly sunset. The geese were far out on the grass plain. Loping across the grass was a Dingo – the third we had seen. He was about 200 yards away – he didn't go in the direction of the geese, but trotted on upwind. Out of the sunset flew a pair of Native Companion Cranes. As they passed I saw that both had their bills slightly open. Perhaps they always fly like this – or perhaps only in hot weather. As we walked back two large mobs of Magpie Geese got up as if going to roost, but they settled before coming to the trees. Nevertheless it was the evening flight at Humpty Doo. It had a great peace and a great beauty about it.

SUNDAY 11 NOVEMBER
Mr Fallon brought us a doodoo (small animal – creepy crawly) in the morning. It was a huge grasshopper – grey with blue underwing, 5″ long. It joined the menagerie on one of the glass shelves formed by the adjustable louvre-type windows against the mosquito gauze.

Our plan was to go further afield to see whistling ducks (which we still tend to call by their old name – tree ducks). There was a lagoon beyond Beatrice Hill – Beatrice Lagoon – lying further north where a mob of *Dendrocygna arcuata*, the Wandering Tree Duck, might be expected.

The road leads to an area of 2,000 acres newly enclosed by flood banks, and along one of them we reached the River Adelaide – a tidal waterway about 100 yards wide. From the trees on the far side came a mournful chorus of wailing screams. These were fruit bats and eventually with binoculars we could make out the creatures hanging like great black pears among the foliage. Harry indicated their size by describing them as pussy cats with wings. The tide was down in the river and the soft grey mud was covered with mud-skippers – gobies capable of remaining out of water and of walking quite rapidly on the mud. There were evidently two species, one quite large – up to 5″ long, the other blotched with black, a different shape and not more than $2\frac{1}{2}$″ long.

The big fellows had a large spinelike dorsal fin with which they made much play. Whether it is actually a spine I was unable to discover. They appeared to be feeding in a curious way sweeping the head from side to side and every now and then rolling first on to one side then on to the other, presumably to keep themselves wet. I also saw one big one retire down a hole backwards and then re-emerge from it, and twice I noticed them get a foot or so from the water's edge, turn round and go down the last little bit backwards.

The little kind had a curious arched tummy and seemed able to hop about more actively than the big ones.

There were lots of little crabs in holes along the edge. Some of the holes were up to mousehole size but the largest crabs I saw were only as big as a thumb nail.

We began to drive across the plain and in due course came to a long lagoon. We saw a new bird here – a particularly beautiful stilt of which there were quite a number, together with Masked Plovers. And beyond them we came to the geese. This was the hottest day since our arrival and by now it was noon. We had driven past some of the geese and now we came to an arm of the lagoon which had a fine concentration of birds. Almost simultaneously a party of shooters came from the opposite side. We could hear their shots getting nearer. Stephen was dispatched to go round the main lot of the geese and bring them past us for flying shots.

Beyond and among the geese were some ducks – lots of Burdikins, a few Blacks, and some tree ducks which we took to be Wandering, but they were distant and the heat haze shimmered.

Eventually Stephen put up the main lot of the geese, 1,500 in the air at once and I hope I may have a splendid shot. Stephen waded across the billabong and met one of the shooters who was not best pleased.

When Stephen returned most of the birds had left and we withdrew under a shady tree for lunch. Phil spotted another Frilly Lizard on a *Pandanus* trunk about 300 yards away and filmed him. He froze, but edged to the side of the trunk where no-one was. But he was strangely inert and refused to react at all when prodded with a stick. Meanwhile I was pulling down a branch so as to keep a clear view between the camera and the lizard but had failed to notice that it had a nest of green leaf ants on it. In due course the lizard jumped down on my side and made off at a good speed on two legs towards a large tree about 30 yards away. When he reached it he climbed slowly enough that had I realised his limitations I might well have caught him. Instead I found myself covered in sharply biting green ants while the lizard disappeared into the higher branches of the great tree.

Goanna, Stumptail, and
Bearded Lizard.

We had another look at the ducks which had accumulated during lunch again in the lagoon and I found a small party of Grey Teal (*gibberifrons*) which were at once identifiable when one saw them with Black Ducks in company. There were also 36 Burdikin Ducks. In silhouette the Grey Teal looked like little pintails and even the Blacks looked lean and pointed of tail, so that I thought for a moment I had found some pintails. Here too was an unidentified wader of common sandpiper size and further up on the dry plain were several Black-winged Pratincoles.

In an effort to get back to Humpty Doo we tried to circumvent the swampy part of the plain by driving through thick *Pandanus* jungle and it was here that we came upon a Goanna (monitor) which crept into cover and froze. We got out a camera and gradually worked round the cover. At first I thought he must have gone on, but then suddenly he moved and we could all see him. He was quite big – say three and a half feet long – and his head was rather small on a long and rather thick neck. But the most striking thing was his extremely long purplish pink tongue. We kept him encircled for a bit and Charles got quite good films, but when I got out the 3″ lens on my little camera he broke through the cordon and made off.

By now we had driven into jungle so thick that we had no choice but to retrace our track and finally we decided to go back all the way by the track we had come out on. 'Who knows?' we said, 'maybe we shall see something nice on the way!' And so it was – for we came to a small lagoon which somehow we had missed on the way out. It was covered with geese which were feeding on both banks, but down at the water's edge there were lots of tree ducks. And so far from being the expected Wandering they were all Plumed. I counted 130 and there were more in dead ground.

For a while we watched them from a couple of hundred yards and then we decided to go down and build an impromptu humpy. So we walked behind the truck as it went down to a small tree at the edge of the billabong. Here we broke down enough branches to hide Charles and me, climbed inside and let the truck drive away. Two groups of tree ducks landed on the far side of the water about 150 feet away and provided some kind of picture. Unfortunately just when things were beginning to look rather good Harry tried to move some more closer to us and raised them all in the process, but we got some flight shots as well.

Plumed Whistling Duck.

Wandering Whistling Duck.

From then on the day developed its troubles and frustrations. We were to go to Darwin for the night so as to fly in a chartered plane early next morning to locate and count the geese and to visit the famous mission station at Oen Pelli. When we arrived at Darwin there were no rooms for the night and we were too late for food. After all kinds of special pleading we finally got a meal at a quarter to ten at the Airport.

It was finally agreed that Phil and I should go to a Mrs Nixon Smith, whose husband is deputy head of the government Plant Development Department. She was very kind but the beds were pretty hard and there were legions of mosquitoes and no nets. Charles and Harry had to sleep on the beach (where there were no mosquitoes).

The nicest things about the Nixon Smith house were the geckos which called incessantly and the huge dull-green tree frogs – at least 4″ long – with binocular vision and enchanting expressions on their faces. One was fascinated by its own reflection in a beer bottle. But by and large we were glad when the alarm went at 6.0 am and it was

MONDAY 12 NOVEMBER

At 7.15 we were at the airport and soon after were boarding a De Havilland Dragon. I swung the props for the pilot (whose name was Doug) and we were off. The plan was to fly low over certain parts of four or more rivers and estimate the numbers and distribution of the geese, then fly on to Oen Pelli ('the beautiful lagoon') for lunch and return by way of other known goose concentrations, particularly one called Goose Camp.

The low flying was immensely interesting and enjoyable. The goose flocks looked wonderful rising below us in the sunlight. The buffaloes sniffed at us with laid back horns, and we could identify every reasonable sized bird we had seen during the previous days, and saw several more including black and white pelicans, a Brahminy Kite, and Black Cockatoos. We saw the bustard which is called the Plain Turkey – in one case a pair with a striking difference in size. We saw the white Torres Strait Pigeon with black wing and tail-tips, the White and Straw-necked Ibises looking like geese, and even two lots of Glossy Ibis. And everywhere we saw Magpie Geese and buffaloes.

Of the ducks we saw lots of Burdikins, Blacks, a few Teal, occasional Green Pygmy Geese and at various times whistling ducks, which looked dark enough to be Wandering. In some of the swamps grew a scarlet duck weed which gave bright splashes of colour down below.

Suddenly we came to steep hills with rugged cliffs and nestling at the edge of them was the Mission Station beside its beautiful lagoon. As we came in to land a large flock of geese rose from the lagoon in company with undoubted Wandering Tree Ducks.

It was very hot indeed when we emerged from the plain to meet the Missionary, Mr Ash. Under the flaming blossoms of the poinsiana trees were a crowd of coal black natives each wearing a red loin cloth.

We were taken to meet Mrs Ash, a gentle much freckled lady with two small children, in their new house overlooking the lagoon, and from its first floor balcony I discovered that the surface was dotted with Green Pygmy Geese among the water lilies – there were perhaps 200 on the whole lagoon.

Besides these there were several groups of Magpie Geese, perhaps

Oen Pelli.

300 all told, feeding on the banks or upending among the weeds, and there was a tight bunch of several hundred Wandering Tree Ducks diving for food just opposite to us on the far side of the lagoon.

We were drinking tea and discussing a plan of action when a native went by below us with a gun heading for the lagoon. Mr Ash called to him and stopped him from going. He stood for a long time when it was suggested he should go up to the other end of the lagoon but there were no ducks at that end anyway. The Missionary was a brisk little man with a capable manner and a vein of hearty backchat with the black people. He took me down to the edge of the lagoon and called in a dug-out canoe which had two boys in it. Jacob was the one who was to

Oen Pelli bilabong.

23

accompany me. I set up the tripod in the canoe and we began a most memorable hour cruising on the lagoon.

It was desperately hot with the sun almost directly overhead and the glare off the water. I was pouring with sweat after only a few minutes, and yet the scene was so full of interest that I entirely forgot the discomfort. I found that we could get quite close to the geese and even closer to the pygmy geese, but that the tree ducks were very much wilder.

When I had filmed Jacob paddling the canoe we returned to the shore and three other little black boys joined Jacob in a bathe which included standing on their heads in three feet of water. We then ate goat stew, with goat's milk in the tea, and drank 'fruit salt' and had salt pills.

The saddest thing was that there was not to be time to cross the lagoon and climb the rocky hill beyond to the famous cave paintings of Oen Pelli. The plane had to leave at 2.30 if we were to avoid thunderstorm risks and it just could not be fitted in. But in the storeroom Mr Ash got out a dozen or more bark paintings in the characteristic style of the Aborigines – in browns, reds and white – mostly animals – emu, fish, tortoises, and some scenes with men in them. The bodies of the animals are filled in with patterns (apparently imaginative) which, especially in the case of the fish are reminiscent of an x-ray picture. They are very decorative and well composed.

We had been only about $3\frac{1}{2}$ hours at Oen Pelli during all of which it had been desperately swelteringly hot – but in spite of that it had left an impression of great beauty and peace. I felt we had seen an unforgettable place and the whole visit seemed to be under the influence of a rare perfection.

The wind through the open windows of the plane brought coolness at last. We flew round the edge of the hills to another beautiful secluded lake called Red Lilly Lake, but it had very few birds. From there we went to an area known as Goose Camp – being where the geese are in the habit of concentrating. The most we had seen on the morning flight had been what I called 10,000 and Harry called 8,000 – but this group of lakes contained four or five times that number. On one smallish round lake there cannot have been less than 20,000 and in the whole system, say in an area of about 5 miles square, there were at least fifty thousand. In some places they rose in clouds from dense concentrations round the lake shores. Flying at between 50 and 100 feet we saw them marvellously well.

And so we came back to Darwin to a desperate evening of chasing the Qantas Agent, the CSIRO entomologist, Lindsay Crawford, who had been buying film for Charles to use, the Macrobertson Miller Airlines Manager to deliver our air tickets, and supper at a 'continental restaurant' (where a huge yellow-underwinged moth with amazing cryptic upper wings came in and eventually settled on a curtain).

The air tickets were finally delivered at a very convivial party to a manager who was in splendid form; I had to remove a tree frog from the pillar of the banister at the top of the steps so that he could hold on to it.

All this made us late and sleepy by the time we reached Humpty Doo (seeing a stone curlew in the headlight beam and turning back to examine an Echidna which proved to be a cow pat – black mark Scott!).

Echidna.

24

TUESDAY 13 NOVEMBER

Our last day at Humpty Doo. We set off with our Frilly Lizard in the sack towards the Green Pygmy Goose creek. We stopped near where we had originally caught the Frilly boy, and filmed him sitting on a *Pandanus* trunk. He spread his frills superbly and Charles got some absolutely splendid shots. We re-enacted the catching and finally our friend ran off on his hind legs. We found that the way to hold him (and perhaps to catch one), was by the base of the tail which was too close for him to turn and bite and which was out of reach of his hind claws. The gape is extended, to make the mouth look larger, by an orange triangular patch in the corner which appears when the mouth is open. Below the frill and behind the enlarged head were colonies of parasitic orange mites. He was one of the finest lizards I have ever handled, a splendid creature who had given us a splendid interlude in our film.

Frilly Lizard.

The next morning we drove into Darwin to take the plane to Perth.

WEDNESDAY 14 NOVEMBER

We had been 6 days in the Northern Territory – six memorable days thanks to Harry Frith's excellent organisation and his great patience. Had we had Charles's cameras with us all the time we should probably have had rather better material, but even without we have not done too badly. Charles stays behind as his gear has at last been located. It is at Perth and will be sent to Darwin so that he can spend two days getting 12″ lens shots to complete our film record.

We stopped 5 times on our air journey to Perth and at each place we looked for any animals that might be on view near the airport buildings.

At Derby there was a bird described by an old chap working on a water tank as a 'Purple Martin' (it was one of the wood swallows). A pair of them had a nest with young in the framework of the tank and the chap said the parents attacked him when he climbed his ladder to do the work. There were curious trees with bottle shaped trunks and large fruits with a dry pithy kernel which rattled inside. In the branches of a bush we saw a little bird with a curved bill which was panting with the heat. The sun was almost exactly overhead and we had no shadows at all. It was very hot – but a dry heat.

At the next place, Broome, there was a sea breeze blowing and a pretty garden with sprinklers on the lawn and cotton bushes and bougainvillea. In the surrounding hedge were lots of lizards of a handsome species in which the male had a large white stripe across the face. No doubt this was a skink of some kind, though it looked quite lacertine (the genus *Lacerta* apparently does not occur in Australia). These were 18″ long.

Flying over land in this region is a very bumpy business. Thermals are strong and numerous and the cumulus clouds have flat or concave bottoms which are more marked than anything I have seen in England. With cloud base at about 6,000 feet, it would have been a marvellous place for a cross country soaring flight in a sail-plane. These conditions must be more or less similar (apart from seasonal differences), on every flight – a tough assignment for the stewardesses with a good deal of air sickness to deal with.

Port Hedland was the next stop. Here the sea breeze was blowing briskly. I walked out across some low scrub and discovered a very swift agamid lizard, in which the males were beautifully patterned in orange and black. It was quite small – about 8″–10″ long – and moved so fast that one was not quite sure one had seen anything at all. This is the fastest moving reptile I have ever seen (for its size) – most impressive.

By the time we had reached Carnarvon it was late in the afternoon and of course we had flown a good way south. The fresh breeze was cool and in a walk round a small garden (equipped with an electric fence against kangaroos) and the nearest scrub bushes we found a small blackcapped finch with a red bill.

And so, in the evening we arrived at Perth, and were met by Dom Serventy and a reception committee consisting of Carol Serventy (wife of Vincent, Dom's brother), a young biologist John Callaby, and Harry (and Mrs) Shugg (Secretary of the Bird Club and also of the Conservation Advisory Committee). Dom was about to fly – an hour or so later – to the east. He is one of the senior men in the Commonwealth Scientific and Industrial Research Organisation (CSIRO) Wild Life Section, of which Francis Radcliffe is the head and Harry Frith is another member.

THURSDAY 15 NOVEMBER

Perth. From the balcony of our hotel room in the early morning I could see a part of the Swan River with a flock of about a dozen pelicans – strikingly black and white – fishing almost in unison. Beyond them were gulls and avocets, which we did not see close to until next day.

Australian Pelican.

We were called for by a group of four ornithologists including a bluff and hearty individual called Joe Trainer who works for the Fauna section of the Fisheries Department. His opening gambit was a classic example of how to win friends and influence people: 'I went to Slimbridge last year,' he said. 'It was looking terrible – you had some drought on or something – all the ponds were dry and I thought how dreadful to have all those birds in such a terrible place!' He bands large numbers of ducks each season and it was, I think, he who angered Geoffrey Matthews [Deputy Director and Director of Research for the Wildfowl Trust and Director of the International Waterfowl Research Bureau] when he was showing him the duck decoy by explaining how many more ducks he could catch with his traps and how much too complicated was the decoy.

Phil and I were travelling with Clee Jenkins, a Government entomologist. The others in the party were John Callaby, who turned out to be a remarkable naturalist, and Harry Shugg. Our first destination was a suburban pool called Butler's Swamp, more recently renamed Lake Claremont. This was perhaps 40 acres of water with many dead trees entirely surrounded by houses, rubbish tips, ruined and half flooded buildings and roads. And yet in the space of less than an hour we had seen four new species of *Anatidae* which I had never before seen alive. These were Musk Duck, Bluebill (stifftail), White-eye and finally Australian Shoveler. There were also Grey Teal, Black Duck and Black Swan. The rest of the list was as follows:

Musk duck.

Dabchick	White-fronted Heron	We had also seen
Coot	Banded Plover	Australian Magpie
Moorhen	Silver Gull	(which is a small
Porphyrio	Stilt	black and white Rook)
Pelican	Little Black Cormorant	in King's Park.

It was really astonishing to find so many new birds on such a small and unpromising looking lake. But of course the star turn was to have seen four new ducks. I cannot remember the last time when such a thing could have happened – perhaps on my first visit to Walcot Hall (Shropshire) or my first visit to California – anyway not less than 20 years ago.

The most peculiar of the four was the Musk Duck, *Biziura lobata*. This is a huge stifftail in which the males are half as big again as the females, with a large pendulous pouch under the bill, perhaps twice the diameter of a halfcrown. The female has no pouch or only a very small one. Those we saw with half and quarter sized pouches were almost certainly young. Musk Ducks were very common on all the waters we visited and we had a good opportunity to see them and in one case (at Mongers Lake) to watch the display which is accompanied by a curious single whistle. It is a typical stiff-tail display using the tail, and characteristically complicated, with a splash of water thrown up, I thought, by the feet, although apparently some hold that it is done with the wings. The effect is rather like the Goldeneye display. Musk Ducks look more or less black, and only at close range with binoculars can one see the paler spotting. They have an untidy dishevelled look but the most striking impression I gained was the extraordinary resemblance in shape and position in the water to the African White-backed Duck, *Thalassornis*. Even the feathering of the head and neck was immediately reminiscent, and the position of the head, held slightly back with the bill pointing slightly up, was strikingly similar. A young Musk in silhouette was almost indistinguishable from a Whiteback, and its extremely aquatic habit, swimming very low in the water, always diving, virtually never flying (except to move from waters which are drying up), all showed a close similarity. Of course it may be a case of convergence and there may be no close relationship; on the other hand the impression of resemblance was so strong that I am inclined to think there must be a not too distant common ancestry.

The next species we saw was the Bluebill – the Australian Ruddy Duck. This looks exactly like the Maccoa or the two South American species; it has a complicated display quite unlike the North American and very amusing. I have so far only seen it once, and the first part of it a second time. The first part consists of slightly raising the body in the water and pointing the bill down the breast as if to try to preen neck feathers. On one occasion this was immediately followed by a dive. I am not quite sure how this fits on to the second half which consists of bringing the tail over the back, submerging the head and flopping the wings in the water as if the bird were *in extremis* and about to drown. At some stage in this a jet of water is thrown up by the foot. I hope to see and perhaps film this display at a later stage. The female is much more heavily marked than in the North American Ruddy Duck.

The third duck we saw was a White-eye and the fourth was a pair of Australian Shovelers.

Next we went to a lake in the grounds of a country club called something like Karrinyup and here met a handsome little dabchick called the Hoary-headed Grebe, with white streaks on its cheeks and a black chin. The common Australian Dabchick had the same pattern and colouring as our dabchick, but seemed to be a little brighter. It was here that we saw the first young White-eyes and later we saw Grey Teal and Black

Australian White-eye.

Ducks with broods. Six seemed to be the standard number of young.

At one end of the lake was a flooded wood, and we sat for a while waiting for ducks to come close enough, which they never did. Joe Trainer had cooked some excellent chops and spread a tablecloth on which a couple of tiny brightly marked black and white toads appeared.

Back near the city was Mongers Lake, a great expanse of open water with reeds round most of it, but park paths and grass banks in places. This was a stronghold of Musk Ducks, Black Swans and Black Ducks, with a very few Bluebills.

SATURDAY 17 NOVEMBER

Early in the morning we set off on an excursion into the bush to the south east of Perth. The party consisted of Vincent and Carol Serventy (who has a small daughter just weaned in time to be parked with grandma), John Callaby, Joe Trainer, Harry Shugg and a fairly wild character called Harry Butler, teacher of Natural History and a first class general biologist, with a special penchant for reptiles, particularly snakes. We had a journey of 160 miles to go, much of the first part through virgin bush – more lush and thick than the eucalypt forests of the Northern Territory.

In one place we stopped to look for doodoos. There were great rocks with little loose ones on top and here we found the most beautiful fat tailed geckos, not quite the same species as the ones I know well in the zoo but obviously of the same genus. These were the Barking Lizard, *Gymnodactylus milii*, a deep velvety purple with white dots forming a most beautiful cryptic pattern. Most of those we found were about four inches long, but Vin found one big one, which bit and held on to my finger. He was about 7″ long.

gymnodactylus milii

As we returned to the car we made the acquaintance of a delightful and gorgeous little bird, the Fairy Blue Wren, which Harry called with a chittering squeak. There were two males and a female. One of the males was the most brilliant blue in two different shades almost all over. The second male was no doubt a younger one and not so brightly coloured. They refused to come out and be photographed, remaining in the middle of a bush with a red flower called the Bottle-Brush bush.

After this stop we transferred to John Callaby's truck in order to pass through the Numbat country. John has been studying Numbats and has a special eye for them, so our best chance of seeing one was with him. The Numbat or Banded Anteater is a marsupial about the size of a Grey Squirrel with a bushy tail, transverse stripes across its back, large eyes and pointed ears. It lives exclusively on termites and was believed to be on the verge of extinction. It is on the IUCN [International Union for the Conservation of Nature and Natural Resources] Survival Service's list of vanishing animals. In this particular area, however, Callaby is convinced that it is still relatively common. But it depends on virgin bush and a sufficiency of dead timber providing hollow logs for its shelter. Thus even though there may be some thousands still in existence, its future may nevertheless be precarious. Apparently the day was rather too hot to see the Numbats out and we were unlucky.

It was a long drive on through Wagin to Dumbleyung where Ray Aitken, the local schoolmaster, had been waiting for us for three hours. He was a delightful man, a good naturalist and a forthright character.

He had arranged for a farmer, Ernest Brown, to bring his boat with outboard motor on a truck. Ernie had made good use of the three hours' wait, in the Club. We set off from the Aitken home in Dumbleyung to the river leading down into Dumbleyung Lake – a very large expanse of water. We stopped on a bridge about three miles up the winding river from the lake. Here the boat was launched, I was installed in the bows, Ray amidships and Ernie at the outboard motor. We departed to the accompaniment of much barracking and the outboard motor was reluctantly persuaded to start after Ernie had nearly thrown himself and us into the water in half a dozen abortive attempts. Then away we went down the river among flooded bushes and tree stumps. The river was stagnant – a creek which in many places was spanned from bank to bank by dead bushes and trees. Grey Teal and some Black Ducks kept flying in front of us and occasionally breaking back where the river curved round. The commonest water birds were coots. A pair of Australian Great Crested Grebes had young. One was riding on its parent's back. Two others were lost and unafraid, briefly following the boat *in loco parentis.* A few Musk Ducks dived in front of us. Black Swans swam ahead and two pairs had small downy young. We had been going for more than half an hour, and I was beginning to think that maybe we weren't going to find any Pink-eared Ducks which had been promised in good numbers on the river, when we came round a corner and there at once were some among the teal.

Pink-eared Ducks.

Pinkear habitat.

There was hardly time to look at them as we sped on with the outboard motor, getting quite close to a few which seemed to be flightless and probably well grown young. One was evidently an adult and flew only a few yards at a time apparently intending to lead us away. Some others had by this time taken off. It was all very hurried and I had been so busy getting slow motion 6″ lens shots, all of which will be underexposed and out of focus, that I had had no time to look at the birds at all. Round the next corner, however, in a big lagoon was a party of four or five and a pair. We stopped the motor and tried to approach silently, but they would have none of us. The impression was that they looked surprisingly like what I had expected, and the illustration in Phillips's *Ducks* (which is by Louis Fuertes, I think) is quite good, especially the distant ones. This time when they flew I heard for the first time the little plaintive clicking whistle which is so characteristic of them. Also in this open bay of the river were Mountain Ducks (*tadornoides*) many of them young ones in a surprisingly dull and nondescript plumage, so much so that for quite a while I gazed at one in the fond hope that it was a Freckled Duck.

It seems that the Freckled Duck, *Stictonetta naevosa*, is by far the rarest of the Australian Ducks (possibly excepting the Cotton Teal). Next seems to be the Chestnut Teal.

On the far shore of the lagoon were some Wood Ducks (Maned Geese) and a couple of Greenshanks.

We turned back from here, having much trouble with the outboard motor, and we found the Pinkear doing a distraction display in the same place. We also found two well grown young Pinkears diving and swimming away low in the water like water-rats.

The moon came up soon after the sun set. It was cool, indeed cold, so that the river water felt warm to hold one's hand in. Ray Aitken told me that he had served with Freddy Chapman [climber and author] in the war, and had spent a long time 'being chased round Timor by the Nips' but I gathered that these were different occasions.

Pink-eared Ducks.

Our camp was on a sandy point jutting into the lagoon. Out on the water Pinkears were whistling and in the track of the moon I could see one, and make out his long bill as he swam off. Two fires were lit and Carol Serventy with swift efficiency was preparing supper. It was quite cold so that Phil and I were glad of our parkas, although the most the rest of the party did was to put on pullovers. So we sat round the fire. Harry Butler hunted nearby for Aboriginal flints, because this was evidently a native camp site of perhaps prehistoric times. The frogs croaked in chorus – one rather like a goose calling (a Greylag perhaps) another exactly like a banjo being plucked. It was exciting, romantic, memorable.

We slept in sleeping bags on camp beds beside the car. It was cold, but no mosquitoes. Ray Aitken and Ernie Brown returned from town at half past midnight with happy shouts of 'Wake, wake rise and shine' together with much banging of car doors, which might well have led to murder.

It was broad daylight when we awoke on SUNDAY 18 NOVEMBER and the bees were already at work among the feathery blossoms of the gum tree close by. On the sandy shore beside me were a pair of Red-capped Dotterel (like Kentish Plover).

The campsite at
Dumbleyung.

After lunch we were on the road again, with John Callaby, on our way back to Perth. We were to stop at Lake Gundearing which was reputed to have a flock of 300 Pinkears. But our attempts to get close enough to film them were completely unsuccessful. Thus we had not yet seen Pinkears close enough to see the pink ears. The characters of colour and plumage which were visible were the black head marking, the striped flanks, the white forehead and a warm buff on the under tail covers. Above this is a noticeable white line passing over the base of the tail. In flight as the bird comes towards you the white front is conspicuous, as it goes away the white trailing edge to the secondaries and the rather narrow white transverse line across the rump. As the Pinkear flies past the most noticeable feature of its appearance is the raised head, and the slightly down pointing bill.

Just before we left we had one last view of some more Pinkears with which one shoveler was swimming. The comparison was most interesting. The head and bill were almost exactly the same size.

CHAPTER 2

Australia: Victoria, Tasmania and New South Wales

DIARY 1   1956

Our camping excursion to Lake Dumbleyung made a sharp contrast with the pomp and splendour of our surroundings for the next few days which we spent in Melbourne for the opening of the Olympics.

MONDAY 19 NOVEMBER
We have a small room with bath at Scott's Hotel, looking out onto a well so that we cannot see the sky.

From then until THURSDAY 22 NOVEMBER which was my darling Phil's birthday, a bright shining day, we were madly yachting, and opening the Games.

As President of the IYRU (International Yacht Racing Union), I am to be Chairman of the International Jury. The other members are William Higgins (whom I made Vice-Chairman) from Australia; Neville Goddard also from Australia; Julian Roosevelt, USA; Captain Count Giulio Figarolo di Gropello, Italy; Commandant Marcel de Kerviler, France, and Soren Wiese, Norway.

We had our opening meeting – I went to a pompous lunch for the Representatives of International Federations given by the organising committee.

Incidentally, the organisation is remarkably good, and the yachting for which Mr Tadgell, Mr Alick Rose, and Mr Lloyd Burgess (sec.) are responsible is quite excellent.

Phil and I went to the opening of the Games in the stadium. We did not expect to be moved and were. The day was perfect – the counter-marching of the Navy band was most exciting. The arrival of Prince Philip, and the teams – with a wild cheer for Hungary and waves back from the Czechs and finally the climax of the torch arriving, were all memorable – and sharing any experience with more than 100,000 other people always has a special quality of its own, so sociable an animal is man.

The three of us, Phil and I and Charles, flew off to Canberra on FRIDAY 23 NOVEMBER arriving in the early afternoon, to be met by Harry Frith. It was a hot day. We had circled Canberra before landing. From the air it seems very beautiful, well laid out, spacious – and indeed it seems that from the ground too. We were only an hour, or less, in Canberra, but in the time it impressed me as exciting.

After a quick change, we set off on the 297 mile trip to Griffith, NSW the capital town of the 40 year old irrigation area out in the desert of western New South Wales. Here Harry had lived and worked until recently, and we were to join one of his boys there and to film Pink-eared Ducks and Mallee Hens.

On the journey we became acquainted with a purplish blue flower of the *Anchusa* family, rather closely related to Viper's Bugloss. This plant is so common and widespread that great areas of the hillsides and the valley bottoms were quite blue with it. It is usually known as Patterson's Curse, but there are areas in which it grows at drought times when no other plants will, and there it is called Salvation Jane. It is certainly strikingly handsome.

Late on a hot evening we passed through Wagga Wagga and stopped for a meal at Narrandera, where we had steak and eggs and orange squash, and flying crickets buzzed round the mercury vapour lamps in the town. Only 60 miles on to Griffith, but we were quite tired when we arrived; we met tall, dark, echo-voiced Geoff Booth, who was supposed to know just where all the Pinkears were.

SATURDAY 24 NOVEMBER

Also a cold grey day – a rarity in Griffith. We made our way to a place called Gum Crick where Harry had a study area, marked out with wire netting fences. We spent a good deal of that day and the next trying to film Pinkears on this lagoon. It was flood water from the Murrumbidgee River about 10 miles away. The floods had come up originally nearly a year ago, and had remained fluctuating for many months, with hundreds of ducks, indeed thousands, breeding all over the area. Here there was thick tall grass and other vegetation – hay-field height – round most of the water, frequent trees – most of them eucalypts but some pines, and a lot of the trees dead and standing grey and barkless in the water. Most of these trees were hollow and it was in these that the ducks had been nesting 6 weeks ago.

The bulk of the ducks – perhaps a thousand altogether – were Grey Teal but there were probably 200–300 Pinkears, a few Blacks (one of them a flightless adult) a few White-eyes, two Musk Ducks and a few shovelers.

SUNDAY 25 NOVEMBER

It was a bright and sunny day but there was a horribly cold wind blowing early in the morning. We had breakfast beside Gum Crick (apparently not to be confused with Gum Creek – quite a different place) and we were all perished. After breakfast we built a humpy using an axe and some string, and cutting branches from a neighbouring tree. A plant called roly-poly with adhesive seeds formed the principle cover. Charles and I both sat in this hide. With wet feet and a whistling wind we were perished sitting in the shade of the humpy. At first the teal and a few Pinkears returned only to an island about 60 yards away, but later, with Harry and Phil hovering about on the far side of the flood a small group swam up to less than 20 yards, feeding away at great speed and practically without pause. They are much more rapid feeders covering much more ground than the Grey Teal.

Pinkear chick.

One of the new birds we had seen earlier in the morning and saw subsequently quite often in pairs and small groups was the budgerigar which Harry pronounced 'boodgerigar', the first syllable to rhyme with 'could'. This is apparently the Aboriginal pronunciation and the word means 'dainty morsel of delicious food'. Apparently the young were speared in the nest, removed and eaten, and tasted very good.

Pink-eared Ducks.

So far all our time in Griffith had been spent on the flat plain. Between Griffith and Leeton is a huge irrigation area about 40 or 50 miles square in which oranges, peaches, olives, vines, rice and many other crops are grown on what was previously arid desert. About 40 years ago the project was first developed and many a fortune has been made there since. There are long straight canals about 30 feet wide bringing water from higher reaches of the Murrumbidgee River. The river itself and its flood plain lie along one side of the fertile area and the recent floods encroached in many places. On the other side there are low hills, and a

Cock Mallee Fowl.

Mallee Hen.

part of them consists of virgin expanses of scrub growing about 15–20 feet high. This is the Mallee and the scrub is formed by two species of *Eucalyptus* which are entirely characteristic of this type of country. We drove along the straight tracks running north and south and east and west which divide the sections, through many miles of Mallee, the home of the fabulous Mallee Hen or Mallee Fowl. This is one of the megapodes which incubate their eggs in huge mounds of sand and decaying vegetation.

Over the past 4 years Harry (Frith) has been making a study of these birds and we were now in his study area. In a square mile he has recorded 58 nests of which only about 17 are in use each year. He has used special instruments for recording nest temperatures, and has watched and filmed the birds at work at the nest. His work on the bird is certainly a major contribution to science. The first nest we went to was No. 3 which this year was the home of a particular male called Joe.

Briefly, the Mallee Hen's year consists of a short period of courtship and nest building, on an existing mound usually, which may be four or five feet high and four or five yards in diameter. The male does all the building, then digs a hole in the top into which the female lays one egg which is then covered up and in the early part of the season incubated by the heat of the decaying organic matter. A week later she lays another egg, and so on throughout the winter and early spring – until more than 20 eggs have been laid. Apart from laying the eggs she has nothing further to do with the nest or the young. The male alone controls the temperature, thrusting his head into the nest and probably using his tongue as a thermometer. According to his findings he either heaps sand on to the huge nest mound or scratches it off. There is an intricate interaction between the heat of the decaying Mallee leaves and twigs and the heat of the sun. Towards the end of the 6 months' laying season almost all the heat is derived from the sun, as the vegetable heat is expended, and the midsummer sun is so hot. The chicks hatch in mid-heap and somehow or other fight their way to the surface. They are entirely independent and neither parent pays any attention to them. They have to rear themselves singly – as, of course, only one hatches out each week. The introduced fox (brought in, believe it or not, for

35

hunting!) which is now immensely numerous in Australia is the principal enemy of the Mallee Hen, as it digs up and eats the eggs.

In the course of filming the Mallee Hen Harry had found this bird Joe, which was exceptionally tame and confiding. He told us that Joe would come up to the nest against an old rabbit fence while we stood by. Harry went on to the nest and began shovelling the red sand with his hand. In a few moments he said 'It's OK – Joe's there – all's well.' He had been worried because it was already 4.00 pm and Joe, like all other Mallee Hens, is usually active in the morning and up until the early afternoon only – after which he wanders away to feed. But Joe was still here, and almost at once I saw a dark shape about 30 yards away in the deep shade of the Mallee bushes. I was immediately amazed at how much larger Joe was than I had expected. He was a great big bird as big as a female turkey and when he emerged into the sunshine we could see the beautiful grey and brown patterning on his mantle.

Harry sat on the edge of the nest throwing sand up into the air. The red dust floated down in cascades which were too much for Joe. He advanced to the nest, looked over the edge at the hole which Harry had dug, turned his back and started to throw the sand back in again. He was 5 feet away from Harry as he worked and I was 10 feet away and in full view as I filmed. Charles was filming from 10 yards away and Phil was taking stills. Nothing seemed to upset Joe.

For half an hour we filmed him. Each time he came up it took 2 or 3 minutes for the urge to cover the eggs to be satisfied, and then he would withdraw for a few minutes only to return again. Harry uncovered 3 of the eggs. They were numbered. I sat on the side of the nest for a bit and Joe came up to me two or three times while Charles filmed. Walking alone the fence we came upon a Bob-tailed Lizard, *Trachysaurus rugosus*, which assumed the typical aggressive position with mouth wide open and blue tongue showing. He always faced one's hand and could therefore be persuaded to circle round following the movement. He was fairly easy to pick up without being bitten. Later Harry caught a fine sharply banded blue-tongued lizard – it was a *Tiligna* but not the familiar species (i.e. not *scincoides*).

Then we set off along the track in search of Emus before dusk. But the Emus failed us. We saw Mallee Parrots and a pair of Mulga Parrots and we filmed a young Peregrine and a pair of Galah Cockatoos in the rosy evening light, and we came upon a pair of Red Kangaroos and later saw a distant trio of Blue Kangaroos, and then, as dusk fell we motored back to Griffith and a meal of steak and egg.

FRIDAY 30 NOVEMBER

We flew in a beautiful DC6 to Launceston, Tasmania. We had two hours to wait there and we had planned to hire a 'drive-yourself' car and go out to the edge of a river we could see as we came in to land, film such birds as we could find, hunt for doodoos and generally take it easy. But such was not to be. We were met at the barrier by a reception committee from the Fauna Protection Board and others. The President had come specially from Hobart that morning (starting at 4.00 am!). We were whisked away to be shown the most English things that were available.

We went to a fine old country house called Clarendon belonging to some hospitable people called Menzies who keep race horses and cattle, kangaroos and ducks (Mountain – Black – Cape Barren Geese). We filmed the native Tasmanian Wallaby (locally called the Kangaroo) which was tame and approachable and took leaves from Phil's hand. Then we were taken to tea – at a picnic beside the river, where finally 80 year old Mr Reynolds, President of the Fauna Board, made a formal speech. It had an extraordinary quality of unreality about it all. Then back to the airport to take our Dakota for Flinders Island.

During the flight we hit the strongest bump (downdraught immediately after a surge of thermal lift) that I have so far experienced in an aircraft. The contents of the tea cups in the hands of the passengers in front appeared like small fountains above all their heads, which, from our seats in the rear, was an exceedingly droll spectacle. I think even the Dakota would have soared in that thermal. I went up to the cockpit as we flew over the island of the Bass Strait and was allowed to stay there for the landing which I very much enjoyed.

On landing we were met by Dom Serventy and at once introduced to Dr Eric Guiler, member of the Fauna Board and lecturer in Zoology at the University of Hobart, and a most delightful Irish Australian with a powerful sense of humour. Next, we met Doug Gibson studying under Serventy, who came from Sydney and was growing a beard. Finally we met Mr Langley who kept the store at Lady Barron. Mr Langley drove the truck which carried all our baggage behind in a large freight space, and all of us in two rows of seats in front. He took us, past White Mark (so called by Matthew Flinders) the town of the airport, over a Blue-tongued Lizard basking in the road – the only living one we saw on Flinders Island – to his weekend farm house up in the foothills of the southern range of mountains. It was a delightful and romantic place, overrun at night with the local kangaroo – Bennett's Wallaby – the very one which does so well in parks and zoos in England. Mrs Langley gave us an excellent lunch after which we established the place in film and found a beautiful and very large spider with sharp radial black marks on the thorax.

The commonest birds on Flinders Island appear to be the Goldfinch and the Starling, both introduced from Europe. Flinders Island is a beautiful place with low windswept trees but very green and lush. There are big areas of the grass tree (black boy) but mostly it is short *Eucalyptus* scrub, and near the shelving shore in Lady Barron Bay the trees are deep green, leaning to the east, with bare white stems, and look incredibly beautiful in the evening sun. At Lady Barron there was a sick Black-faced Cormorant sitting on the counter in the local store (which we afterwards released on Fisher Island).

We went first to the top of a neighbouring hill where the whole landscape was spread out majestically before us. The sea was a brilliant incredible green-blue. The islands famous for their part in the Mutton Bird industry were pointed out by Dom. Away to the north was Babel with a low flat island next to it on which the gannets breed. To the south were Little Green Island, Big Dog, Rabbit Island, Rifle, and beyond as a mountainous backcloth Cape Barren Island itself. Looking westward to the right of the tiny dot of Fisher Island was Little Dog and beyond it Tin Kettle and Big and Little Woody Islands. These are the islands of the Furneaux Group, the home of the sea birds and the Cape Barren Geese.

Immediately below us on Flinders Island was a lagoon and beyond it various others stretching away northward. As elsewhere in Australia, the water is high on Flinders. The nearest lagoon was called Scott's Lagoon and it was here that we were hoping to see Chestnut Teal. But when we got down to the edge of it there was surprisingly little bird life. Three Black Swans, a few Pacific Gulls and that was all. We walked with care along the flooded edges because there were said to be many snakes, but we did not see any. By squeaking at one point we called up a number of small birds including Grey Fantails, *Rhipidura fladellifera*, and Blue Wren, *Malurus cyaneurus*. We tried one other lagoon, but a burn had recently blackened the scrub across the end of it. Once more a few Black Swans were the limit of its avifauna.

Back at Lady Barron in the clear evening sunshine we filmed embarkation in the Fisher Island row boat and then went to have tea with a charming lady called Miss Barrett who lived in a dark little house in the middle of a dark grove of bare stemmed trees opposite to the landing place. It was she who had prepared our room in the hut on the island, and another lady also there had prepared and cooked the salted Mutton Birds we were later to eat.

Later we crossed over and landed on Fisher Island after transferring all our baggage and camera equipment from shore to dinghy to fishing smack (belonging to a delightful weatherworn character called Tuck) to dinghy to shore again, for a journey of about 200 yards to the tiny 2-acre island. The hut consists of two rooms, one of which is the living room with 4 bunks and the other a store room with two camp beds, which was allocated to us. Then there is a small ablutions building, recently added, containing a shower and Elsan.

This is the headquarters of 9 years of research into the biology of the Short-tailed Shearwater or Mutton Bird, *Puffinus tenuirostris*, conducted by Dom Serventy for the CSIRO. Only a very small number of Mutton Birds breed in the two small rookeries on Fisher Island – just over a hundred nests, but every bird is known and most have already been marked for many years. On the nearby islands many hundreds of thousands of Mutton Birds have their nests. Dom thinks that there are not less than a million nests on Big Dog, and as many on Babel. But the Mutton Birds were not in evidence when we landed. We were welcomed by a pair of Black Oystercatchers (Sooty Oystercatcher) which are larger than the Pied. The Pied is also in the Bass Strait – a subspecies of ours, *H.o.longirostris*. There was also a Black-faced Cormorant on the shore to welcome us. On a tiny reef 70 yards away were more cormorants and on top a sitting Caspian Tern. There was only a light wind blowing, which is very unusual in the Bass Strait, and out beyond the reef were two Musk Ducks diving.

It was not until late in the evening when, after supper, we went down in the dusk to Pott's Point and saw our first Mutton Birds. They came sweeping in low over the sea, swerved upwards over the lip of the island and dropped out of sight into the tussock grass of the rookery. They were no more than dark half-seen shapes against the light that had almost faded from the west. But they were to be counted because the numbers indicated the stage which had been reached in the nesting cycle. Mutton Birds all lay their eggs within a 4-day period. When they are laid the males come in to start an incubation period of 13 days after which the female comes for 13 days. The eggs take about 70 days to hatch. After we had watched the flight and counted in 84 birds we wandered over the island paths looking for stray birds still outside their burrows. Dom found several and we checked their ring numbers. Most of them were immature non-breeders. We also caught a Fairy Penguin at its nest burrow, and a little later one of its young with a feather boa of down round its neck. It was rather exciting working over the rookery with torches coming upon occasional birds among the tussocks.

I woke very early, about 3.30 am on the morning of SATURDAY 1 DECEMBER. It was already almost daylight and there was a weird croaking coming from the burrows. The shearwaters were making much more noise than they had made in the evening. The sea was like glass, a very rare kind of day for the Bass Strait.

After breakfast Trooper Lou Bailey brought the police cutter to take us to the islands. She was a fine boat – 37 years old – with a good cabin, a large cockpit, a mainsail bent on the spars but not used and an auxiliary. We transferred the gear by dinghy, and set off at once for the islands to the west.

Cape Barren Island from Fisher Island.

39

It was on the westernmost end of Big Dog Island that we saw our first Cape Barren Geese. There were three pairs widely scattered on the rocky shoulders of the island. The pairs stood close together and often on a rocky eminence. They looked huge and majestic, and somehow supremely appropriate in their setting. On the next island there were three more pairs, and finally we came to the island where we were to land – Little Woody Island. Here were several geese on the crest of a central ridge watching us. But they were very spry and mostly moved off, either to Big Woody Island or to a small reef in between. We found one hatched nest full of down and the pile of droppings where the ganders had stood. We saw several other such piles but were not sure if these also indicated nests or were just favourite roosting sites. The plan was for us to signal back after we had got all the pictures of the geese on the island, and then build a humpy. When we signalled the rest of the party were to walk round Woody Island and drive the geese back to our island.

We made our signal and then settled ourselves in a group of large rocks which provided only moderate facilities for humpy-building. We planted rows of branches of a low shrub, fixed between stones but we were, at the end of it, much less than well hidden. However, the sun had come out and it was all very beautiful and pleasant. We could see the 'beaters' walking over Woody Island and the geese moving in front of them. Not many came our way until at last, when the accumulation on the reef was disturbed, a flock of nearly 40 swept over the edge of the island and low over our heads. The birds seemed huge and floppy as they passed over with heads sideways looking down on us. They saw too much to allow them to settle and went away, ultimately to Tin Kettle Island. So we were left with the strange grunting calls ringing in our ears and the feeling that we had been properly introduced to the Cape Barren Goose on his home ground.

Earlier from our humpy we had watched a Swamp Harrier hawking over the island, seen a Brown Hawk and had a magnificent view of a Wedge-tailed Eagle being mobbed by the Brown Hawk and by ravens. The Wedge-tail is closely related to the Golden Eagle and apparently replaces it in Australia.

Goose photography now being over, we turned to a splendid doodoo which we had found when building the hide, a very large rather flat spider which was negatively phototropic – *Delina cancerides* – well named, as it had a certain unmistakable crabbiness in the flat sideways movements and the forward curve of the anterior legs. The abdomen was bluish grey. Charles found an exactly similar one under another stone half an hour later.

Before building the humpy we had seen a family of 5 geese running in front of us to the far end of the island. We decided to explore this before leaving. I found a goose skeleton with a perfect skull which I decided to keep. A minute or two later up jumped three full sized goslings still unable to fly. They went down among some big jumbled rocks just above the shore. Two of them hid, but the third one stood in full view evidently undecided on whether it should run or crouch. I walked almost up to it, talking to it all the time, circled round it and walked it back past Charles who had been filming it, and up on to the top of the island where both of us increased speed until I finally picked the bird up – a great big gander gosling. Phil held the gander and I went to the place where the other two goslings had hidden. They were still sitting in a rock pool. I persuaded them both out and caught one – a female – while Charles filmed. We decided to take them back to the boat so that they could be banded.

Charles and I stayed behind at the top of the island to film the views, and while doing so I found a very nice lizard – a skink occupying the niche of our Sand Lizard. We had seen several small ones, but this was about 9″ long with a yellowish brown back with three black irregular stripes down it. There is some doubt about its identification, but it is believed to have been *Egernia whitii*, the Smooth Rock Lizard. While filming it I held it by the base of the tail, but just before we had finished it twisted round sharply and broke off its tail at the base. I had not realised that this type of skink had a breakable tail.

We returned to the boat and upon our arrival in the shallows at the edge of the rocky shore I spotted a large octopus – a very bright orange – trying to hide in the weeds. Eric leapt out of the boat into 18 inches of water, ran and seized the animal and brought it back to the boat, where it slithered and flowed across the floorboards in an appropriately sinister manner. As we filmed it, it changed colour from dark chestnut through orange pink to pale flesh colour and back again in a matter of seconds. It swam quite a lot and we found it quite possible to redirect it so as to keep it within range of the shore.

Part of the return journey was spent in removing Bidgy-Widgy from our clothes. This is a burr-like seed head which comes off a low plant as a ball and then proceeds to disintegrate so that the whole of one's socks become covered with it as if they were made of green matting. It is only slightly itchy and bears no relation to the agony created on ankles and feet by the two kinds of adhesive grass seeds we met with in Western Australia.

On the return route the sun fell full upon the pairs and small groups of geese we had passed on the other islands on the way out. There was something statuesque about them as they stood on their rocks and surveyed us as we passed by.

Mrs Bailey – dark and rather attractive – had produced a great meal (provided, I think, by Dom) consisting of more crayfish than we could eat. These are superficially very like the European crayfish – though apparently belonging to a different genus. (Part of the cutter amidships was a tank contaning lots of very large live crayfish). Lou Bailey himself was quite knowledgeable about the geese. He had caught 22 for the Sydney Zoo just after the war and one of our ganders at Slimbridge, which I think came from Taronga Park, was probably caught by him.

We were tired and replete with filming when we got back to Fisher Island, and I spent the evening making a drawing for the front page of the new Visitors' Book at Yolla (the Aboriginal name for the Mutton Bird after which the hut is named).

This was the evening on which we were introduced to cold salted Mutton Bird. The bird was about the size of a teal – cut in two halves like a kipper and filled with sage and onion stuffing, then roasted. It was served cold with a piece of string tied round it. It was rather oily, and vaguely fishy, but when that has been said it was really quite good, I thought. Phil had graver doubts. We had them again for lunch on the following day. The Mutton Bird you eat is of course the downy young or rather the half feathered young at its heaviest – which is considerably heavier than the adult.

SUNDAY 2 DECEMBER

Neither so calm nor so clear as Saturday morning had been. But otherwise it developed upon the same pattern and soon after 8.30 we were embarked once more in the cutter and chugging down the straits towards Rabbit Island and the open sea. When we reached Rabbit Island it seemed already rather rough for landing and the wind was freshening. We decided to go back to more sheltered waters, and eventually landed with Doug Gibson on a small reef with a tiny harbour of calm water between Little Green Island and Flinders Island. Here was a colony which we estimated at 300 pairs of Silver Gulls. We found their nests with 1, 2 and 3 eggs, and one nest with a dead chick, maggot ridden. The gulls were fairly tame and there is no doubt that the Silver Gull is an extremely beautiful bird with its bright red bill and legs and the smooth grey of the mantle, somehow softer than in the Herring or Common Gull. The whole effect indicates relationship to the Kittiwake. We sent the boat back, rowed by the redoubtable Dan, aged 70 odd, to the cutter to get the tape recorder to record the gulls, but we found after getting the birds to call incessantly within 2 feet of the microphone that we had nothing but a hopeless distortion on the tape and my identification note was incomprehensible. We hauled 2 young Fairy Penguins out of their burrow. They had charming ruffs of thick grey down, but the plumage was brilliant steely blue. They pecked at anything, including each other and their own feet and flippers and could really only be handled with gloves.

The mosquitoes on this island were quite fierce and I was bitten to such tune that my hands began to swell up so that I had to go down and dabble them in the sea, to cool them off. I'm not sure whether the Australian mosquitoes are a special brand affecting me, or whether I have recently become more allergic to them than I used to be. Anyway I have been bitten more than Phil since we have been in Australia, which is unusual.

We knew that a pair of Caspian Terns, *Hydroprogne caspia*, was nesting on the island as the bird, with its characteristic croaking call, was hovering overhead among the gulls. On our second exploration of the far end of the island (total length 70 yards) we crept over the crest and surprised a parent tern on the ground. Hiding at the spot we found a well feathered young bird with bright yellow bill – perhaps as big as a wigeon with a huge bill. In due course we put him down hoping that his mother would come to him, but she didn't, so we withdrew.

On the island we also found a starling's nest with young, and a broken shell of a Paper Nautilus (a small cephalopod), of which there was evidently an unusual abundance last year. We established that two kinds of *Mesembryanthemum* were present on all these islands, a large one with a greenish leaf and a small one with a purplish leaf and a much smaller flower.

When we got back to the cutter, well pleased with film we had got, the wind, contrary to expectation, had fallen off a lot and we decided to go back and have another shot at Rabbit Island. The landing was now quite simple and it was a beautiful island. Its visible avifauna consisted of a swath of white breasted penguin-like Black-faced Cormorants which were not breeding but had a special roosting place, white with guano, and a colony of the large Pacific Gull, a brightly coloured version of our Greater Blackback. These and the Silver Gulls are the only two Australian gull species. The cormorants took off with our landing and we saw them no more. The gulls also took off from their nests but hovered, complaining, in much the same tones as a Blackback would, at a safe distance over our heads. Their nests – some with eggs, some with downy young – were scattered through the straggly scrub.

We extracted some penguins and marked them with flipper bands – a process which we filmed before leaving the island. But as well as a large number of penguin burrows there were hundreds, probably thousands of much smaller holes and from one of these Dom brought up a most beautiful little petrel with white underparts and a very pretty grey and white pattern on the head. This island was a breeding colony site for the White-faced Petrel, *Pelagodroma marina*. We filmed the bird and its egg. All over the island were the remains of these petrels (starling size) which had been swallowed whole by Pacific Gulls and then disgorged as complete birds, mostly with skull, legs and feathers – a complete sausage shaped pellet consisting of a complete dessicated petrel. There were hundreds of them all over the island. There were also remains of a fish called the Leatherjacket which looked to me to be a species of file fish. Many of these were in and around the nests and so were the eggshells and even recently cracked fresh eggs of the Mutton Bird, which Dom suggested were those laid by mistake on the surface. We found one each of the remains of a Blue-tongued Lizard, *Tiligna scincoides*, (probably brought from Big Dog Island like the Mutton Bird's eggs) and a quite large sea horse, *Hippocampus* sp.

The gulls were so standoffish that we finally hid Charles rather ineffectually behind an old stone wall (function and origin obscure) so that he could get any pictures of them on the ground at all.

By the time we had finished it was again time to return to Fisher Island. The reembarkation from Rabbit Island was quite spectacular as the wind had freshened. Dom fell in up to the neck while embarking which occasioned much levity.

On MONDAY 3 DECEMBER we had to leave in order to catch our plane back to the Olympic Games. Our departure from Fisher Island was timed for 10.30 and we had a list of film sequences we wanted to make which was as long as your arm. The most important were close ups of Mutton Birds themselves which so far we had only seen at night. We found all the shots we needed within 15 yards of the hut and should have nice films in spite of a 25–30 knot wind. These shots are important to us because we plan to use a film (or parts of it) made by Dom on the Mutton Bird in *Look*. Introductory shots of Phil and me at the island will therefore be essential if I am to introduce Dom's film with any authority.

Dom's work on the Mutton Birds is really a wonderful study, with many parallel problems and solutions to our Pinkfoot study. Very briefly, the story is as follows: Many millions of Mutton Birds breed on the south and east coasts of Australia, nowhere in greater profusion than in the Furneaux group – Babel, Big Dog, Chapel Island and others being the main rookeries. On migration they follow almost a figure of

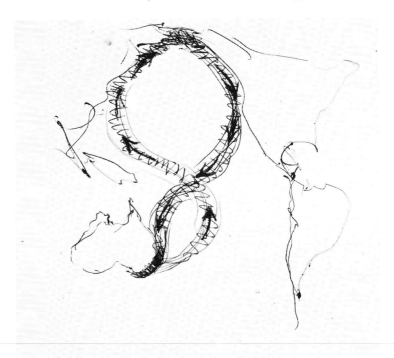

Migration route of the
Mutton Bird.

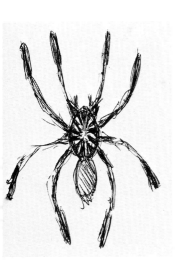

On our last morning
at Fisher Island
we filmed this
fine spider
we had caught
on Flinders Island.

8 in the Pacific Ocean and the Behring Sea is one of their main feeding areas. They return on very precise dates each year, choose their burrows where apparently copulation takes place, after which the female lays a single egg representing about one-sixth of the bird's weight. All egg laying takes place within about 4 days in all the rookeries. The male immediately (next night) takes over incubation, and sits for about 13 days after which he is relieved by the female who incubates for a like period. The egg can be cooled and hatching is merely delayed thereby. The total incubation period is about 70 days. The main food is krill (*Euphausia* sp.). The young grows until it is larger than the parents and is then abandoned. It lives on its fat until it is fully fledged and can make its way to the sea. The Mutton Bird industry therefore has a very short season when all the young are at their peak weight. In some seasons about half a million birds have been taken on one island alone. The 'Birders' who live in special sheds and have other processing sheds – little groups of three or four shacks at the shore in each suitable bay – take about 60% of the hatch (shown by Lincoln index sampling of ringed birds), and it appears that the species can stand the harvesting in spite of extensive 'wrecks' of the birds every few years. The resilience of the species to this fairly heavy predation by man is one of its most remarkable features. Dom has now had rings on the small Fisher Island rookery of about 100 nests for 9 years.

Even as Tuck's boat arrived at the island to take us away Charles was still filming the cormorants and the Musk Duck and the Caspian Terns on the little reef 70 yards away with his 12″ lens. We noticed an interest-

44

ing piece of behaviour. Two cormorants, one only slightly smaller than the other, did a food pursuit (exactly analagous to food pursuit in the Adelie Penguin) the young chasing the adult with flapping wings and begging attitude. The chase led past the Caspian Terns' nest and the male tern (or off duty parent) gave chase. The cormorants flew off, still pursuing and being pursued, and eventually returned to the island when the tern had given up and gone to chase two Pacific Gulls. Then the young cormorant began the pursuit again and this time finally persuaded its parent to regurgitate a meal by thrusting its head half way down its throat.

So finally we came to leave the romantic little island, and very sad we were to be doing so. The wild winds of the Bass Strait were blowing, the sun was shining; it was certainly one of the unforgettable places – and there are not so very many – which we have been to in pursuit of birds.

Upon arrival at Launceston we had arranged for Charles to do some filming – especially the Spur-winged Plover of which there were numbers on the aerodrome.

The rest of us however were whipped off to a reception. In spite of driving out along a suburban road and having to turn back as soon as we reached open country, we were early at the Town Hall by about 5 minutes and so we were driven round the block.

However it all went off quite well except that I forgot to put in a plea about the rarity of the Cape Barren Goose in my speech and the need for watching its status, the Mayor forgot to give poor 80 year old Mr Reynolds, Chairman of the Fauna Board, a chance to make a speech, and Doug Gibson thought he had left all his camera gear in the wrong car which held us up in the town until we risked missing the plane. At the airport we found that Eric Guiler had rescued them so all was well. And so back to Melbourne.

TUESDAY 4 DECEMBER
A beautiful day for a Royal Occasion. The Duke of Edinburgh was to watch the yachting from the Melbourne Harbour Board's converted B class ML [motor launch]. We assembled at the Station Pier at Melbourne – with the Lord Mayor, Sir Frank Sellick; the Premier, Mr Bolton; and about 20 others – organisers of the yachting mostly – including Alick Rose, Reg Tadgell and Lloyd Burgess (three men who deserve great congratulations for the way they have organised the yachting events).

We steamed to Brighton where HRH came off in a barge. He seemed genuinely pleased to see a familiar face. Mike Parker [Equerry to the Duke of Edinburgh] and Jim Thomas (Lord Cilcennin) were with him. Jim was still feeling the effects of last night's ball which went on till 4.0 am and we both had a 'horse's neck'. Admiral Abel Smith was there too. He had hauled Jim over the coals for not wearing a black tie with RYS [Royal Yacht Squadron] buttons (he was wearing a Britannia tie). Jim deflected the Admiral's attention to me and pointed to my squadron buttons and RYA [Royal Yachting Association] tie. I had to claim divided allegiance. As Vice President of an organisation of which HRH was President, was I not in duty bound to wear the Association tie when meeting my President – especially when I had designed the tie myself!

I had about an hour with Prince Philip almost entirely on sailing topics.

At lunch I had Mike Parker who was interesting about Sweden's underground harbours and airfields. Admiral Abel Smith on the other side told me about *Britannia*'s route to the Antarctic, weather and fuelling problems.

We watched the start of the Finns after lunch. Paul Elvstrom who has the Gold Medal in his pocket was far more upright than anyone else and looked firm and comfortable with his back 2 inches from the water continuously for the whole of the beat – not just occasionally. He is very good.

I had another long talk with Prince Philip about catamarans and hydrofoils. He would have liked *Fairy Fox* to have been a cat. I told him of my keenness to develop cats as an item of progress in yacht racing, and that we'd need his help. He indicated that he would give it.

It had all gone very well, and I think he had enjoyed his day. I had certainly enjoyed mine. And so by car from Sandringham, where we caught up with the Duke driving his own car, to St Kilda and the meeting of the Jury.

WEDNESDAY 5 DECEMBER

A rushed day in which we met Harry Frith off the plane from Canberra and took him out to Healesville to record the openings of the Mallee Hen, Magpie Goose and Pink-eared Duck programmes on sound film. It was a lovely sunny day and Healesville sanctuary was hopping with noisy school children but we found a wild place and used it as a studio. We also recorded a piece with Gasking and the Platypus on sound film, and then at 3.45 we dashed back to Melbourne, arriving late for the Jury meeting to find that luck was with us and the meeting had been postponed from 5.0 to 6.0. We had a distasteful job – to disqualify the Australian sharpie, Tasker, who would otherwise have won the Gold Medal. He was caught port and starboard at the weather mark by Tirian, the Frenchman, and claimed that he couldn't give way because of the Canadian on his weather. All were agreed that the Canadian could have – and in fact did – cross the Frenchman and so Roley Tasker had put himself in an impossible position. His lack of realisation of this basic principle of the rules suggests that he was not really of Gold Medal standard. Even with disqualification he was still equal top on points with New Zealand, but the New Zealander won by reason of his three firsts to Australia's two. The general feeling was that Tasker had got away with one 'port and starboard' and couldn't expect to get away with two! When spoken to afterwards by me in friendly condolence he was talking loudly of how he was going to appeal (further evidence that he was unfamiliar with the rules under which he was racing, as there is, of course, no appeal from an Olympic Jury). After this incident no further sympathy could I find.

I was booked to give a lecture after the jury meeting. By the time we got there (I with no dinner) it was nearly 10.0 and the 20–30 ornithologists had been waiting for $1\frac{1}{2}$ hours. After the lecture (with Phil's slides) we had tea and cakes in the house where I had lectured. It was very hot in the crowded room and I very nearly fainted, only just getting outside into the cool air in time. I was very tired.

THURSDAY 6 DECEMBER

The medal ceremony for yachting was performed at St Kilda at 11.0 am. Avery Brundage [President of the International Olympic Committee 1952–72] presented the medals. I had a useful half hour with him before it. He asked about the rules and why there were 2 sets. I asked him about including a 6th class in the next Games and he said it would be worth putting in for it.

After lunch and shopping and airlines offices, we went to the zoo. They do not know how to show animals in Australia. They have not many animals to show because of their absurdly strict animal importation laws. The flowers were pretty but otherwise the zoo was not very good. It was a desperately hot day, and the Koala bears were flaked out in their tree stumps. In the evening we went to a cocktail party in the *Britannia*. There was a long queue because the Duke was talking to everyone as they arrived. He asked me about the Australian sharpie and I told him that Tasker was lucky not to have been put out before.

FRIDAY 7 DECEMBER

I called on the head of CSIRO – Sir Ian Clunies Ross – a most delightful man, who really knew what his organisation's objects were and pursued them. I was greatly impressed. I fixed the films for *Look*, furthered Harry Frith's plans (I hope), put in a plea for the Cape Barren Goose, and another for a duck survey – especially Freckled Duck.

SATURDAY 8 DECEMBER

We drove out to Philip Island about 70 miles south of Melbourne on the east side of the bay. Wilma Dennis was our driver and Max Downes of the State Fish and Game Service, with wife and small son, followed us in convoy. It was a dull day to begin with, but it brightened up in time for some excellent photography. The objective was wild Koalas. No sooner had we reached the appropriate eucalypt grove than we saw a Koala in a tree by the road side – and another and another. There were perhaps a dozen on either side of a quarter of a mile of road. There were also a great many very determined mosquitoes. I got quite badly bitten – indeed these were the worst and most numerous mosquitoes we have met in Australia. Some German Olympic team members stopped and interfered with our filming. They spread out into the wood, and one returned saying he had seen two snakes. We still have not seen a wild snake in Australia.

Koala.

We decided to go on to Cowes, buy insect repellant, have lunch and then come back to the Koalas. We tried a different road after lunch and almost at once found a mother Koala with baby in a very small tree about 8 feet from the ground, with papa in the next tree. After much photography I climbed the tree and could stroke the mother and baby with impunity. Later the baby climbed round on to her back and I tried to remove it, but it clambered up scratching the top of my head and climbed into the top of the little tree. The mother then started towards me and as I was between her and the baby I thought it best to descend without ceremony. The baby then climbed down again and we filmed the reunion.

Later I found another nice Koala which was feeding, and driving home that night we came upon one on the ground. Once more it was

PS with Koalas.

absurdly tame and made no attempt at any kind of aggression. There can be very few mammals, large or small, which appear so completely indifferent to the presence of man.

We went from the Koalas to a Penguin Sanctuary – a rookery of Fairy Penguins in the sand dunes of a bay with a sandy beach. There were well marked paths worn by the penguins from the beach into the rookery. The main path was flanked by a fence to restrain the crowds who come nightly to see the Penguin Parade. We went into the rookery and found a number of sitting adults and almost fledged young. Some penguins were nesting quite close to the car park, and one adult sat under a bush, not in a proper hole at all.

We had a quick dinner (very good) at a hotel in Cowes and rushed back in time to see the Penguin Parade – the return of the adults to the rookery. It was late dusk. About 50–60 people were assembled on either side of the main route. We could dimly make out black blobs far out on the wet sand, for the tide was low. These blobs were clusters of thirty or forty penguins which seemed to wait at the edge of the waves until the party was big enough to make the crossing of the beach. They stood undecided at the foot of the steep upper beach and stood again at the edge of the dunes and the marram grass, and while they stood half a dozen torches illuminated them. How much their indecision could be attributed to the lights or the people was hard to tell. Smaller parties going up the beach further along seemed to walk on without pause. The birds which had been sitting and were returning to sea were going down singly over the beach, and did not form up into mobs. On the way back by the fenced path through the rookery there were young penguins – almost fully grown – outside most of the burrows. They paid no attention to the torch light or to the people passing and parents were already with many of them though we didn't see any feeding them. Many adults were streaming across the path close to the hot dog stand beside the car park. They seem delightfully oblivious of man.

And so, in the dark, we drove homeward, pausing only to talk to the only Koala we met, to get petrol and change drivers.

Koala.

SUNDAY 9 DECEMBER

We were met in Sydney by Sir Edward Hallstrom with a car and conducted first to the terminal where poor Charles was dropped to cope with the baggage, then briefly to Taronga Park Zoo and finally to our hotel. Sir Edward, a business man who has made a great fortune selling refrigerators, is President of the Taronga Park Zoo and also owns a rather famous little zoo at Nondugl in the Wahgi Valley in New Guinea, where Fred Shaw-Meyer, the well-known naturalist and collector, keeps and breeds birds of paradise and many others. We are to visit Nondugl at the invitation of Sir Edward.

He told us that he proposed to present us with 3 pairs of Salvadori's Ducks.

The zoo is on a steep hillside, overlooking the harbour and the trees and plants are beautifully done, but the animals are almost all on concrete and the architectural aspect is deplorable. No, they have no idea how to show animals in Australia. Modern ideas of sunk ditches, invisible barriers and so on are virtually unknown. Sham rockery is usually in distressing taste. It must be admitted that we only had a very short time (45 minutes) in the zoo, and that the animals were, as far as we saw, in excellent condition.

MONDAY 10 DECEMBER

Sir Edward Hallstrom sent a car which took us to his office where, in a chair carved realistically as a brown bear hugging him, the great man sat holding court. We met his son and several of 'the boys' all of whom seemed to be quietly efficient. The secretary sat in another brown bear and was invariably addressed by Hallstrom as 'Miss'. Pictures of black cockatoos were on the walls, and of birds of paradise under the glass on the table. Phil got some letters from home and I tried to advance our plans against irrelevant telephone calls and the Hallstrom morning mail which the old boy was trying to read at the same time. It was all very difficult. Finally we were driven into the city, had an hour to wait in the Qantas office and then found that extensive papers were needed before we could enter New Guinea.

SALVADORI'S DUCK
ANAS WAIGEUENSIS

Swimming
when disturbed

CHAPTER 3

New Guinea

DIARY 1   1956

WEDNESDAY 12 DECEMBER

Off to New Guinea at last. The taxi failed to turn up at 1.45 am at the hotel outside Sydney as ordered and we had to knock up the proprietor to open the office, so that we could telephone. We finally got the chap who said he'd been ordered for 2.40 so when he came we had to take him all the way to the airport instead of just to the city air-terminal. Waiting for the cab, before we telephoned, was memorable in its minor anxiety. It was a still starlit night, the lights wriggled at us in reflection from the harbour. A hissing noise was a late ferryboat steaming past. After three hours' sleep we were in no case to greet the situation with the fatalistic resign which it required.

And so we embarked with hordes of schoolchildren returning home for Christmas. We left at 4.15 am and flew north along the Queensland coast. We had our first view of the coral atolls of the Barrier Reef, green in the shallows, so green that after a while the little cumulus cloud looked pink. And then in the afternoon, with a deal of turbulence at low altitude we landed at Port Moresby. This is in arid savannah country with sparse eucalypt bush.

We were met by the representative of the Hallstrom Trust – Barry Osborne – who was helpful and pleasant and saw us into the DC3 which was to take us on to Lae. It was a freighter and we sat on benches along each side. We flew through thin and wispy cumulus, over steep wooded ridges and swamps. It was green and lush and jungly. And at 5.00 in the evening we circled round Lae, seeing how the town has surrounded the airstrip, and how the waters from the Markham River, laden with mud, sweep round the north shore of the Huon Gulf (in spite of the clean waters of the little river at Lae itself) so that a Japanese ship beached in the war is now so silted up and around as to be entirely surrounded by land. Only from the air can the new bulge in the coastline be detected.

At Lae it was not unbearably hot, being evening. We were met by Mr Cunliffe – among other things Veterinary Officer – and by Mrs Taylor of the Department of Agriculture. It seems that Hallstrom had given no prior notice of our arrival to anyone and his telephone message by radio had become considerably garbled. They were expecting two of us – me and Director Severn [of the Wildfowl Trust, Slimbridge]. Where, I was asked, was Director Severn? 'That's me!' 'Oh, then where is Mr Scott?'

We were last through Customs and Immigration and rooms were finally arranged for us all at the Hotel Cecil – the only hotel in Lae. I was suddenly excited by the whole prospect. This was New Guinea. It looked strange and exotic. It was superbly tropical. It was the

Naturalist's paradise as I had always read, and I suddenly felt sure it was going to live up to its reputation. Besides it was the home of the mysterious Salvadori's Duck which I should soon be seeing for the very first time. It was dark by the time we were established in our rooms, but I could see at once that the population of geckos was higher than anywhere else I had ever been. Phil found a tiny baby in the bath – newly hatched, young and adults were all over the ceilings and around the lamps. The passages were full of them. Every few minutes we heard the delightful little clicking call, 'Tche-tche-tche-tche-tche', not unlike the noise one makes to persuade a horse to go faster. The call gets softer and the repetitions quicker at the end. During the night I made a round of the passage and bathroom lights and found a large stick insect which flew like a daddy-longlegs. It was about 7 inches long and I put it in my mosquito net. I also found quite a nice plain green mantis, and in the morning a much larger brown one.

THURSDAY 13 DECEMBER

After breakfast we went out into the hotel garden where we found that one of the commonest weeds was the Sensitive Plant, *Mimosa pudica*, which sometimes covered several square yards of flat grass and sometimes climbed five feet up in the hedge. There were several fine butterflies about and one particular one was rather special. It was a shade lover with a rich purple glow on the upper side. With wings closed it was brown and leaf like, but at the tail of the hind wing were two little black streamers edged in white. With the wings closed there was a continual very slow movement of the hind wings against each other. This produced a striking movement of the two little streamers in the wind. As the wings slowly moved the streamers passed each other with a little flip which clearly would attract the eye of a nearby predator; the business end of the insect would be overlooked in favour of the moving tails which were exactly like an insect moving at the edge of a leaf.

A young man from the Department of Agriculture was to come for us with a Land Rover at 2.30. Before he arrived I went out towards the shore to get some film establishing New Guinea. I found a pair of quite pretty vanessid butterflies copulating and a catamaran with bamboo sails coming across the Gulf of Huon, with steamy mountains beyond. But it was very hot and I was pouring with sweat as I returned to find Phil and Charles bathing in the swimming pool. They were trying out the mask, schnorkel* and flippers we had bought ourselves in Sydney. I got mine too and had my first experience of the technique. The water was so thick and green that I could see practically nothing, but the equipment seemed quite comfortable. We found a little freshwater crab in the pool and filmed him. Then the new escort arrived and took us first to a chemist and then to the Botanic Gardens and the War Cemetery. There was a fine orchid house, with quite a lot of fascinating wild orchids in bloom. In the trees were some pretty parrots with orange breasts, scalloped with black, a purple blue head, pale green ring round the neck and bright orange bill. This was the Coconut Lory, *Trichoglossus haematodus*.

*Schnorkel is a German word which was applied to a special 'breathing tube' developed by German U-boats to renew air supplies without surfacing in World War II. As used by skin divers the word is now spelt without the 'ch'. But in the early days of my underwater adventures the diary uses the German spelling.

The cemetery was a lovely place, brighter and gayer than the general run of such, full of gay plants with the parrots overhead, and butterflies all over the place. But, oh, the ages on the little grey stones, so many below 20. If there is any comfort in the surroundings of a grave, then certainly the cemetery at Lae should provide it.

Our young guide took us to a quarry almost in the town, if Lae can be so described. There were two ponds – one large and one small, said to contain crocodiles though we saw none. On the larger pond were half a dozen ducks, and I had a moment of excitement and I put the glasses on them, but rather dully they turned out to be *superciliosa* (the local Grey Duck). I had hoped to see tree ducks at least. There were also quite a lot of Little Grebes which looked just like the Australian Dabchick. On the small pond behind us was a single white egret with yellow bill. We filmed a rather lovely and moderately oblivious butterfly and a dragonfly with scarlet body, and we found some pretty little toads down at the water's edge. The quarry was in line with the runway of the airdrome and a continuous stream of aircraft came in to land, maybe six or seven DC3s. There was talk that Lae had at one time been the busiest airport in the world and was still the third busiest in Australasia. Anyway it seemed quite busy then.

When we got back Charles and I decided to film some doodoos in the hotel garden. We started by taking out the large stick-insect which promptly flew off into the nearest tree. So we turned to the small mantis which Charles had found in the garden after breakfast. And then began the mantis saga. I had both mantises – the small green one and the large brown one which I had caught in the gents' lavatory in the morning – in a bunched-up piece of mosquito netting. I was trying to get the small one to the entrance, but the large one came too, and suddenly, even under the pressure of the netting the male found himself near the female, seized her, and copulation began. I did not immediately realise what was happening and still tried to pull him away from her but it was impossible. He had grabbed her like a vice, and almost at once the abdomen twisted round. Both insects have a pair of feelers at the end of the abdomen, which are used at this time for mutual location.

We filmed the couple walking over Sensitive Plants and then we took them upstairs again and I put them back in my mosquito net. Before dinner Phil saw them separated again but when we went to bed they were together but the male was headless. Could she have eaten her husband's head while he was perched on her back, or did the cannibalism take place when they became detached, after which the headless male proceeded to further copulation?

Next morning the male was still quite 'alive', still gripping the female and the abdomen still working and contracting. During our landing at Goroka on the way to Nondugl we filmed them. The female was trying to escape from the male – indeed she had done so in the camera box, but if placed in contact with her the male resumed his position and copulation began again.

Two days later the male was still moving although no longer attached to the female. He knew it if he was placed on his back and the legs struggled until he was turned over when they stopped struggling. He was by now very sluggish. This was about 54 hours after copulation began and 50 hours after he had lost his head.

We tried offering him to the female who was obviously hungry, but although he still moved she was not interested. A beetle was grabbed at once followed immediately by two grasshoppers. It seems therefore that the murder of the husband is a 'ceremonial' affair.

In the evening Charles and I went into the garden with his torch to look for nocturnal doodoos. Charles showed me how creatures' eyes showed up if you held the torch against your forehead. The lawn was covered with large toads whose eyes glowed red. Pinpoints of white light turned out to be tiny spiders whose eyes were amazingly reflective. A moth's eyes showed brightly in a tree.

When we got back to the 'arbour' we saw a very large hawk-moth hanging on a light. Near it was a gecko stalking a smaller moth, which it caught from behind. The moth fluttered and the gecko's head was rattled about but a little later we heard its triumph call when presumably it had finished eating the moth. I fetched some mosquito net and, putting a table upside down on a chair, Charles climbed up and the great hawk-moth dropped off into the net. On a leaf quite near was another of the same species but even larger – probably a female. Unfortunately, although Charles got her onto his hand, she took off and was lost. We found yet another hawk-moth in the arbour, rather like a Pine Hawk, but it eluded capture. The one we had caught was like a very large brown Oleander Hawk with yellow underwings. The head and eyes were enormous. I put it in the mosquito net over my bed and during the night the female mantis attacked it twice. I finally had to persuade it to go under the bed.

FRIDAY 14 DECEMBER
We left early for the flight to Nondugl. At the airport Charles had Customs difficulties. It appears that we had not been properly cleared on Wednesday evening, and the Customs Officer now wanted a deposit of £250 on the value of Charles' cameras and film. Honour was finally satisfied with the gloriously illogical arrangement that Charles was to leave one half of his Letter of Credit as guarantee of the deposit! Then we boarded our DC3 freighter with a great pile of furniture and other freight in the centre and a bench of seats along one side only. There were six passengers including us.

It was a calm flight – being early in the day – and our first landing was at Goroka, already in the highlands at several thousand feet. It was cool here, and delightfully informal. We sat near the aircraft while some of the freight was unloaded, and filmed the mating mantises. During the

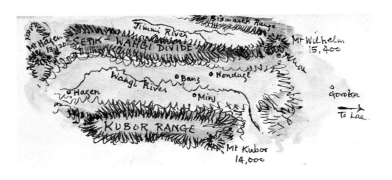

half hour we were there a three engined Junkers 52 flew in, and a few minutes later out again. It was airborne in about 100 yards. This was one of the war-time machines, but it was in the prototype that I had made my first flight in an air liner – and I think my second flight ever – from Munich to Berlin in about 1932. Having talked to the pilot at Goroka he invited me up to the cockpit on the next leg of the flight. This was through steep country, along narrow valleys and low over passes where round native grass huts lined the crests of knife edge ridges. The whole country was thickly wooded here, and then suddenly a great wide valley stretched out in front of us. This was the Wahgi Valley, bounded by high mountain ranges on either side. It is about eight miles wide and consists mostly of open grassland. The loading of the plane was such that we had to pass our destination in order to get rid of our cargo before we could get into (or more important, the plane could get out of) the shorter runway at Nondugl. Thus our next port of call was Minj. Here we wandered away and I found some small creeping tomatoes going bad in an unkempt flower bed on the far side of the runway. They were the size of marbles and very good. There were quite a lot of busy looking white folk clustering round the plane as it was unloaded, with their wives and even a small baby in a pram.

All these runways are on the sloping shelves of the valley so that, whatever the wind, you land up hill and take off down hill. Half an hour later we took off and flew across the valley to Banz. We were hardly airborne before we were coming in again with the flaps down.

Banz had some more decorative, or at least more highly decorated, natives with great crescents of pearl shell through the septum of the nose and head-dresses of extended birds' wings – notably Barn Owls. One had a head-dress of cassowary feathers. There was an apparently half-caste boy with straight hair and dark skin but strikingly handsome. It was amusing to see these natives, all in their finery, pumping fuel into the tanks of the Dakota – amusing enough to be filmed.

The next stop was Hagen (pronounced to rhyme with bargain) which was larger than the others. There were big crowds of natives including a pale skinned one – leucistic, like a 'white Pinkfoot'. These natives are rather fearsome of visage – real wild men to look at. They have big drooping noses, thick lips, a deep notch where nose meets forehead. They wear only a belt on which hangs in front, a small net in the case of men, a fringe in the case of the women. Behind, the men wear a branch of *Pandanus*. Round their arms they often wear a woven band – made of cane or grass. In their hands they carry either an axe or a jungle knife. They are certainly fearsome until they smile. But they are gay and cheerful – though apparently without much loyalty and no good, we are told, in a tight place.

At Hagen the District Commissioner named Skinner came up and introduced himself. He told us his son had shot two Salvadori's Ducks with one shot – at eight years old. Skinner called over and introduced Ned Blood as the most knowledgeable person on ducks. He had been at Nondugl for some years. He said the only other ducks in the Wahgi Valley were Black Ducks, but that over on the Sepik there were 'lots of ducks including the Harlequin Duck'. Just then the plane was about to take off, so I never had a chance to find out what the New Guinea Harlequin Duck might be.

Nondugl.

I liked Nondugl the moment we were down. It was near enough to the northern foothills to have dominating hill features as a backcloth and somehow the broken country and the trees made the whole landscape just right. Nondugl was at once apparent as a lovely place. Frank Pemble Smith, manager of the station, arrived on a motorbike, and soon after a tractor and trailer arrived with Fred Shaw-Meyer to greet us. These were two very different men. 'Pem' thickset, self-assured, a pioneer, an Empire builder. Fred, tall, quiet, a scientific collector and ornithologist, now in his late 60's, burned dark by the sun, slow of speech, courteous of manner.

We went down to the Fauna Section which is Fred's zoo. He showed us round and it was an utterly delightful afternoon. The zoo, perhaps

Salvadori's Ducks.

better called the sanctuary, covers about 10 acres. It consists of three ponds formed by dams across a shallow cleft. Around these are lawns and flower-beds and flowering shrubs and bamboos, and dotted about are eight or nine aviaries beautifully planted up and somehow fitting most appropriately into the whole landscape. The collection consists of about 200 birds of paradise, some bower birds, parrots, three cassowaries, and twenty Salvadori's Ducks and a dozen or more tree kangaroos of three different kinds.

It was not unnatural perhaps that we could hardly wait to see the Salvadori's Ducks. Fred took us in the enclosure round the top pond and there at once was a pair of them about 15 yards away at the edge of some sedges. The bird was more striking than I had expected. The yellowish flesh coloured bill with no black tip was prominent and there was quite a sharp dividing line between the dark brown head and the pale creamy yellow ground colour of the spotted breast. The barring of back and flanks however was less precise and neat than I had painted in my illustration for Jean Delacour's *The Waterfowl of the World*. Nevertheless it was quite a handsome bird. More surprising were its movements. It swam with a rapid jerky backwards and forwards movement of the head, caused apparently by nervousness, or watchfulness, and the tail which is very long, was carried at times almost vertically. After a while we saw the display. It was the only true courtship display behaviour we saw, though later we saw 'dashing and diving'. The male's head is stretched up and moved only slightly in unison with a whistle. The whole of this is reminiscent of the shelducks. The female meanwhile pumps her head up and down violently emitting a series of croaking barks which are clearly analogous to the Mallard's quack.

In the next few days we had ample opportunity to become familiar with the bird. In feeding it frequently 'up-ended' like any other dabbling duck. But it dived much more readily and went under from a 'low-in-the-water' posture without making a ripple. It is obviously a very accomplished diver. It is also of skulking habit and largely nocturnal, as Fred told us of various occasions when he had seen them about the pens at night. Later I had a chance to handle three live birds – two males and one female. The female's head was much paler on the crown and forehead, and more streaked. The wings are quite short, but the speculum is very well marked, though the green is only on the inner half. The line of the white tips of the secondaries is extended to the tips of the inner primaries.

From all that we saw of the bird I have no doubt that it is a dabbling duck and should correctly be in the tribe *Anatini*, though certainly not just another teal like the Cape Teal or Chile Teal. It is quite highly specialised for living in mountain streams, the long tail and the jerky head movements are reminiscent of *Merganetta*. The eye is rather further forward than in most dabbling ducks, suggesting the requirement for increased binocular vision in order to catch living prey. Fred thinks that tadpoles form the basis of their diet in the wild state. He feeds his tadpoles during most of the year, but in the wet season, when they are harder to get he augments this with meat – sometimes tripe.

Later in the day a Land Rover was sent over from Minj for our use (though as we afterwards discovered it was really for the use of some botanists who arrived later on(!)).

Breast + flank feathers of
SALVADORI'S DUCK

♂ whistles

♀ head pumping accompanied
by harsh creaking bark
analagous to quack.

Commonest form of
display.

This is a correction of the bird at top
opposite.

It is not a display
posture but the
normal surviving
position when
disturbed and
nervous, with the
head moving
backwards +
forwards like a
moorhen.

Salvadori's Ducks.

SATURDAY 15 DECEMBER

In the morning the boys brought in a young phalanger on a large branch. This was an adorable ball of chocolate-coloured fur with a tail which was bushy for half its length and bare for the other half which was prehensile. It climbed about its branch quite actively, hanging by its tail, peering at one with boot button eyes. It could easily be stroked but it took a nip of my finger as soon as I gave it the chance. This animal was the Silky Phalanger, *Phalanger vestitus*. We filmed him overlooking the gorge at the back of the zoo and then filmed the enchanting tree kangaroos.

Later Pem took us for a drive in the Land Rover round the estate. We went first up the slope to the site of a new Training College which is to be built. From here we looked down the easy sloping side of the valley across pastures dotted with *Casuarina* trees. The Hallstrom Trust ground is a narrow strip half a mile wide and two miles long. At right angles to it further up the Wahgi Valley, and detached by a couple of miles, is another narrow strip of about 800 acres. These lands are bounded by native holdings. The native population is very large and yet one is hardly aware of it. Nowhere can a dense human population blend more perfectly with its environment. The little low grass houses are hidden away in the shade. Only occasional glimpses of banana trees, or sugar cane, or the squared beds of sweet potato on the hillside show that the landscape is subject to man's influence. There are 6,000 Awahgas in the immediate vicinity of Nondugl. Minj – only 17 miles by road and 5 by air across the river – has a different native tribe. The road we took to see the detached part of the estate was the main road from Lae to Hagen. This road has only been open for about 18 months. It has been built by the owners of the land through which it passes. Pem surveyed and built the section on either side of Nondugl. It has some excellent pieces of engineering, including a cutting through the steep rocks of a river bank. It was dug in two months by native labour and without explosives. It is about 20 feet deep, 60 yards long, one track wide with vertical rock walls. Even now no heavy freight can come through by road. The whole of the development is still supplied entirely by air. Hagen, Minj, Banz, villages now, towns of the future have been built from supplies carried by DC3s. It is an exciting thought.

SUNDAY 16 DECEMBER

Charles got up early and recorded the howling of the wild dogs. The pair of New Guinea Wild Dogs kept in the zoo are the most delightful animals. They look like a cross between a fox and a Dingo. (We filmed them later.) I think they might well become a highly successful new breed, if properly introduced. Phil and I were also up early and filming Salvadori's Ducks on the lower pond before breakfast.

Later in the morning we filmed the female mantis eating grasshoppers (she had refused the still moving but headless male). The first doodoos were brought in by the natives – mostly tree frogs. A lot of tadpoles are brought in daily for feeding the ducks. There were at least three species among these – two of which had sucker mouths with which they attached themselves to the buckets and basins containing them. Another doodoo brought in was a young Red Bird of Paradise. Fred and I were filmed feeding it on fresh ants' 'eggs' on paw-paw, with a bamboo spatula. While we were doing this a wild female Lauterbach's Bower Bird, *Chlamydera lauterbachi*, flew along the *Casuarina* hedge.

But the main occupation of the morning was filming the Salvadori's Ducks. They behaved fairly well, although they usually retired in the shade before displaying. Later, in the afternoon, Phil took some stills from the same hide, while Charles filmed Gowra Crowned Pigeons.

MONDAY 17 DECEMBER

The day's objective was to see Salvadori's Ducks in the wild. For this we were to go up the Ganoigle (pronounced Gonigel), a river flowing fast past Nondugl from the north. We set off in the Land Rover and drove as far as the road went – a timber road cut for getting out logs. Our guides were Aroba or Roba – the Pemble Smith's house boy and two young lads who worked for Fred Shaw-Meyer called Aggis and Kahboon who were supposed to have located some ducks the day before but hadn't found any. It was still grey and cloudy when we got to the end of the road, and indeed it remained so all day. The road ended at the river and we were supposed to ford at this point, but the first of our band of a dozen or more natives who had assembled found the crossing too deep.

So, having removed shoes and socks it was decided we should try a few yards upstream. This few yards developed into quite a climb along a cliff face, over a ridge, through a *Pandanus* swamp and eventually to the river about a quarter of a mile further up. We squelched in our bare feet through the mud pools along a scarcely detectable path.

At last a crossing place was found and Charles filmed us all wading thigh-deep in the white waters, making a chain across the river. Once across I filmed Charles following. On the far side we put our shoes and socks on again and started up the side of the river again. Soon, however, we joined a more major path, leaving Roba to follow the river and report if any ducks were seen. We met natives along this path, which wound through high timber, past native grass huts and gardens, up into the moss forest. Here, mosses and lichen grew on many of the trees. There was surprisingly little in the way of animal life. The only bird I saw to identify was a Yellow-faced Honeyeater. It was quite pleasant climbing and the boys were carrying all our camera equipment, coats and so on. By now we were quite hot although the valley was still overcast. But the cloud had been receding up hill ahead of us, so that we were never walking in mist. Eventually we reached a bridge across the river and not long afterwards the stream divided.

At this point Pem suggested that we stop for lunch sending the 'monkeys' (small boys) on ahead to find ducks. It was an excellent lunch of grilled chops, tomato sauce, excellent home made biscuits, banana and pineapple. During, before and after lunch various small doodoos were seen and I filmed two colour phases of a fine balsam – *Impatiens* sp., one of which was purplish pink and the other orange scarlet. A rather nice beetle with yellow tail was brought in by the 'monkeys' and I watched a very beautiful red, yellow and blue tiger-moth trying to find somewhere to lay an egg. She landed for a moment on my shorts. After laying an egg under a very large leaf, the culmination of a couple of minutes of hovering, the insect swept up and away with unexpected speed.

The boys returned after lunch, standing round the fire to keep warm. They had seen no ducks. They now said that it was no good up here in the rainy season, the river was too swift, the ducks had all gone down to the swamps along the Wahgi. 'Yes', Roba said, he knew the duck well. It was called Koorang or Koorund. We got them all to say it, and finally it was Toolund. I did a drawing for them and they all agreed. There were two kinds down on the Wahgi – the big ones which were dark and the little ones which were paler. If we were to go down to the Wahgi he would show us that he was not telling lies. All this was communicated in New Guinea Pidgin which is just understandable when Pem talks it, but quite incomprehensible when spoken by the natives.

After lunch it seemed that nothing remained but to turn back, especially as the rain might soon be expected to start. We stayed on the main path which finally led down to the ford opposite the Land Rover. When we got there Pem and Charles were already across. It appeared that Pem had been swept off a rock and had fallen in completely, and that Charles had filmed the whole thing. They suggested that we should go a few hundred yards further down stream where there was a bridge. This we did and were met there by the Land Rover. Charles was wading about in the stream below to film the crossing of the bridge which consisted of three *Pandanus* trunks lashed together with vines, with a single branch like the prong of a fork as a hand rest for balancing. Once safely across the bridge we were soon embarked in the Land Rover with a mass of natives piled in the back with Charles and the cameras, and on our way down the valley to Nondugl.

During the night it rained and it rained, so that the next morning . . .

TUESDAY 18 DECEMBER

The cutting on the road was blocked by a landslide and our trip to the Wahgi had to be postponed. Instead we filmed and recorded the yodelling call by which news is passed round the valley. In this case the cry was to bring in 'buatang' ('buatang' is the Malay pidgin word for doodoos). The cry was answered and there should be a very nice recording of it. Then we rigged up a moss and orchid covered log and a *Pandanus* head behind Fred's house as a background for filming the various small animals which by now were coming in fairly well. One of the best was a huge web spider covering perhaps 8 inches with legs extended. It was dark grey with red and yellow markings and spun yellow silk of extraordinary toughness. Unfortunately, this first one brought in was missing two legs, but later we filmed a complete female with a much larger abdomen. There was a rather charming leaf grasshopper with a face like a bishop, a very large cicada with laced iridescent wings, several more mantises including an apterous larva with a turned-up tail. We established that cannibalism was certainly not the standard procedure in this species although a large one made half hearted attacks on a small one.

Several lizards had been brought in and the natives were strangely frightened of them. There were two species of skinks, the larger had recently changed its skin and was patterned with iridescent pink. Then they also brought a fine Agama with a crest of spines down the back of the neck and an immensely long tail. This beast although not very large must have been nearly 2′ 6″ long. The natives were scared stiff of him and said he would bite, which no doubt he would have done, but I soon tamed him down by handling him very gently and he was no trouble. Unfortunately he escaped before we had really finished filming him. We also filmed a medium sized dull brown tree frog and a very large *Rana* with a pointed nose. Altogether we filmed nine doodoo species in the day – and that was keeping at it pretty hard.

WEDNESDAY 19 DECEMBER

Pem and Phil and I made the trip to the Wahgi in the Land Rover, while Charles stayed behind to film birds of paradise and doodoos. It was a very hot sunny morning. We went down the main road for a few miles and then struck out along a ridge to the edge of the last ledge above the river. Here we looked across the bends of the meandering river, café-au-lait coloured after the rains. The river flowed fast, but there were some swamps which were the remains of ox-bows, old river channels. One of these which was almost overgrown was immediately below us and Roba suggested we should go down past a little homestead and its pigs and see if there were any ducks. Another ox-bow on the far side of the river had an egret beside it – *Egretta garzetta nigripes* and a couple of black dots which were almost certainly Black Ducks.

What would there be in the much thicker swamp below us? Accompanied by two little girls we got down to the edge of this swamp, but could find practically no vantage point from which we could see what

Wahgi Valley.

open water there was. A large bird in the distance flying over the river was pronounced to be a duck, but was in fact a cormorant. We saw a pair of rather pretty little shrikes with red backs. These were *Lanius schach stresemanni*. There was also a pale harrier-like hawk with black shoulders of which we saw two or three during the day. It is *Elanus coeruleus wahgiensis*. The 15 foot high reeds were full of little brown finches, the males with smart black heads – the Wahgi Munia, *Lonchura spectabilis wahgiensis*. Roba and a local who had joined us were sent to look for ducks on the next bit of swamp. It was half an hour later when our spirits were a bit low that conversational quacking began in the reeds quite close by. This was evidently a Black Duck, but it showed that there were ducks about.

We were now about 1,500 feet below Nondugl (5,500) and it was becoming very hot indeed. The prospect of a 500 feet steep climb back to the Land Rover was not inviting, but we decided to make a start, having persuaded the little girls to call to Roba. Half way up the hill we stopped to rest and were joined first by a very attractive 15 year old girl and then by a charming old man – father of all the children who came up – making a most peculiar and excited noise like 'Eeee-eeee-eeee' which was evidently an expression of extreme pleasure at meeting us. He was quite delightful. Roba explained his joy with the phrase 'Big fella master, big fella Mrs'. It is a commentary on the size of these natives that Phil should be regarded by them as 'Big fella Mrs' (at 5′ 3″).

We decided to have one more try at the Wahgi swamps by going round and over the bridge and then coming back on the other side so as to overlook the pool on which we had seen the pair of Black Ducks. So, extremely hot and deliquescent, we got back to the vehicle and set off up stream towards the bridge. One of the nicest features of the roads is that they are planted with flowering shrubs, especially plants with red leaves. Among them is a pink flowered balsam with red leaves.

62

The Wahgi bridge is a suspension bridge on wire cable which produces a wonderful wave action as the vehicle advances across it. In a garden we saw a tiny dark quail, *Turnix maculosa giluwensis*. Then on to Minj where we turned back down a track leading to the river again.

But the trouble with the track was pig fences. The first one we came to had two natives beside it, and Pem decided we should dismantle it; the natives were a bit sullen about it but eventually they helped Roba with the job. Two more fences were dismantled and then we came to a stream with a *Pandanus* trunk bridge and the car could go no further. Then began an endless walk along a black single track footpath between hedges of *Crotaleria anagyroides*, a shrubby yellow leguminous plant with leaves rather like laburnum. The flowers are about the same size too, but on a spike instead of hanging. Frequently we thought we were getting near the river only to find that another long stretch of level path opened out in front of us. At one place where there was a dip in the path we came upon a most colourful muster of a dozen or more natives with fine head plumes and looking magnificent against the mountains at the crest of the rise. We wondered if this was their everyday wear, or had the bush telegraph given warning of our coming; certainly we had heard no yodelling shouts.

Salvadori's Red Bird of Paradise.

In the bushes beside the path we came upon some very beautiful little birds with sickle shaped bills. They were very small – about the size of blue tits and mostly blackish except for the head and throat which were brilliant scarlet. These were honeyeaters – *Myzomela adolphinae*.

At last we came within sight of the three trees which we had marked from across the valley and a few minutes later we were climbing the last ridge to look over at the swamp below. At first we could see no birds on the water at all. The pool was two or three hundred feet below us and as many yards away from us. But we sat down with the glasses and quite soon I saw a Black Duck, then another and later a third. Over on a more overgrown part of this marsh were two Swamp Hens, *Porphyrio* sp. and beyond on a small stream two more Black Ducks swam into the open. A little later the egret which had been there in the morning reappeared. Flitting over the water were several Willy Wagtails and screaming down among the trees on the slope were some little parrots – probably *Neopsittacus pullicauda*.

Honeyeater –
Myzomela adolphinae.

As we sat there an extremely exciting moment arrived. From the rushes on the right of the pool swam out two small ducks. Any small ducks there should have been Salvadori's but these quite certainly were not. These were Grey Teal, *Anas gibberifrons*. As they swam out across the water they passed behind a tree in the topmost branches of which sat a bird looking large and prominent and reddish. This was a male Red Bird of Paradise (*Paradisaea apoda salvadorii*) though not in full colour. As we identified him the Grey Teal swam behind him.

It was one of those great moments in ornithology when two exciting things happen at once and there is not enough time to think of both. After a while the Red Bird flew away and the Grey Teal went ashore on the left hand bank of the pond. There they preened and finally went to sleep. They seemed to be stained reddish on the breast which was very pale. It was disappointing that they were not Salvadori's Ducks, but the Grey Teal has only been recorded once from the valley. No native

had ever reported *three* kinds of ducks in the Wahgi Valley. Evidently they did not differentiate between *waigiuensis* and *gibberifrons*. This immediately suggested that the swamp habitat for Salvadori's Duck was an error and at once the whole story began to make more sense.

Salvadori's Duck is a bird of highland streams and lakes. It is analogous in habit with the South American torrent ducks, and the long tail is an adaptation for the swift mountain streams. It has never lived in the Wahgi swamps nor is it likely to occur below 5,000 feet.

We saw two more birds from our look out point. A pair of coots *Fulica* sp. swam into view on the pool and twice we saw a chestnut brown pigeon, *Macropygia nigrirostris*, with greyish head and a long fairly wide reddish tail.

Macropygia nigrirostris.

The Brown Pigeon.

THURSDAY 20 DECEMBER

This was the day of the 'sing-sing'. Phil had a nasty septic place on her ankle. In spite of this she went riding with Pem in the morning while Charles and I filmed doodoos. Soon the natives were assembling in full regalia for the 'sing-sing' (chanting and dancing) which was to be laid on especially for us. There is no doubt that the head-dresses made largely from the plumes of birds of paradise are superbly colourful.

There is a striking variety in the form and structure of each head-dress. The most typical has a fan of plumes – virtually the whole bird stuffed and flattened onto a piece of bamboo which is then attached to the head band. Three forms of the genus *Paradisea* – all I believe races of *P. apoda* – were in evidence, the Lesser, brilliant yellow when fresh, whitish when faded, the Red Bird, a rich pinkish orange, and an intermediate one of which I saw only one skin. It had what Fred rightly described as 'glorious sunset tints'. The long tail feathers of the Princess Stephanie Bird were fairly common, but one head-dress had even longer ones from another species and some which were black and white from the Ribbon-tailed Bird. Across the forehead of several head-dresses were the 'breast-plate' feathers of the Magnificent Bird.

The wire spring tails attached to the red skins of the little King Bird I only saw once, and there was only one head-dress with the plumes of the Blue Bird, but many used the curious aural feathers of the King of Saxony Bird. Sometimes these were bent round to produce a circular motif, sometimes worn horizontally through the nose. Also worn through the nose were the blue tail feathers of the local kingfisher – with a little white oval at the tip, or the wing feathers of a parrot. Sometimes these horizontal plumes shared the pierced nasal septum with a large down-curved crescent of shell, or a round disc of shell.

One man, not dressed up for the sing-sing had a boar's tusk in his nose. Parrot plumes were also in evidence on one old chap, an ex-chief of the Awahga, deposed by the Administration, who was wearing the blue wing of a Red (South American) Macaw given to him by Hallstrom. It was interesting that the only false note of colour in all these head-dresses were some puce pink dyed feathers from Japan, which we were told were not at all liked by the natives. Their innate good taste saw to it that in all the others, form and colour were marvellously well blended. 'All the others' consisted of thirty of the thirty one men finally assembled for the dancing. The close decoration of the head-dresses consisted of bands round the forehead. Some of these were of small cowrie shells, others were of rows of brilliant green beetles encased in a network of woven grasses. Round the necks of some of the men were 'necklaces' of tails of the phalangers, furry for two thirds of their length and then bare skin at the tips.

When a good number of the dancers were assembled we set off for a special place half a mile away. On the way we met Phil and Pem on their horses (which did not much like the plumes). The actual performance of the dancers was a little disappointing. It was under the direction of the present chief who was dressed in a dirty shirt and shorts with an American peaked sports cap with a transparent green eyeshade under which, across his forehead, he wore the medal of chieftainship issued by the Administration. He flitted about, acting each part, like a producer at a dress rehearsal. Most of the dances were mock charges, but it seems that they never really got worked up and it was all a bit hot and a bit boring for them. However, in spite of that we got what should be some very fine pictures. We filmed from various angles, I at one time from a hollow dug for a banana tree, Charles from a huge timber platform which was brought up on a tractor about half way through the proceedings. At times the boys jiggled up and down in time with a drum carried by one of them which was shaped like an elongated egg-timer and covered with the skin of a monitor.

Although most of my film was taken of the dancers, I tried from time to time to record the hordes of women and children – and men, who were onlookers. These crowded round us in an odoriferous cluster. There is a very strong, a wholly characteristic, smell given off by these natives, which becomes almost overpowering when they are up wind or in bulk! Many of the onlookers had their faces asymmetrically painted – as indeed had the dancers. One red half, one black half; a red patch around one eye; yellow across the forehead; or an all coal black face, ending in a black beard – all these were quite common, and lent additional colour to what was really a marvellous scene. And at the same time we recorded the sound of the drum and the chanting.

By lunch time it seemed that we had had all we were going to get. Pem had promised them some money. When we got back to his office he gave me a bag of silver and through the window, as at a school prize giving, I presented each with 5 shillings. Only one of them, a youngish rather good looking one who had been rather sullen about the whole affair, appeared to check how much was being given and then to refuse to come up for his – on the ground, one supposed, that it was not enough. But when Pem asked him if he had had his yet, he immediately came up to get the money.

And so we assisted, if only in a small way, in the degradation towards the white man's level of the Awahga natives. There is nothing that Australian civilisation (or indeed any civilisation) can do to make the New Guinea native remotely more happy than he was before his existence was discovered. There is only one way in which the white man could play absolutely fair with the New Guinea natives and that would be by declaring huge areas completely out of bounds to any white men at all, and leaving them entirely alone. I have no doubt whatever that they are the better without us. But as this would be putting the clock back, and as the grasping stupidity of man is such that for all his loudly proclaimed ideals he cannot resist exploiting new lands without thought for their original inhabitants, the natives of these lovely highlands will be spoiled, debauched, and degraded by the processes of civilisation.

After lunch came more filming of doodoos and such until the rain came, after which I made a pencil drawing of the young (14 year old) house boy whose name was something like 'Oungl'. He sat very still, but dark skin with an HB pencil on foolscap is plain hard work, and the tone balance was pretty dicey by the end.

Phil's ankle had become very swollen and I began to be very worried about it. A nice chap called Frank, who is second in command at Noudugl and had once been a hospital assistant, came and gave her a shot of penicillin.

FRIDAY 21 DECEMBER

Phil's ankle more swollen. Frank thinks there is an abscess as well as a tropical ulcer. The original poisoning came from a scratched insect bite.

This was the day of our departure by the weekly DC3 mail plane. We were to be ready after lunch, so the morning was spent with birds of paradise and tree kangaroos. Charles was very patient – waiting in the aviaries with black and white film because of the overcast sky and finally getting good shots of Princess Stephanie's Bird, *Atrapia stephaniae ducalis*, and MacGregor's Bird, *Chemophilus macgregorii sanglimeus*, which used to be regarded as a bower bird and has a flowing orange yellow crest on an otherwise blackish bird. Meanwhile I turned my attention first to Lauterbach's Bower Bird and then to the Blue Bird, *Paradisea rudolphi margaritae*, and finally to the tree kangaroos who were much more enlightening than before. I got some very funny shots of the family which includes the now grown up twins, and mother with a smallish joey. If offered not very much carrot or lucerne they went through quite entertaining antics, pushing in each others' faces and grabbing. Charles joined me later. A small native boy had attached himself to me as camera-bearer and he and a group of half a dozen other children with two women made up a delighted audience making the high-pitched 'eeee-eeee-eeee' sound of pure enjoyment. Certainly the kangaroos were marvellous to watch. One mother, eating the tops of a carrot, allowed one leaf to fall down whereupon the joey grabbed it and had a mouthful before the mother pulled it away. Another joey had both hands gripping the edge of the pouch and suddenly out came a foot on which he then rested his chin in the most nonchalant manner.

After lunch we were told suddenly that a Norseman would be with us in 15 minutes. Frightful panic as we had an hour's worth of packing to get Charles' gear properly stowed. Then we heard that the Norseman had gone somewhere else – panic over. By about 3.30 a plane buzzed the station, and was obviously for us, so down we went with all our gear in the Land Rover to find a De Havilland Beaver, pilot named Brown, with a red-bearded passenger already aboard named Crouch. Glancing to the eastward Brown said 'My God, it *has* clagged up hasn't it', and we saw the Dakota bound for Madang to the north, which had been circling to get out of the Wahgi Valley, turn back towards Minj. We loaded the gear aboard, said goodbye to Pem, and climbed into the back seat, three in a row with Phil in the middle.

The way out of the Wahgi Valley to Lae, by way of Goroka is through a winding pass. This had been quite hair-raising on the way up in good visibility. Now a huge inky black cloud lay right across the pass with a curtain of rain below it. We flew on towards it hoping for a way through. 'Just a wall of water', said Brown, then he turned to us and said 'I hope they've got plenty of beds at Nondugl.' For a bit we weaved to and fro looking for a passage through the hills. We remembered being told that the Duke of Edinburgh had not been allowed to go to the highlands because the flying was too dangerous. Brown was now doing steep turns and it had become rather bumpy and turbulent. He said 'We'll just have one more look', and I said 'We'd much rather go back if you have any doubts about it at all', to which he replied 'Oh, we won't take any risks, don't worry.'

I was pleased to see that he had been circling occasionally in order to make sure that the cloud didn't close in behind us and cut off our retreat. It was the only thing which was worrying me at all. But the whole aspect of the sky and the dim black hills disappearing into the black cloud was so forbidding that one couldn't blame Phil for being alarmed by it all.

Eventually it became obvious that we weren't going to get through and so we turned back. On reaching Nondugl we flew round the valley where we thought Pem had gone to collect the botanists and then landed, to find Pem already there with the Land Rover. While we were there the Junkers 52, with a little fat pilot called Bob something or other, who was clearly a character, flew in with an enormous American Catholic Missionary. He was going to push through to Goroka, but by now it was too late for us to go to Lae even if he had found an improvement, so we made our plan to start at 6.00 the next morning and we had confirmation that the DC4 would be held for us.

Then back up the hill to the homestead. Frank came to give Phil some more penicillin, her fourth injection (250,000 units a time in oil). The ankle is still swollen but apparently giving her less pain. Supper was a buffet affair, very good, but not till nearly 9.00.

SATURDAY 22 DECEMBER

Up at 5.00, another injection for Phil, the fifth, and it seems that the stuff has worked – three cheers for Sir Alexander Fleming. The swelling is definitely down, and there is much relief from anxiety. One trouble affecting our flight was the possibility of low cloud (morning mist) lying in the valley. There was some in the floor of the valley but Nondugl strip seemed to be just clear. Fred Shaw-Meyer was standing at the entrance of the Fauna Section to wave us farewell and to thank me for a drawing of a pair of Salvadori's Ducks which I had left for him at our false departure. I have an inescapable conviction that he is a great man, and with it all a charming modesty and courtesy – a manner rare in this part of the world. The saddest thing is that he has not recorded enough of his unique knowledge and experience. Certainly his zoo with its beautiful gardens, pools and aviaries, his 200 birds of paradise, his ducks and tree kangaroos, parrots and cassowaries, is a piece of creative genius which has a rare perfection about it. He has much in common with John Yealland [ex-Curator of the Wildfowl Trust, and of Birds at London Zoo], the quiet conscientious approach, the knowledge – without 'knowing it all', the patient good manners. Meeting him was one of the nicest features of our New Guinea trip.

A large black rain cloud still hung over the eastern end of the Wahgi Valley. To be sure it was nothing like so black as it had been the night before, but it was enough to arouse gloomy forebodings. As it turned out, however, it was nothing but a small shower half way down the valley. We climbed into the sunrise, we flew close to great wooded bluffs, and skirted thin white patches of cloud, and eventually came out into the Markham Valley with a clear run down hill to Lae. We did the journey in under the hour and were in time to catch the DC4 to Port Moresby and Cairns. The heat at Lae, Port Moresby and Cairns was all pretty over-powering after the comparative cool of the Highlands.

Queensland coast
at Cairns.

It was after 1.00pm when we arrived at Cairns hoping to find Vincent and Carol Serventy. But they were not there. Instead we were met by a Mr Reid who had been detailed to look after us. He had been given a list of things we were to see and film by Vin – this included White Pygmy Geese, Fiddler and Soldier Crabs, breeding sea birds etc. etc. Meanwhile he had arranged a reception at one of the finest homes in Cairns for afternoon tea that very afternoon. There was to be a day on the Cook Highway, a day on the table land, a day at Michaelmas Cay – a breeding island of Sooty and Noddy Terns and half an hour on the way back at the famous observatory on Green Island. Our hearts sank. Our Christmas was not to be the holiday we'd hoped for, but a round of tours to a tight schedule.

The trip to the bird island was official, by invitation of the Cairns Harbour Board with a party of 20 or more, including the press. We were like sardines in the taxi, what with all our luggage but the cab driver – a member of the Natural History Society of which Reid was an officer (Dr Flecker the President, having gone south a few days before) – was keen to show off Cairns, which it must be admitted had a fine show of flowering trees, especially the Scarlet Poinsiana and the orange Flame of the Forest.

While we had lunch Reid went off to telephone to a doctor so that Phil's foot could have professional attention. He came back to say that the doctor had gone to bed and that he had said she didn't need any more penicillin till 7.00 pm. As the doctor had not seen it, nor had details of the treatment given, this seemed a pretty incredible report by our standards, but apparently is quite normal practice in Australia. Not taking this for an answer we sent the man to try another doctor but he had no success, so I decided that we should go to the hospital. On the way we stopped to send Christmas cables from the GPO, a huge and imposing edifice with only one clerk behind the counter, because of Christmas hols.

In the evening Mr Reid brought his son Hughie, a rather nice looking boy of 20 who runs a 'Termite and Wood-borer business' from which one supposes that he is 'against' rather than 'for' these animals! We had a useful talk and gradually altered most of the plans until the future looked more rosy. We decided that more time should be spent on the Barrier Reef and less on Cook Highway and Fiddler Crabs. And so next morning it was agreed that Hughie should take us to Double Island where we could explore a coral reef which Reid père assured us was just as good as Green Island or any other part of the Barrier Reef.

CHAPTER 4

Australia: Queensland and the Great Barrier Reef

DIARY 1 1956

SUNDAY 23 DECEMBER – TUESDAY 25 DECEMBER

For a part of these three days I have been in a new world. Nothing I have done in natural history in all my life has stirred me quite so sharply as my first experience of skin-diving on a coral reef. Konrad Lorenz said, when I saw him in Bavaria in September, that this was one thing 'you *must* do before you die' – and now I have done it, or rather started to do it. The dramatic threshold which is crossed as soon as one first puts one's face mask below the surface is, to a naturalist nothing less than staggering in its impact. Much has been written about the scarcely exploited new continent of the ocean; I have read these descriptions in the works of Cousteau and Diolé, and yet I was unprepared for the visionary revelation when I first saw the real thing. I must try to describe it chronologically and in some detail, but the effect on my mind is still rather kaleidoscopic and bewildering.

First it should be explained that the adventure falls into four chapters and an appendix – and by the way I have no hesitation in using the word 'adventure', for this type of swimming cannot fail to be high adventure; nothing less, for any naturalist, indeed for any imaginative person who has never done it before. The four chapters were four separate dives – two on the first day and one each on the next two. The appendix is two visits to the Underwater Observatory on Green Island. As befits such a sequence each chapter was a little bit more exciting and more moving than the one before. The final effect was overwhelming, so that in spite of trials and tribulations with ill-designed equipment, and intense discomforts arising therefrom, I cannot see how I can escape from its lure. I am already an addict and I have not yet used an aqualung.

Chapter I began when Hughie Reid came to fetch us in a beat up Vanguard estate car with no back seat. We drove north to a beach to pick up a boat which we put on top of the car and then drove yet further north to Trinity beach off which lay Double Island.

We launched the boat and Hughie rowed us across to the edge of the reef. Hughie couldn't explain where we were going or why to one spot rather than another. Nor did he bother to mention that the water was unusually muddy because of the recent cyclone which had struck further down the coast but whose repercussions had set up strong winds in this area.

Charles, who has done quite a lot of skin diving, knew that it should be better than this, but when I slipped over the side of the boat and adjusted my mask and snorkel I looked vertically down at just visible coral about 5 or 6 feet below me and saw fish going comfortably about their business among it. In those first few minutes I saw a dozen kinds of fish; I was shown the blue and purple edges of the mantle of the clam – a curly line of colour which narrowed in sudden jerks at the approach of my shadow and I had my first chance to differentiate between hard coral and soft coral. There were too many different kinds of coral for them to be catalogued in the mind, each and every one seemed different from its neighbour.

I borrowed Charles's New Guinea arrow which he was using as a probe, and touched some of the soft coral. In one large 'bush' of flesh coloured soft coral when I touched a twig the whole branch drew in its tentacles and the fingers looked darker and thinner. There were about four branches in the bush which, in my ignorance, I supposed to be four corporate coral 'animals'. Already I was having some difficulty with my mask and the mouthpiece of my snorkel. Charles was saying that if this was the Barrier Reef it wasn't a patch on Indonesia, but still Hughie did not suggest that it was unusually cloudy.

We went ashore on Double Island. It was blazing hot and one could hardly walk on the beach. There were little mouse holes in the sand and these were apparently the homes of sand crabs. I dug one out. He was surprisingly large and handsome with eyes on long pointed stalks which could be carried horizontally or raised comically one at a time. We took our lunch across the point to a little table under a tree beside a tumble-down shack, and ate sandwiches and water melon.

Our picnic place
on Double Island.

After lunch we decided to dive on the other side of the point (Chapter II of my new adventure). There was not much coral here but there were rocks along the steep shore. The water was much clearer, so much so that I could see the fish quite a long way ahead – say 20 feet or more. This gave much more of a side view and less of a top view of the fish than I had had before. But the absence of coral was more than compensated for by the fish which were more in number and in kinds than earlier. It was here that I saw my first *Chaetodon*, a square fish with a long snout and a beautiful zig-zag pattern – otherwise known as a butterfly fish. There seem to be a lot of different kinds – slightly different. To what extent this indicates different species, I have still to discover. Maybe there is a sex difference or polymorphism or just plain individual variation*. Growing on the rocks here was a curious shell with corrugated edges and clustering so as almost to cover some of the large stones.

There must have been at least 20 different kinds of fish round these rocks. The largest and most exciting I saw was a parrot fish. This is, I think, a wrasse. I saw two together, one larger and more brightly coloured than the other. The mouth is parrot-like, the colours are green and blue and red and the bright blue pectoral fins flap up and down just like a parrot in flight. In fact it is a very good vernacular name.

I was having quite a lot of trouble with the rubber mouthpiece of my snorkel but so intense was the enjoyment of what I was watching that I hardly noticed that my lips were being quite badly damaged by it. I swam between stratified near-vertical sheets of rock – I was in the nave of a leaning church. Although there was a slight swell I did not feel in serious danger of being swept onto them. The only times that I scratched

*I was later to find out that there is no external distinction between sexes, virtually no polymorphism, and that in fact up to fifteen or more different species of butterfly fish may be found on the same reef.

my fingers was when I tried to hold onto a rock in order to adjust my mask and snorkel. I chased a small fish up a rock passage and finally he went to ground under a stone. Later I found a shoal of tiny sardine type fish, and showed them to Charles. We cornered them against the shore and they dashed past us. In the shallows near the rocks were quite large dark blennies.

The last excitement was a shoal of about 20 round fish like vertical dinner plates, about 8 or 10 ins across which stayed in a decorative and sociable cluster about a foot above the rocks. They were brown and marbled and their sociability was vastly impressive. I think it was this shoal which was quite slow moving and often stopped which suddenly showed me the immense possibilities of all these fish in terms of comparative ethology.

Only the intense pain in my lips made it possible for me to stop cruising among the fish. The greater clarity of the water on this side of the island had opened up new vistas, and cruising in the very shallow water had a rather distant association in my mind with a bathing delight of my early youth when I enjoyed cruising in a shallow sandy pool of warm water pulling myself forward with hands on the bottom.

A very curious feature of swimming with a snorkel is that although one's eyes are only an inch or two below the surface, there is no feeling of being on the edge of the world one sees. On the contrary one feels very much part of the scene, and of course one *is* in among the fish, for one's hand reaches out towards them, and some are hardly scared by it and move quietly only a foot or so in front; one's feet sink down to the rock or the coral below and the nearest fishes dive for cover into the crannies. It is as new a sensation as gliding or skating, and with it all is the almost agonising thought to a naturalist of how much there is to learn before one can begin to know or use all that one sees. And above all there is the incredible beauty of it.

MONDAY 24 DECEMBER

Christmas Eve, and an early start. We were collected by the Secretary of the Cairns Harbour Board and conveyed to the harbour where a fine launch was waiting and soon we were off to the reef. Including us and two or three journalists, there were about twenty people on board.

It took $3\frac{1}{2}$ hours to get to Michaelmas Cay, past Upola Cay. As we approached we saw first Sooty Terns, next Noddy Terns (mostly immature) and also a single frigate-bird. The island is very small, two acres of rough grass and marram above a dazzling white beach.

This was my first introduction to the tropical terns: the Noddies which are sooty and Sooties which are not – indeed they are very handsomely marked, and inappropriately named. The top of the island was indeed a remarkable sight.

The Noddies were nesting on the marram and *Mesembryanthemum* sward – three nests to the square yard. The Sooties were in thick masses but not nesting. On the far side of the island was a round patch of white – about 100 Crested Terns on their nests in a six or seven yard circle. There may have been 60–80 thousand birds (certainly not a million as we had been told) and we duly filmed and tape-recorded them, which took about an hour, and made our hosts happy.

Now the decks were cleared for Chapter III of my underwater adventure. Putting on the mask and snorkel was agonisingly painful. My mouth was now swollen greatly and my lips were raw inside, but somehow I managed to get started and from the moment that I dipped the goggles under the water I was too fascinated to notice my discomforts.

The water here had a totally new clarity so that Chapters I and II were blurred and muddy preludes to a crystalline brilliance which I had never believed possible. It was as if the water were air – or so it seemed. This was particularly true in the shallow water where the coral began about 20 yards off shore. The next thing I noticed was that the fish were all quite different from those I had seen at Double Island – perhaps not all, but certainly most of them.

Almost at once I saw the first 'blue fish'. There were two kinds – one about 5 inches long in which the male had an orange yellow tail and the female was all blue. They lived in pairs and their blue was of such brilliance that it appeared iridescent like a butterfly wing. The other kind was smaller with no orange tail and of a slightly different shape though the blue was no less brilliant. These lived in shoals and were not, I think, the young of the larger species. When I saw the first shoal of a dozen or so I found myself exclaiming with astonishment out loud – it was a sort of shout of joy at seeing something so incredibly beautiful. I was to discover much later that these two 'blue fish' belonged to different genera – they were *Pomacentrus coelestis*, the Neon Damsel, and *Chromis caerulea*, the Blue-green Chromis.

Breeding colony of Sooty Terns at Michaelmas Cay.

73

Charles swam with me for a good deal of the time. We found some huge clams – two I think – which were not much less than 3 feet long. Then there were the deep ultramarine blue starfish. Charles dropped one into a big clam which closed convulsively, but without pinching the starfish, so that he later retrieved it. In deeper water the numbers of fish were greater but there was still nothing to compare in beauty with the two blue fish. One of the small disc shaped fish had bold black and white vertical bands and a long white streamer from its dorsal fin. And so gradually we swam out until we came to the launch. I had been swimming in a shirt so as not to get sunburned too much. I was now fairly tired, as we had been swimming for about an hour. We had seen nothing big in the way of fish but, oh so many different small ones, such profusion, such variety! My mouth was very painful so I decided to climb out on a rope which was looped over the side.

In due course we were under way and heading for Green Island. This is quite a different kind of island. It is much larger than Michaelmas Cay – about 32 acres, inhabited, tree-covered and has a jetty at the end of which is the Underwater Observatory. The above-water-part of this Observatory is as trippery and vulgar as one would expect to meet in any tourist resort. Highly coloured postcards, horrible ornaments made of dyed coral, knick-knacks of unexampled bad taste. We were let in free and while Phil quickly bought some postcards for sending to the children I went through the turnstile and down the stairway into the underwater chamber which had been brought to the spot. It was a large room with round port-holes in all the walls. I took a quick look through the first two and was running up the stairs again to collect Phil so as to share this newest thrill with her from the start.

In a moment she was following me down and we began to watch the fish. Eye level was about 10 feet beneath the surface. Although the effect was very much like an aquarium, the 'tanks' were in fact the open ocean. Some of the corals had been brought to augment the existing reef – brought from elsewhere round Green Island, but there was nothing to retain the fish, which were free to come and go as they pleased. Here the profusion of fish and of species was once more amazing. There were large parrot fish, and Coral Trout, shoals of striped and spotted fish with huge eyes which lay hiding in the fronds of coral, chaetodons with 3 or 4 different patterns and bright yellow snouts, busy little wrasse, large shoals of tiny fish looking just like the hatchet fish of freshwater tropical aquaria which hung motionless opposite two of the portholes, the whole shoal swaying gently forwards and backwards with the movement of the waves. There were shoals of blue fish, not so bright as the ones on Michaelmas Cay, with sharply forked yellow tails; in the background shoals of larger fish which looked like silvery pike and were all the same length – about 18 inches (barracudas). Outside some of the portholes were huge sea anemones with their attendant anemone fish, the most brilliantly coloured of all. There were 2 species of anemone fish – one was the common one – orange with pale blue stripes edged in black, the other was dark chocolate with yellow fins and tail and a single brilliant opalescent blue stripe behind the head.

So impressed were we with Green Island and its potentialities that we decided to come back to it on the morrow, which was Christmas Day, sacrificing the chances of seeing the White Pygmy Goose.

TUESDAY 25 DECEMBER

Christmas Day we set off again, this time in the tourist boat, *Mingela*, for Green Island. We had arrived at the jetty more than half an hour early, so as to get seats, but the boat was not really crowded. It left at 9.30 and was over at Green Island by 11.00, a calmer and quicker passage than yesterday. Immediately on arrival Phil went off to get tickets for lunch and came back with some bottles of orange. Charles and I took the gear to the observatory. For the next $\frac{3}{4}$ hour we worked in the underwater room, filming mostly in black and white to get depth of focus. These two visits (today and yesterday) to the observatory constitute the appendix to our underwater adventure.

It was very hot down in the observatory – so hot that Phil couldn't stay there very long, but I did not feel it so much, and Charles filmed away nobly. At noon we went up the pier to the restaurant in the trees. Here were coconut palms and many species of trees. We had a lunch of fried fish and immediately after we set off to the beach on the north side of the island. Here we found a place to undress under the trees from which big drops of 'rain' were falling. Only later did we discover that these big drops were excreted from scores of large cicadas perched all over the branches.

The decks were cleared once more for the fourth and last chapter of our underwater adventure. It consisted of about $2\frac{1}{2}$ hours in wonderland. Phil was doing it all for the first time and she had some trouble with her mask and snorkel, also her flippers gave her cramp. All this happened close to the beach. About 10 yards out in $4\frac{1}{2}$ feet of water there was a species of *Zostera* (sea grass) growing which had quite a few

Green Island, from the jetty leading to the underwater observatory, from which, looking out into the sea, I once counted 70 species of fishes.

75

fish, but the coral did not begin for another 10 or 15 yards in a depth of about 5 feet, which was just too deep for Phil to stand and adjust her mask. At first I stayed with her but later I realised that she would prefer to work it out for herself so I set off to join Charles on a protracted cruise of the nearby coral. Just as each of the preceding chapters had outshone the last so now this cruise was far and away the best of all.

Once again most of the fish were new – different from those at Michaelmas Cay, not even identical with the ones at the observatory which was about 200 yards away (or at least not all of them). One of the first fish I saw, and one of the most colourful and amusing was one which looked rather like a pig, with prominent blue stripes between the eyes and across the tip of the snout, and yellow patches elsewhere with a very characteristic black pattern. These ran up to about 10″ long and were quite charming in their manner.

This was the first fish that Phil ever saw through a face-mask and was, we were later to discover, the Pig-Snout Trigger Fish (*Rhinecanthus aculeatus*) which is widespread in the Indo-Pacific Oceans and is known in Hawaii by the delightful name of 'Humu-humu nuku nuku apu-a-a'.

Cruising very close to the beach was a large fish, perhaps 2 feet long with a very blunt head – Hump-head Parrot Fish? Also near the shore I came upon some grey mullet which looked just like the ones one might see in England. On the way out to the coral there were some sand gobies, more or less white with black spotting. There was a similarly marked blenny and another all black blenny, which lived in the coral and sat with tail bent in the typical blenny attitude, and yet it was surprisingly flattened and very conspicuous. Superficially it was very like another black flattened fish and I wondered if this was merely convergence or perhaps a case of mimicry. Charles showed me a browny grey starfish, as well as the ultramarine blue one. He found a grey one with two regenerating arms and a blue one with only 4 arms – they seem usually to have five.

One of the loveliest sights were the shoals of blue fish – not the very bright ones I had seen at Michaelmas Cay but a soft blue fish which was in shoals always near a coral the tips of which were just the same colour. This was so delicate and in such perfect taste that I lay for a long time looking at this gentle combination. Presently Charles came and said he had seen what he thought was a young hammerhead shark, which had 'scared the daylights out of him' but if two of us went back . . . but alas he had gone – Charles thought he must have been about five feet long – I swam on out and came upon a large ray flapping lazily along. He was pale brown and spotted and had round ended 'wings'. Later Charles and I found another hiding under some coral near the edge of the reef.

I went back to see how Phil was getting on. She had discarded her flippers because they gave her cramp, but she had mastered the mask and snorkel and had reached an area of coral where she could see quite a lot. I went off again further out on the main reef and found first a new kind of anemone fish, brownish with three pale blue vertical stripes. This was to some extent intermediate between the two we had seen from the observatory. Whether these are different species or polymorphic phases I do not yet know. (They were in fact three different species). Next I came upon a pair of razor fish floating with head vertically downward. I gave chase to see whether I could scare them into any other swimming position, but I couldn't. They kept ahead of me still vertical, apparently by the use of a well developed anal fin. Then I went out to the edge of the coral. Crawling slowly up and down over the sandy ripples of the sea's floor was a hermit crab in a tall shell about five inches long. Near the edge of the coral there were shoals of parrot fish – one or two rainbow coloured males among a dozen drabber females. They flapped their wings up and down just like bright parrots. Among them at the edge of the coral were some even larger deeper fish with little horns above their eyes and snouts like pigs. Charles joined me out here and we looked at his watch and decided it was soon time to go back.

On the way back we met pipe fish, small and spotted, a large blenny with a pearly lustrous eye, and finally a moray eel – white with black spots which scuttled away under some soft coral and weed and later went further still when I fanned him with my flippers. There was also a little fish with pouting mouth which fed along the coral in a vertical position head downwards. He was not so well adapted for this attitude as the razor fish, and when swimming from coral to coral he came down to about 45°. When we got back to the shore we had been in the water for $2\frac{1}{2}$ hours.

I had finally adjusted my snorkel in such a way that the whole mouthpiece was inside my mouth and my teeth gripped the breathing tube. It was the only possible way with my lips as swollen and lacerated as they were. As I walked up the beach I felt quite groggy and unbalanced, but it soon wore off.

While dressing Phil pointed out the cicadas in the tree above our heads. There were dozens – on every twig they sat squirting out a little jet of water from time to time.

We only just caught the boat and had a pleasant homeward journey, upon which we saw a flying fish scuttering over the surface. It had been a wonderful and memorable Christmas day.

BLUE MOUNTAIN DUCK
Hymenolaimus malacorhynchus.

CHAPTER 5

New Zealand

DIARY 1   1956–1957

On Boxing Day we flew south from Cairns to Sydney and thence on the following day by TEAL (Tasman Empire Air Lines) in a DC6 to Christchurch, New Zealand – a five hour flight for part of which we had a following wind of 105 mph. At Christchurch Airport was a fleet of huge and ugly American Globemasters which were serving the US Antarctic expedition 'Operation Deep Freeze'. We were met by the press in force, and then flew on to Wellington in a DC3 of the rather 'one horse' National Airways Corporation – New Zealand's internal airline, which suffers from lack of competition. The name of our aircraft was *Papango*, which is the Maori name for the New Zealand Scaup.

For the next two nights we stayed with Sir Willoughby and Lady Norrie at Government House. Dr Bob Falla, who is head of the Museum in Wellington, and his wife came to dinner and we talked extensively about New Zealand's birds – Blue Ducks he thought only in hundreds (maximum 1,000), and Brown Ducks only in scores (maximum 300).

The Norries have bought a number of my pictures down the years, and many were hanging in Government House. Next day we discussed our itinerary with the new head of the Wildlife Section of the Department of the Interior, and in the afternoon I gave a slide lecture at the Museum to which the Government brought a large party. Afterwards we bought new skin diving equipment, including masks which cover the whole face – made in Italy.

SATURDAY 29 DECEMBER

Flew away early on a sunny morning to Dunedin with Gordon Williams as guide and mentor. He was at Slimbridge five years ago. He is a nice chap – a good biologist in charge of the *Notornis* studies. He is rather serious minded with thick spectacles and going prematurely bald.

We arrived in Dunedin at lunch time and after lunch we were taken out by a Warden, Stan Sharpe, to see the breeding Royal Albatrosses. On the way we drove along the shore of the Otago Peninsula, seeing the New Zealand Stilt, breeding Dominican Gulls, Pied Oystercatchers, and young Spotted Shags.

We stopped at Sharpe's house to pick up his son (one of three) Ernie, aged about 13. Our destination was a headland at the mouth of the approaches to Dunedin. When we got there it was blowing a gale from the North. We walked up the last steep slope to the Signal Station seeing a colony of Spotted Shags on the way up, and a Dominican Gull soaring on the slope with wings half closed and legs down but still going up. We were introduced to the coastguard look-out, and then led down to a fence beyond which, sitting deep in the grass was a huge white bird

Incubating male
Royal Albatross.

79

with black wings. It was about 20 yards away, impressive in size, but otherwise it was an unrewarding view.

There are six nests in this Royal Albatross colony, which is the only one in New Zealand and which began with one nest about 20 years ago. Because it takes 11 months before the single young one leaves the nest, albatrosses only breed once every two years. The nests are so greatly valued that all access to the colony, which is surrounded by a barbed wire fence, is prohibited by Act of Parliament. While we were looking at the sitting bird from outside the fence the Coast Guard called down that a bird which had been sitting on the hillside opposite earlier in the day had returned, so we set off immediately to see this one.

Mr Sharpe went past the bird and upwind of it to prevent it from taking off. At this critical moment two gentlemen of the press arrived for an interview. I could scarcely remain civil but eventually we began to film the huge bird. Sharpe stayed within a few feet of it to prevent it taking off, and eventually without warning pounced on it, and read the numbers on the two rings it carried. When released it wandered about and finally climbed a steep slope before taking off. Once airborne, which it achieved with great difficulty, it soared away shaking itself two or three times and eventually sailing along the cliffs to the eastward.

The light then improved and it was decided to visit one of the nests in the sanctuary, but only Charles and I were allowed to do so. (It was particularly annoying and embarrassing that Phil was not allowed in as part of our team, and we told them so when we got back to Wellington.) Much secrecy was involved. We waited until cars had gone from the neighbourhood and then sneaked in through a padlocked gate and walked along a path thick with Bidgy-Widgy (the burr-like seed we had encountered in the Bass Strait) – here known as 'Biddy Biddy' and apparently imported, no doubt unintentionally.

The cart track ran horizontally round the steep face of the hill and slap in the middle of it, in a clearing of the tall summer grass sat an albatross. It was a male and it looked slightly embarrassed and snapped its bill with a resonant rattle and a little grunt. We took its egg from under it, looked at it, and put it back. The bird was quite extraordinarily steady and did not seem to be at all resentful of us. So close were we that we could see the feather lice wandering among the feathers of the head. We filmed the bird extensively including large close-ups of the eye and nostrils.

Stan Sharpe had been looking after the colony for six years. He knew a very great deal about his albatrosses. A large part of the diet is squids which have been identified from the eye-lenses cast up by the birds round the nest.

So we finally left and on the way home Sharpe told us the history of his colony and many other things about these great birds, whose wing span is commonly 10' 6".

Back in Dunedin there was just time for dinner and then a new adventure was to begin.

After special pleading I was to be allowed into the famous Takahe Valley to see the recently rediscovered Takahe, *Notornis mantelli*. It is a huge flightless moorhen the size of a large domestic hen. Neither Phil nor Charles Lagus were accorded permission. Two conditions were attached to this concession. The first was that no publicity whatever

Notornis mantelli. The Takahe.

Notornis mantelli. Between 1949 (when the Takahe/*Notornis* was rediscovered) and about 1965 surveys indicated that the total population of the species was probably as high as 500. Over about the next 3 years the population fell to about 250 and the reason for this is unknown; it could have been a combination of bad breeding seasons, an upsurge in predation by stoats or a result of grazing of the Snow Grass by deer. Numbers then seemed to remain stable until about 1980 when another decline began and the 1983 estimate for the total world population is now down to about 125. Attempts to breed the Takahe in captivity are still not very satisfactory and only about 6 chicks have so far been raised; transferring birds to another suitable island may be the best hope. (These figures were kindly supplied by my friend Gordon Williams who for many years was head of the wildlife department in New Zealand.)

should be given to the visit in New Zealand, the second that I should give advice on methods of increasing the Takahe population. The first condition led to a great deal of tiresome and embarrassing subterfuge. A cover plan had to be invented that we were going to see Black Teal (scaup) which in fact we expected to see as well.

Gordon and I set off after dinner in a Standard Vanguard driven by the Warden from Queenstown, on Lake Wakatipu, whose name was Marsh Small. In the back were his wife and black dachsund and a couple of mattresses. We proceeded very slowly, and before it got dark we passed a lake with Black Swans on it with cygnets. Later on I offered to drive and found that the reason for our slow progress was that the car had no brakes. In spite of this, however, I managed to push up the speed, and on good straight roads we did 55 miles in the next hour. Then we changed back and I stretched out on one of the mattresses in the back – Gordon on the other – and slept reasonably well. Before we arrived it had begun to rain heavily. Small and his wife got off as we passed their home and Gordon drove the 8 miles on. Eventually we found the home of the local Wild Life Administrator who had tea and biscuits for us, and took us across the road to a guest house where at 12.45 we crept into bed.

Primary
of
Takahe
found near
hut.

SUNDAY 30 DECEMBER

It was raining hard when we woke up without any apparent promise of better to come, but after breakfast it looked as though it would clear. We were in Queenstown overlooking Lake Wakatipu, a very big lake, long and narrow and winding, lying in the lap of fine mountains. As the day cleared we could see snow well down the mountain sides, and eventually the sun shone out. On the left was the dark wall of the Remarkables, still in shadow. The valley ahead was only just clear of cloud, but it should be possible to get through to Takahe Valley.

We went to see the pilot of the Grumman 'Wigeon' amphibian which was to take us. He was Jim Monk. He said to come back in an hour and he would have the met. report. So we parked and paid for our night's lodging and then went down to the waterfront. Here was a small pier and a jetty with a lake steamer alongside. There should have been quite a flock of Black Teal (New Zealand Scaup) but for some reason there were hardly any! All I saw were males, though there had been a distant female with brood opposite Monk's house. The first male was fairly far out among some Grey Ducks, but the next was in full wing moult sitting on a sloping groyne. I filmed him and a Grey Duck at about 30 feet. When we got back to the pier there were two more drakes and these finally swam ashore among some Grey Ducks, so I filmed both species at 25 feet, over the wall of the esplanade. Then we went out onto the pier to see the semi tame trout – some up to 15 lbs which were sailing majestically round in the clear water. After that we had a quick drive into the local park, to see a granite memorial to my father – not very good but in a lovely park.

Soon after 9.00 we were back with Monk and being ferried by his small boy across to the 'Wigeon' which stood in a couple of feet of water just off the shore. I sat up beside the pilot and in due course we took off. The technique of warming up and running up the two engines was interesting and the whole of the flying side was intensely enjoyable even though we had to dive through a pass in which the visibility was pretty poor. It was also extremely turbulent and bumpy. After 40 minutes flying among snow mountains with their peaks in cloud, we came out over a wide valley with a lake at the far side. This was Lake Te Anau. We were now at cloud base and heading straight for the wall of hills on the west side of the lake. I could see no way through this wall, so I asked the pilot who said 'Takahe Valley is just in there' and pointed to a dimly paler patch in the dark mountain side ahead. Then I saw two clefts and we started by flying into the right hand one. It cleared for a few minutes as we entered the side valley and there was a lake about half a mile along – Lake Orbell. We turned left round a high buff and over a low septum dividing the Orbell lake basin from the valley of the Point Burn.

Then we flew 'round the block' again, this time much lower, and came in over the top of the lake to settle safely onto the peaty water, lined with squally bubble rows. We taxied back towards the outlet, above which a shining new aluminium hut stood – the new head-quarters of the Takahe Study. As we came to the shore the rain descended on us again, heavy and relentless like a curtain. I had been lent some thigh boots and had my parka so we decided to sally forth, Gordon wearing his oilskin and with bare feet and rolled up trousers.

As soon as we were out of the plane and on our way round to the most likely area for Takahe the rain eased and the sky brightened, so I went back for camera and tripod. The easy slopes beside the lake were covered with reddish buff tussocks of Snow Grass, *Danthonia flavescens*; above this were various shrubs, notably one with leaves arranged in a pleasant pattern called I believe, *Dracophyllum uniflorum* (Turpentine Shrub). Above this again was luxuriant forest mainly consisting of a beech, *Nothofagus cliffordioides*. Gordon said the Takahes had very acute hearing, and that we should go quite silently forward. Very soon we had to negotiate the crossing of the river, which was apparently about a foot higher than usual. The stepping stones were far under water. However with the tripod as a staff we managed to get safely across and very soon after we heard the characteristic bumping noise which is the alarm note of *Notornis mantelli*. Gordon and I were some distance apart and the noise was well ahead.

Presently. I saw a movement in the Snow Grass and then a great dark bird crept across an open patch under a Turpentine bush. I had a brief glimpse of the heavy red bill and a suggestion of blue green on the back and it had gone. From time to time I could see a dark shape showing dimly through the yellow grass. Then there seemed to be two, one much closer to Gordon who was making a piping noise designed to attract the birds. I came down to join him, and the nearest bird hung around close by, but it turned out to be a Weka, the much commoner and smaller rail – *Gallirallus australis australis*.

The Takahe had moved over towards the forest and presently we heard it call, and its mate reply – a most unexpected, loud and characteristic cry. Gordon thought they were calling to a small young one, but one large enough to follow them out of the Snow Grass. After searching around for a bit we found the nest with the membrane of a hatched egg in it. All around the Snow Grass had been pulled out and was lying about in the hollows between the tussocks. The nest was under a tussock with two entrances, but not very well hidden. About six feet away was a large pile of droppings. The droppings are somewhat gooselike, green when fresh, but mostly washed whitish by the rain and consisting of sharply chopped up lengths of the grass stems.

We decided to move up the lake shore to an area of Snow Grass where the second pair was likely to be. Gordon believed there to be about 50 *Notornis* in the whole of this valley area, a lower figure than had been formerly estimated. It rained very hard with a strong wind blowing in our faces as we made our way up the valley. But Area B produced no Takahes, only freshly cut Snow Grass and fairly fresh droppings.

Gordon told me what I had not realised before – that Orbell had made two expeditions especially to look for *Notornis*, believing it to exist in spite of the current belief that it was extinct. On the first he found footprints, on the second he found and caught the birds. Since then many people have come forward with stories of seeing it in the intervening 50 years but in his view none of them is reliable. One farmer described the bird in great detail in an area in which it just might have occurred. It was sitting on a fence post – unusual, but not impossible, and what did it do then? The answer was 'It flew away'. *Notornis* is, of course, flightless.

Back in Area A we heard the bumping alarm note again but we

Egg membrane of *Notornis mantelli*. Taken from nest in area A.

couldn't find the bird, nor did we see anything more of *Notornis*. By this time it was past 1.00 and we were very wet and cold. Gordon's teeth were chattering. From the little shiny aluminium hut's chimney rose a wisp of blue smoke. Evidently Jim Monk was brewing up some tea. So we made our way across towards the hut. Suddenly we came to the river and there was a family party of Blue Ducks. It was very sudden and unexpected, and to me *very* exciting. I could see at once that there were four or five birds at least, and the nearest were about 25 yards away. We afterwards found that there were five well grown young, fully feathered with their parents. The only differences in the young were that their bills were grey blue instead of whitish flesh colour and that their breasts were not spotted with chestnut as in the adults. They were also, of course, a trifle smaller. The drake sat on a rock in mid-stream, the duck was on the shore with the young and making nervous head movements surprisingly reminiscent of both torrent ducks and Salvadori's.

It was still raining heavily so we turned a little way up-stream in order to cross without upsetting them, and went on to the hut. Here was a lunch of cold tongue and hot peas, bread and honey and tea. Here also was a good fire in front of which to dry off some of our sodden clothes. It was all very cheerful and Jim Monk told stories of flying the hut, in pieces, into the valley, and of Charlie, the Takahe who habitually came to the edge of the lake and walked up and down on the beach consumed with curiosity over the amphibian aircraft standing in the shallows 20 yards away.

We decided to give it an hour to clear up, and if it didn't to cut our losses and quit. By 2.30 it had not improved; we gave it a quarter of an hour more and still it rained, though a little less heavily. We decided to try filming the Blue Ducks holding an oilskin over the camera which Gordon was prepared to do. So once again we advanced upon the Blue Duck family which still sat in precisely the same place. Very soon after we had begun the rain stopped and the sun broke fitfully through. The closest shots were made at under 30 feet – I think in one case about 24 feet. The male swam off the first rock and landed with the whole family on another rock from which all of them jumped in and out of the water most obligingly for the next ten minutes. At one time the drake made a rush attack towards Gordon.

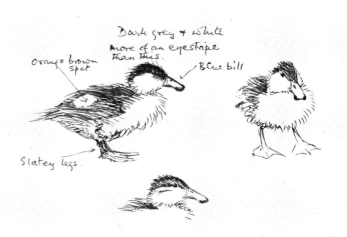

Blue Duck chicks

I was so busy filming that I did not have so long as I should have liked to look at the birds critically with binoculars. So I did not form any opinions about its relationships. The bill was pinker, less yellow than I had expected (in the adults), the tail was long as in Salvadori's or torrent ducks, the yellow eye was sharply contrasted with the blue grey plumage. Although none of the birds flew I noticed that both parents had full length primaries – at a time when one might have expected them to be moulting and flightless. The complete lack of speculum (the 'wing mirror' which in many duck species is brightly coloured and irridescent) is a most puzzling feature. I heard the call which is a loud rather rasping whistle, not unlike a wigeon drake's, and which gives the bird its Maori name 'Whio', pronounced 'few'. There is also a croak which the male made frequently when I was at my closest. It would scarcely have been possible to imagine a more confiding or co-operative group of wild birds than these seven Blue Ducks. While we were filming Gordon picked up a moulted Takahe primary which is stuck into this book.

By now it was after 3.00 and our programme left us no more time, so we left the ducks and made our way to the Grumman 'Wigeon' where I changed my boots and socks for shoes, put on my dry coat and took my place beside Jim Monk. There was quite a lot of wind – and consequent turbulence at take-off. It was evidently quite hard to 'unstick' the amphibian and after pulling her off with brute force and a quick climb to 30 feet, Jim put the nose down again to get some speed. Eventually we teetered up a couple of hundred feet which was just enough to get us over the hill into the Point Burn valley. From there we ran down to Lake Te Anau and landed at the village where a motor boat cut across our taxiing path and incurred our pilot's wrath. At Te Anau they were water-skiing in the rain. It was a pleasant flight onward, with a nice young pilot, and in three quarters of an hour we had landed on the grass of Invercargill aerodrome. We had time for an excellent meal at the Peter Pan cafeteria and just caught our train nicely, having no difficulty in getting sleepers. And so at 7.30 on

MONDAY 31 DECEMBER

I found Phil asleep in our hotel room at Christchurch, overlooking my mother's fine marble statue of my father. It looks absolutely magnificent in that setting, and especially good when floodlit at night, as I found out that evening.

Of our two and a half days in the Christchurch area we decided to spend the first going out to the Gliding Club's Camp about 80 miles away at Hanmer in the hills. At lunchtime we reached our destination and saw some gliders flying over a broad valley between fairly steep hills. When we got to the field, which we located below us as we came through the river gorge and emerged on the bluff overlooking the valley, we were met by Dick Georgeson, New Zealand's entry in the World Championships, and a man called Dingwall who was Chairman (or President) of the Club.

I was offered a flight in a T31 with the acting Chief Flying Instructor, John Messing, and had a very good winch launch. There was no lift so we did a circuit slightly marred by Messing telling me 'I shouldn't go too far down wind' with the result that I had to slip off a lot of height and made a landing 100 yards too far up the field with a slight bounce.

With my mother's statue of my father in Christchurch.

85

After this 3 minute circuit I was sent solo in the T31 and made 1,200 feet of the launch which kept me in the air for 4 minutes. I made a peach of a landing 'spot-on' for the next take-off, which was all rather satisfying.

We met Christopher Wills – Philip Wills' [gliding champion] son – who told us the sad tale of the famous Weihe which had belonged to his father before Dick Georgeson brought it to New Zealand. Later Philip Wills had flown it again in waves near Mount Cook and taken it to about 30,000 feet. Christopher had been flying it two days before and had finally landed about $1\frac{1}{2}$ miles away in a turnip field in a 40 mph wind. He had not dared to get out and had sat there for two hours before the farmer arrived. The farmer had been so concerned about his crop that Christopher had promised to carry the glider out instead of bringing in the trailer. He had carried one wing and the tail plane, leaving an inexperienced person to hold down the rest of the glider when a big puff had caught and overturned it, breaking the tail and damaging the wing root facings. All very sad, but she is not written off, and can in due course be repaired.

Later I was offered a flight in the South Canterbury Club's Kookaburra with Peter Cummins (gliding instructor). The Kookaburra is amazingly small for a two seater. The seats are staggered. I sat in front and we had an aero-tow. This was my first experience of aero-tow, and very turbulent it was.

Most of the gliding in New Zealand is based on 'wave lift'. When stable air (which is what the air usually is after it has crossed the sea) comes to a mountain, the wind flows up the hill creating what is called 'ridge lift'. As gliders are always coming down through the air the only way a glider can stay airborne is by the pilot finding air that is going up faster than he is sinking. A variometer measures this and shows green when the plane is ascending, red when sinking. 'Ridge lift' is one way to stay up, another is 'thermal lift' which involves using rising columns of warm air. I shall explain this more fully in Chapter 11 when describing a glider flight in Africa. 'Wave lift' is a third kind for which New Zealand is famous in gliding circles. When a fast river passes over a hidden rock one can often see a wave downstream of it which stays in the same place with the water flowing through it. This is called a 'standing wave' and the same thing happens to stable air blowing over a mountain, the only difference being that there is no surface to show it, as in the river, and the scale is enormously greater. 'Wave lift' on the lee side of mountains – sometimes a number of waves several miles apart – has carried gliders to more than 40,000 ft. The great standing wave with its lenticular arch, which often forms in the lee of the New Zealand Alps, provides opportunities for flying world record distances at high speed along the length of the South Island and sometimes crossing to the North Island as well.

The object of my modest flying at Hanmer was to use 'ridge lift' and a little 'thermal lift' for soaring with a remote chance of contacting a wave. This background may make it easier to understand my first glider flight in New Zealand.

Peter did the take off, and bounced her back on the floor. Then I took over and found it quite hard to keep her down enough. Both we and the Tiger were bouncing about madly. We went up the valley, then turned and headed for the soaring hill. We headed so directly at it that I had no idea which way the tug would turn. At last we turned left along the slope. Here the gusts were very severe and when the tug went hurtling up in front of us and even the tow line was blown into a steep upward bow, Peter suggested we should release, which we did.

We were well below the top of the ridge at about 1,800 feet. The lift was maddeningly patchy, so that we scraped and scraped and only got to about 2,100, which was still barely above the crest of the ridge. After about 20 minutes of this, with occasional bursts of 20 green when we got into a funnel of lift, but plenty of 10 and sometimes 20 red, we were down to 1,500 feet and had to head back towards the landing field. We crossed the braided channels of the river and its wide expanses of grey gravel and then came to a field of brilliantly green lucerne. Here we picked up a thermal and I started to circle to the left. After two or three turns we were out of it. I came out up wind and soon ran into it again, and this time began circling to the right. This was good stuff – much of it steady 10 green. We climbed up 1,000 feet, by which time we had blown back almost level with the ridge, so I turned (probably a little too soon) and went across to the ridge and here we began to soar again. Our maximum height was 2,300 which puts us up among the Skylarks. All the time it was unpleasantly turbulent on the ridge which meant flying at about 45 mph. But the Kookaburra designed by the man who designed the Grunaubaby is very nice to fly, although of course, not in the same class as my lovely Olympia at home.

We could have stayed on the ridge for much longer, but it was already 5.00 pm so we thought we had better go back. I made quite a pretty landing, although 50 yards further up the runway than I should have liked. Soon after we were setting off for the homeward run to Christchurch.

Lake Ellesmere:
Black-billed Gulls
and a White-fronted Tern.

TUESDAY 1 JANUARY

The first two days of January were spent at Lake Ellesmere, which is 15 miles long, trying to film Black Swans – of which we saw more than 20,000 but none came close enough for us to film sequences we had hoped to get. The swans have been introduced from Australia, and it is astonishing that they have been so much more successful here than in their original habitat – at least it would be astonishing if there were not so many other examples in the world's fauna.

With boats we managed to drive 700 swans, out of a flock of about 5,000, between the shore and an island where Charles was hidden in a hide. It did not produce very interesting pictures and they were two very frustrating days. Black Swans are considered to be sporting quarry in New Zealand and locally referred to as 'game'. 'We'll show you some "game" this afternoon', they had said to us. After our frustrations Phil had become rather bored with all the efforts to show us 'game'. 'You know', she said to a nice-looking girl who was walking with her to a vantage point overlooking the lake 'if they show me another Black Swan, I shall scream'. She did not know that the nice-looking girl was a journalist and next morning's paper carried a banner headline, 'Mrs Peter Scott says if she sees another Black Swan, she'll scream!'

WEDNESDAY 2 JANUARY

In the afternoon we flew from Christchurch back to Wellington and boarded the MV *Alert* belonging to Alec Black which was to take us for a two day cruise in the Cook Strait between the North and South Islands of New Zealand. The *Alert* is a converted wartime Harbour Defence Motor Launch of very practical design, and a first class vessel for these stormy waters.

On board we met Alec again – he was at Slimbridge five years ago – and his young wife Coleen. Their two month old baby, known as Mr Fug, was also on board. The rest of the crew consisted of a marine biologist (conchologist) Dick Dell, a schoolmaster, Maurice and two Scouts, Graham and Peter. Gordon Williams was still with us and Dr Falla was one of the party – 11 all told including Mr Fug.

Charles and Gordon had gone on to Wellington in order to collect mail and returned later with quite a lot which pleased Phil who does not like to be without news of the children, especially Christmas news.

THURSDAY 3 JANUARY

Late to bed the night before and *Alert* set off at 4.30. Our cabin was so near the engine room that it meant no more sleep for Phil, although we didn't get up until 7.30. It was a fine calm morning and interesting sea-birds were about. We saw Blue Penguins – also Fluttering Shearwaters, *Puffinus gavia gavia*, which look rather like Manx Shearwaters, brown on top and white underneath.

For breakfast we went to the little bay where Cook made his first landing in New Zealand and to which he subsequently returned three times. We had breakfast alongside the little jetty there, and after breakfast we walked along a path through the sub-tropical forest which came right down to the water's edge. Tree ferns were overhanging the water. There is a little stream which Cook used for watering his ships and beside it a memorial, consisting of an anchor on a great granite pedestal. Up in the bush behind we saw two of the great bronzy green native pigeons with a white belly and a sharp line dividing it from the green breast. This is *Hemiphaga n. novaseelandiae* and it has a beautiful display flight in which it climbs up and stalls diving away deeply, very like our wood pigeon does only more so, and the bird is a good deal bigger.

We had only half an hour ashore and then we were on our way again round the North Island coast en route for the Trios, a group of small islands lying just to the east of Stephen's. On the way we came upon a flock of several hundred dove petrels or prions. These were grey with a diagonal streak across the wings and they ran over the water in the characteristic and utterly charming manner of the storm petrels. This bird was the Fairy Prion, *Pachyptila turtur*, known to the Maoris as Titi Wainui.

Once we saw an albatross which Falla immediately identified as the White-capped or Shy Mollynawk, *Diomedea cauta cauta*. It was, to me, just a white albatross with black wings, and it was demonstrating the principles of dynamic soaring. Later we saw a single Giant Petrel or Nelly, *Macronectes giganteus*, last seen at Rio Grande, Tierra del Fuego. On the cliffs of an island close to which we passed were some Pied Shags, *Phalacrocorax varius varius*, which had a yellow patch in front of the eye and an area of blue skin around the eye – quite a handsome bird. Spotted Shags, *P. p. punctatus*, should have been breeding on this cliff but we saw only one bird in flight.

When we came to the Trios however, on the steep slope of the pinnacle to the north west of the main island was a colony of the New Zealand King Shag, *P.c. carunculatus*. They had finished breeding, the nests had been trodden flat and the young were fully grown. They were fine big black and white birds, the head and neck being black, but they were rather wild and mostly flew off when we were still a few hundred yards away. There had been about 60 to start with which represents more than a quarter of the world population of this sub-species. One or two climbed up the slope away from us but quite soon they had all gone.

So we went back to the main island on which there were nesting colonies of Red-billed Gulls and White-fronted Terns. We found a moulting penguin standing on a ledge, where he may well have been for a fortnight or more, as penguins don't like getting wet during the moult, which involves a fortnight's fast. The *Alert* poked her nose into the little bay where he sat in the shade in a dark corner of a rock. Finally as we began to withdraw he climbed down into the water and swam out underwater close past us so that I could film him.

We spent some time looking for a place where we could land direct from the *Alert* but finally the dinghy had to be launched. We landed at high water on a tiny stony beach. There was a kind of a path leading up a steep earth bank, and this was said to be a penguin and petrel path. It was exceedingly difficult to climb, especially with camera gear. Falla went on ahead to pioneer the route. When we had climbed a fair height – say 100 feet or so, the path emerged from the thick shrubbery – which was open under a thick canopy, and riddled with shearwater burrows and came out onto a ridge. From this ridge we later identified two Reef Herons or Blue Herons, *Egretta sacra sacra*.

Falla had caught a Tuatara (pronounced Tooatera – almost Tooa-

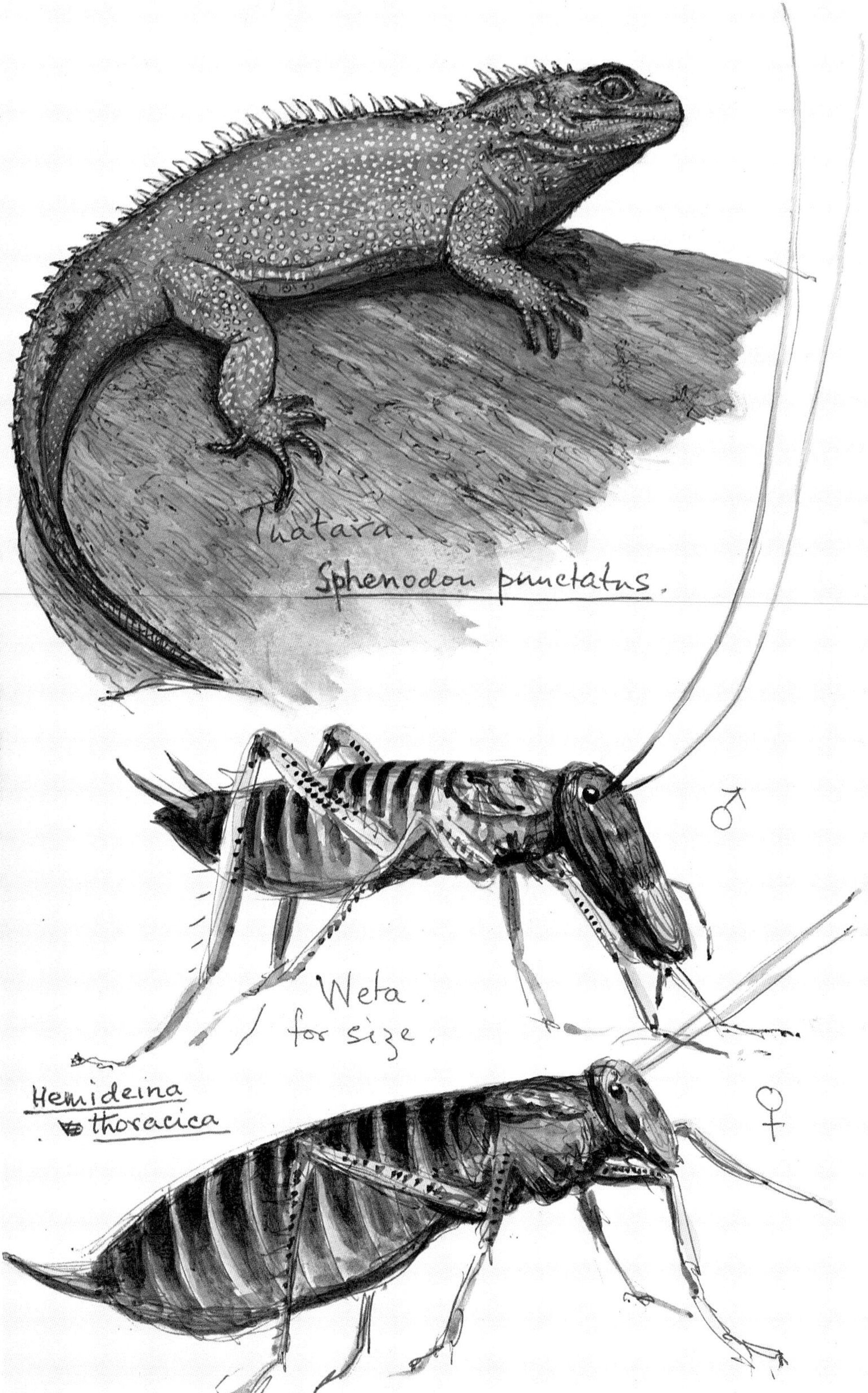

Tuatara.
Sphenodon punctatus.

Weta.
for size.

Hemideina
thoracica

♂

♀

terror) in a burrow and was holding it in his beret. I had not handled one of these miniature dinosaurs since I was a boy at the London Zoo. They are most impressive animals – heavy of head and body, pleasantly green in colour and quite steady if held comfortably. They only bite in the process of capture. This particular animal was blotched with orange, which were colonies of mites. The fringe of drooping white spines on the back of the neck and down the back was unexpected in that the spines themselves were quite soft. Those on the ridge of the tail on the other hand were different and quite hard. The tail was slightly jointed, but rather a crocodile's tail.

Dick Dell came up while we were filming. He had found some Wetas. These are huge crickets – males with enormous heads and jaws, the females much larger and fatter but with a normal sized head. Both sexes have very long antennae. They are reddish brown and shiny with transverse stripes on the abdomen caused by paler joints to the segments. The overall length of the female is about $3\frac{1}{2}$ inches. One of the males walking on my hand bent down and deliberately bit me – not very hard.

One Tuatara was living in a burrow on the path leading up the spine – a penguin path, as few people ever land on the Trios. Falla had seen him sunning himself in the entrance to the burrow. I put on gloves and got him out for the camera. Re-enacting this later without gloves I let him get a pinch of skin on the back of a knuckle, but the bite scarcely drew blood.

Down the same hole we found a penguin which was moulting. We filmed both returning to the burrow. Then we persuaded the Tuatara to stay in front of the burrow and eventually to turn round and go down again – which is just how Falla first saw him. An earlier moulting penguin, when held, had bitten his own flipper in two places, drawing blood. This is a rather unusual thing which I had noticed with this species in Australia. It is strange that the pain did not prevent the bird from biting so hard. Is this a reflection on reaction speed, or an indication of reduced sensitivity or of such extreme aggressiveness that pain is disregarded?

Gordon had been down to the beach and brought the packed lunch up the very steep slope – a noble service to the party – so that we could have lunch and go on filming afterwards. Falla brought a young squab of the Fluttering Shearwater. It was big and fluffy and floppy. We cleared a hole for some sunlight underneath the thick shrub canopy where the main concentration of burrows was, and filmed the baby shearwater in there. We also found several more Tuataras, indeed it would be safe to say that we did not find more than an occasional burrow which was without a Tuatara in it. It has been estimated that there are 7,000 on the much larger Stephen Island, and Falla thinks there must be at least half that number on the five or six acres of the main Trio Island. They are said to live 300 years and only to become

Tuatara.

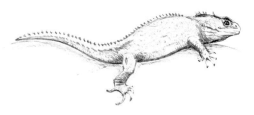

sexually mature at 60. We found two smallish ones with regenerated tails. This was new to me. I had not realised that Tuatara tails would break off. The character is shared by many lizard families – nevertheless it makes Tuatara a bit more of a lizard and a bit less of a dinosaur for me. Do you suppose *Diplodocus* had a breakable tail which wiggled when broken? It was decided to take two Tuataras back – one for the London Zoo. The animal is, of course, protected and there would be formalities, but Falla wanted to take a couple, and I suggested that London should have one of them (it now transpires that two were sent there recently).

On top of the island we were visited by three birds hopping in the bush over our heads. The most confiding was a fantail, *Rhipidura fuliginosa fuliginosa* – the South Island race with sooty body and pure white tail which it fanned constantly within a few feet of us. The second was a Grey Warbler, *Gerygone igata*, (which I had heard only at Takahe Valley). This time I saw fleetingly a little Grey Warbler. Only later (at Hamurana) did I see it properly and take note of its red eye and its white tipped tail with a black subterminal band. The third bird, seen even more fleetingly was a White-eye, *Zosterops lateralis*.

By 4.30 *Alert* was back for us and we made our way down toward the beach. On a white flower were a number of small butterflies showing probably sexual dimorphism. They were coppers, *Chrysophanus salustius*, – very pretty and orange. There was also a black moth with white spots and feathery antennae which appeared to be related to our Cinnabar, or perhaps to our Magpie Moth (probably to neither). *Nyctemera annulata*.

The tide was out on the beach and I decided to have a swim and try out the new mask–cum–snorkel I had bought in Wellington. The mask covers the whole face and has two snorkel pipes with float valves to block them. The water was breathtakingly cold but the mask worked perfectly. The water was fairly clear, visibility about 5 yards (it had been 20 yards at Green Island) and there was tall weed in a great forest immediately off the beach. Amongst it were little perch-like fish of varying size, but obviously all the same species. This was the commonest. But then I found some leather-jackets which were larger – about a foot or 15″ – and grey with a comical expression and a spine which they kept putting up when they saw me. They progressed by a wave motion along the dorsal and ventral fins. In one place I found a great profusion of *Echinus* – a large grey sea urchin – one every few feet. There were also some nice small sea anemones on the rocks – red, and a larger purplish one looking like a large mauve raspberry which grew on the brown seaweed. I swam along the shore for about 150 yards but it was really too cold to stay in long.

As we had tea *Alert* set off to the Chetwode Islands where we planned to anchor for the night. At the Chetwodes we passed a rock with a pair of oystercatchers on it. One was all black, but the other showed some white on the belly and flanks. These were obviously a pair, belonging to the dimorphic form *Haematopus unicolor reischeki*. Apparently the occurrence of individuals with some white on them is commoner in the north but where the name *rescheki* should be used, indicating that subspecific status is justified, seems still to be in doubt. We arrived through a tide race, with little whirlpools, into a bay in Little Chetwode Island and went ashore before supper.

On the beach where we landed was a female skink which I caught. She was under a stone which I wanted to use to secure the anchor of the boat. She was a rich red brown, about $5\frac{1}{2}''$ long and very full of young ones. Also on the beach was a female South Island Robin or Toutouwai, *Petroica a. australis*, which was amazingly tame and also incredibly like a large English robin but without a red breast. It is said to be more of a flycatcher than a robin, but it cannot be far removed from our robin all the same.

Bob Falla and Gordon and I set out to scramble up to the top of the island about 500 feet above. Falla chose a route up a near vertical face and went blinding up ahead. I had to stop and rest a couple of times, and looked down on a gully full of what is locally called flax – which looks as though it might be related to aloe. It is a tuft of sword-like grass with leaves six feet long and an exotic looking flower head, with green and black flowers. On these were feeding Tuis, *Prosthemadera n. novaeseelandiae*, and Bell Birds, *Anthornis m. melanura*. Both had agreeable 'contralto' songs, very rich in tone, and both had their bills and foreheads covered with the yellow pollen of the flax. The Bell Bird is rather a dull little honey-eater but the Tui is very fine and handsome. It is a black bird with white on the shoulders and a white spot under the chin, but when you see it close to it is much more handsome than that. The back and wings are bright glossy green, the neck has a cape of loose feathers which curl a little and each of which has a pale grey shaft line, so that the whole effect suggests a lace collar, and the white spot on the upper breast is really two tufts of curved white feathers, like two round white beads on a necklace. Altogether the Tui is a very beautiful bird.

Also feeding in the gully below were some little green parakeets with yellow heads and red foreheads. These were *Cyanoramphus auriceps auriceps*, the Yellow-crowned Parakeet or Kakariki.

I decided to come down again by way of the gully, while the other two returned by the steep face we had climbed. To begin with my route seemed better, but as I got down near the beach with the other two still far up above me, I ran into trouble. Bracken of a wiry kind was growing to a height of 6 or 7 feet and was so knitted together as to be springy and resilient. Several times I fell forward onto it, clearing my own height ahead of me and then getting up again to fall forward again. Suddenly I realised I had been stung on one ankle and across the back of one hand. Almost at once I saw the culprit, a large and fearsome looking nettle with thick almost spine-like hairs. This was *Urtica ferox* and the sting was certainly ferocious; I could still feel it 48 hours later.

FRIDAY 4 JANUARY

A not very early start to return across Cook Strait to Kapiti Island on the west coast of the North Island about 30 miles north of Wellington. It was not a rough passage but I felt fairly sick. Phil had indigestion and felt poorly too. I took a seasickness pill produced by Charles called Marzine which seemed to work pretty well, so that I wished I had taken it earlier. After about four hours we sailed round the north end of Kapiti into a little bay off the homestead of the Webber family which used to be a whaling station.

Kapiti is about 7,000 acres of which $\frac{2}{3}$ is bird sanctuary belonging to the Government and the rest belongs to the Webbers and is farmed

North Island Kaka.

as a sheep station. Apparently it reverts to the Government in due course. Bob Falla went ashore to make contact with Graham Turbott (an old friend from Uppsala [Sweden, venue of the 1st post wat International Ornithological Congress 1950] days who has been to Slimbridge and was also at Basle). He is director of the Museum at Wellington. Presently Falla returned with Graham in the boat, and we sailed on a mile or so to the house of the warden of the bird sanctuary, Mr Fox. It was nice to see Graham again with his slow quiet voice and dry sense of humour – a first class naturalist and scientist into the bargain, and a delightful chap. Mrs Fox feeds the native birds, and particularly the curious bush parrot, the North Island Kaka, *Nestor meridionalis septentrionalis*. She called to them 'come on birds', 'come on Hector'. In due course three Kakas come to the bird table for dates. Many more apparently came at other times than the nesting season. It is a large dark greenish brown parrot, spotted and barred with a flask of dull orange red as it flies, showing on the wings – particularly underside – and rump. It is obviously a small version of the Kea, *Nestor notabilis*.

While photographing these Kakas, which came and went rather too rapidly we had close up views of a Weka which looks like a cross between a Corncrake and a Water Rail blown up to the size of a small hen and flightless. This female who had two downy young under a bush in the garden, was quite absurdly tame. Some parakeets flew about the garden, but these were different from the ones we had seen at Chetwode Island, lacking the yellow crown. They were *Cyanoramphus n. novaezelandiae*, the New Zealand Parakeet or Red-fronted Parakeet.

Lunch on board, after which it rained and the Marzine caught up with me – so I slept. At 4.00 I woke up feeling like death to find the sun shining; so I went ashore, called on the Webbers, who are of Maori descent, and saw the Black Swans and Grey Ducks and the wild Wekas in their garden. Then, I walked along the beach of grey stones towards a point on which was a breeding colony of Red-billed Gulls. Along half a mile of beach were scattered the nests of the Black-backed Gull, *L. dominicanus*, most of which had feathering young, but the Redbills at the end had eggs and all sizes of young up to practically fledged ones. I sat about 15 feet from them and filmed the parents feeding the young and squabbling away among themselves.

MONDAY 7 JANUARY

We flew to Napier to go to the famous gannet colony at Cape Kidnappers. Land Rovers took us for 6 or 7 miles across farm land by a very rough track. At last along a knife-edge hill, we approached the final headland and drove to its top, where the nesting gannets were less than a dozen yards away. The estimate of nests is 2,000. The Warden was Mr Williams who has organised a number of young lads as a perpetual watch on the birds all through the breeding season. He led us down to the saddle where we sat and filmed for a couple of hours. For the photographer who is trying to conserve film, a gannet colony is disastrous. Charles stayed at the top filming. Between us we shot well over a thousand feet of film. The sun kept coming out just after one had shot something without sun, so that the shot had to be repeated. There should be some nice slow motion flight shots.

The New Zealand Gannet, *Sula serrator*, seems to have a brighter yellow nape and more black on the wings. As usual they were absurdly

94

tame. One sat sleeping within two feet of my arm, only waking when I rewound the camera or changed lenses. We were surrounded by nesting birds, sitting on a guano covered sloping rock, the only nest free place in the colony. The gannet's calls were delightfully musical, pairs were bill-fencing, giving an ecstatic display, fighting, marvellous soaring was in progress in a strong up-draught. It was an extremely beautiful and entertaining scene.

TUESDAY 8 JANUARY

In the morning, at Lake Tutira, I was shown 27 Paradise Shelducks, the first wild ones I had ever seen, and in the afternoon we flew to Gisborne and motored for three hours up the coast, and then for 30 miles inland to the hills at the edge of the unexplored bush, to find Blue Ducks. It was a remarkable road, winding along the hillsides, through sheep stations with a fine panorama of mountains to the north. At dusk we reached our destination – the penultimate farm on the road, called Owhena (pronounced Ofenner) of which the manager was Fred Maxwell, (of Maori extraction). Mr and Mrs Maxwell greeted us with delightful hospitality at their homestead which was very much like an English farm house. Self-made electricity, a bathroom, a radiogram and indoor sanitation were among the amenities, and the beds were agreeably soft. The telephone rang at about 4.00 am and this was a neighbour called Cresswell, whose station we had passed on the way and who wanted to join us on the morrow.

WEDNESDAY 9 JANUARY

One of the best days we have had in New Zealand. We set off at 9.30 by car five or six miles up the valley of the Waitataia (past a junction above which the river changes its name to Ruatatiunga) to the last station, run by Mr Macpherson. It is called Muugawhero – the 'wh' being pronounced as 'f'. Here a cavalcade of 14 horses had been assembled, one

'Horses ready': the Blue Duck expedition.

a pack horse for the camera gear. There were 13 of us in the party including a young journalist called Wisely whose overturned car we had passed on the coast road on the way up. In addition Cresswell, an amateur botanist and geologist with a loud and tiresome voice, attached himself and his two sons, 19 and 17, to the party on foot. Sixteen was too large a party, but even that could not spoil the day.

My horse was a mare called Tui, Phil's was called Sheila and Charles' Satan. We started down the steep slope from the farm leading the horses. It must have been at least 1,000 feet down to the river perhaps more. There was a rough path which in places went down incredibly steeply, and frequently went along the edges of near-vertical hill faces. One had to put much faith in the sure-footedness of the animals, but it wasn't misplaced. There was a junction near where we came to the river, and from here up stream it was expected that we should find Blue Ducks. Instead we found at once a single Grey Duck in this unusual setting. It flew down the valley then turned and went up it again out of sight.

We crossed the river and rode up the far side. Fred Maxwell was following the river itself and was far ahead of us. We were led by Fred's assistant Stan, leading the pack horse. We had various troubles with the party getting stretched out all over the valley with us in the middle, but it straightened itself out a bit after we had read the riot act.

As we rode up the steep valley I heard ahead the call of a drake Paradise Shelduck, above the noise of the river. I was rather pleased with this identification which was doubted by all around me until the bird flew up from the slope ahead. Later he was joined by the female and they flew up and down the narrow valley. I filmed them flying below us, with the white wings showing up beautifully and the white head of the female too. It was a most exciting and romantic setting for the birds. But as we rode on we began to doubt whether we were in fact going to find any Blue Ducks. Phil was already quite certain we should not.

We came, at last, to another river junction and here Fred Maxwell met us with the news that he had been several miles up the main Ruatatiunga without seeing a sign of a Blue Duck. We should stop here and brew up tea while he and Jim Douglas (whose horse had been badly cut by a stake during the first descent so that it had to be left by the first river crossing) went up the little side stream on foot. So we had a pleasant picnic on a grassy flat beside the river, and above on the steep slope of the rain forest we had fleeting glimpses of a pair of the great green New Zealand Pigeons. Someone brought Phil a spray of a small flowered yellow orchid which hung epiphytically from a tree (*Aerina* sp.). As we finished our meal Fred reappeared and walked down leaving his horse tethered at the junction, which was a good omen, and when he reached us he told us of finding a single Blue Duck about $\frac{2}{3}$ of a mile up the little brook – locally a creek! This as we afterwards found was an underestimate. We immediately decided to go up, taking cameras and tape recorders.

The first part of the walk was through forest, through a tangle of moss covered branches and tree trunks. It was very green and lush, mosses and lichens of inumerable species, and many kinds of ferns and club-mosses and liverworts. The canopy above was thick so that it was quite dark underneath, but occasionally a shaft of light came through to illuminate the softness of it all. Everything was padded with the rich green plants, and the branches we had to climb over were perfectly upholstered. It was the most impressive bush we have been through on our whole tour. In New Zealand it is called just 'bush' though it deserved the name 'moss forest' more than the high bush which is so called in New Guinea.

We plunged down a tangled bank to a trickling stream and down it until it joined our brook, up which we turned. At this stage there was nothing for it but to abandon all hope of keeping our feet dry; shoes, socks and trousers were immersed to the knee and above as we waded up the middle of the stream itself. It was a long, tough and wearisome climb up through waterfalls under thick tangles of bush. The rocks were slippery, there were deep pools, big tree trunks to climb, thickly knitted fallen branches to walk over or push through, piles of flotsam left by earlier floods which collapsed under our weight. Phil was marvellous. She went up as fast as the rest so that they were all amazed at her stamina.

We had been going for an hour and a half (and were six hours out from Owhena) when we came to a recent landslide which had been mentioned by Fred Maxwell. One hundred yards beyond it was a small cairn of stones and immediately above this the single Blue Duck was said to be. Roy Cavanagh came back to say he had heard it whistle. We advanced cautiously and suddenly there it was within 15 feet, but very nervous and moving quite rapidly up stream. It sat eventually on a rock about 20 yards away, but half hidden by fallen branches spanning the stream. In appearance it was remarkably different from the two adults I had seen in Takahe Valley. It was hardly blue at all, but a dusky olive colour, with quite a strong metallic green on the back. Perhaps the most striking difference was the iris which was not bright yellow and startled, as I had seen before, but a dusky almost hazel yellow. Evidently this was the dark phase which has been described, but I had forgotten about it, (although I painted both forms in the 2nd volume of Delacour). I fell to wondering whether the North Island and South Island Blue Ducks were distinct races.

Meanwhile Charles had set up a camera but the view of the bird was interrupted by branches and before we could find a clear passage he had swum up stream into deep shadow under the bushes. Roy Cavanagh and one of the two Maori boys with us went round the duck to try and move it back towards us, but almost at once it took wing towards us and passed low over our heads, my first view of a flying Blue Duck, and this was Phil's first encounter with the bird at all.

Jim Douglas took my tripod and went blinding off down the stream, while we followed at a slower pace. This was tedious and unimaginative of him. Even down hill it was a long grind which would have been made interesting had there been a chance of coming upon the Blue Duck, but to know that someone was ahead quite spoiled the return journey for me. I suppose if you are to be 'shown' birds instead of finding them you must expect to follow, not to make the discoveries yourself, but it is not so difficult to make the visitor go in front – which is worth remembering in future, even with reference to wild geese at home perhaps.

We had a cup of tea when we came finally to the lunch place. Then

Hymenolaimus malacorhynchos

Blue or Mountain Ducks.

97

onto the horses and the long ride home. This was enlivened by the discovery of a Blue Duck half-way back and we wondered whether we had missed it on the way up, or whether it had flown down from some unexplored tributary in the interim.

After that Cresswell found two Blue Ducks on the junction pool where we had first crossed the river. We were able to assemble fairly close above them – say 50 yards – and they stayed swimming on or sitting by the edge of the water.

Phil and Charles and I had seen three Blue Ducks in 10 hours of riding and walking and we had not shot a foot of film on them, although we had nice pictures of the horses and river crossings and of 'cutting our way through impenetrable bush'. And so we came home on horses that were in much more of a hurry than they had been on the way out.

THURSDAY 10 JANUARY

A second attempt at filming Blue Ducks. We set off on horses directly from Owhena – not quite so big a party as yesterday – and rode down to the Waitahaia. On the way we disturbed a family of Paradise Shelducks – parents and five full grown young – which flew high up the valley, then down again and up again, and were joined by another pair so that for a while there were nine flying about. Far below was the river but these birds had been sitting on the steep grass slope hundreds of feet above the river and far from any water, but perhaps a trickling brook. Again it was a landscape of large dimensions and of very considerable grandeur which formed the background for these shelducks.

We rode down the river passing a single Grey Duck which sat tamely and watched us from the still water of a pool near the far shore. We crossed and recrossed the river in order to get the best riding and finally came to a party dipping sheep. It was in the next river (the name of which I never discovered) that we were expected to find the Blues. Halfway down the slope towards it we found Stan who had been out since dawn and had found a pair of Blue Ducks with five half grown

Drake Paradise Shelduck.

Blue Duck.

young at the foot of the ridge. He had seen another single bird at the junction pool just above. This pair with young was fairly well known, it seems. They had been observed to hatch 12 young, which when last seen two weeks before had been reduced to 8. Now they had apparently lost more.

We approached the final descent to the river with infinite caution, I being allowed to go ahead on foot. It was not until I was at the bottom that I finally saw the ducks about 70 yards upstream, although they must have been in full view for much of the time. I was climbing down the steep path. I signalled to the others to come down, we crossed the river on horses then dismounted and rigged cameras. The ducks had swum just out of sight round the corner. When all was ready we crept forward up on the slope about 20 feet above the river and came upon the family at fairly close quarters. Originally we had left Charles at river level just round the corner with a view to driving the birds down to him. Phil stayed on top and I was to go forward and round them so as to turn them down stream. I got to within about 100 feet and then began what was to become a $2\frac{1}{2}$ hour filming session with this obliging and long suffering Blue Duck family. The young were still in down, though the first feathers were beginning to show. They had blue bills, prominent white cheeks and a curious golden brown spot on either side of the back. This colour contrasted sharply with the dark grey and white of the rest of the down. There was a vague look of Carolina or Mandarin in the face markings, but also (especially in the shape of the head) a look of baby Goldeneyes, perhaps due to the white cheeks. The parents were as blue as those I had seen in Takahe Valley. The chestnut spots were different however, in the two birds. The female had pale orangey spots, the male's were more maroon, almost chocolate. As before the female was more nervy than the male, but they settled down well in various different pools.

In most of the places the young and sometimes the adults too did

BLACK TEAL

Aythya novae-zeelandiae

Hamurana
Rotorua
11ᵗʰ Jan. 1957

some feeding. In other places they all went to sleep. In between they swam briskly in the white water, and once passed upstream within 15 feet of me. In one place the young seemed to find food on the underside of a stone which overhung them.

When I had shot 350 feet and Charles had shot 500 we decided to call it a day and let the birds depart without more ado. We had a hasty cup of tea, some biscuits and cheese and tomatoes and remounted for the long homeward grind. There is no doubt that our horses were a good deal more tired than they had been the day before. It was, nevertheless, a quick and uneventful journey over which the aura of success hung like a rosy glow.

FRIDAY 11 JANUARY

A five hour drive from Gisborne to Rotorua. On our way we were taken to the mouth of a beautiful clear river which is part of the grounds of a holiday hotel run by an acquaintance of mine, Lovat-Fraser. It is called Hamurana and it is very imaginatively laid out. The river is about 20 yards wide, crystal clear and smoothly flowing with beds of brilliant green weed. On it were groups of Black Teal (New Zealand Scaup) and a few Grey Ducks, one with a brood. There were also some Pukeko (the Swamp Hen or Blue Gallinule).

On a stretch of 50 yards of river, on which there were also boats, we saw perhaps 25 little New Zealand Scaup, and in one place – though alas in the shade – a group of them were displaying. This display and the call which went with it were extremely like the display and call of the Redhead, and quite unlike anything done by Tufted Ducks. The head was thrown over the back, though not so far as in the Canvasback, and when the call – a soft whirring whistle – was made by the drake his chin was enlarged – a thing which I noticed in the Australian White-eye and which is so typical of Redhead and Pochard. Just as the Ring-necked Duck is not so close to the Tufted as might be supposed, so I believe the New Zealand 'Black Teal' is not very close either. How strange it is that characters of this kind seem to be interlaced among the species suggesting affinities between those which do not at first sight appear to be closely related, and showing new differences between those that do. This must mean the loss or suppression of these characters in some species. Thus, surely, an archaic Tufted Duck got bored with throwing its head back and the species lost the habit. And at once we're back with the question 'What is the survival value or true function of courtship display?'

Blue Ducks.

When the sun was too low for more photography we motored on the few miles to Rotorua and pulled up at Brent's Hotel. Mr. Fitzgerald, the old road engineer who used to keep Blue Ducks and many other birds, and who was with us at the New Grounds [Slimbridge] a year or so ago, was on the doorstep to meet us. He was spending the night at the hotel and during dinner he described how he had started the Blues on worms which they immediately ate, and thereafter switched to slivers of meat. He will put all his experience at the disposal of Roy Cavanagh who is to ship the birds to us.

SATURDAY 12 JANUARY

We spent the morning being shown the hot-springs and Maori village by the most famous of the guides – a characterful lady called Rangi.

Her patter was mainly for American consumption, and unfortunately an American party joined us. Rangi was full of philosophy and economics and comparisons, and her Americanised jokes alienated Phil and Charles, but making allowances for the number of times she has to do it, I thought she was rather good. There was some original comment designed for the particular visitor. I wished I could be sure I was doing it as well when I show people round the New Grounds. There is inevitably a boisterousness about the extrovert type of guide, but the alternative is evident boredom with the work, and I prefer the gusto.

The decoration of Rangi's own house and of the houses in the Maori village is very handsome. Black and white patterns on the beams and dark red covering the carved figures, which are of the 'totem pole' type. On one house was a man holding the horn of an obvious narwhal and I wondered where they had seen one. Graham Turbott said it must just be a western influence. Rangi had a different story. The spiral horn was, according to her, a rope and the fish was being towed and this represented some complex conception of Maori origins. But it was still an obvious narwhal.

The main geyser boils up and gushes forth every 3 or 4 hours. We were lucky in that it did so as we passed. Approaching we saw a small fountain of steam, splaying out, and called the Prince of Wales' feathers. This heralds a much higher fountain rising about 40 feet. The spray from this descends as rather cold rain. Perhaps the nicest thing we saw there was the crater of bubbling mud.

In due course we set forth again by car and drove to Hamilton where we were met by a large reception committee of the Auckland Acclimatisation Society. They were mostly elderly shooters, quite ignorant of their quarry. These are the folk to whom the New Zealand Government has delegated its wildlife administration and law enforcement. It is a pretty weak set up, as the level of prejudice and ignorance is very high and a wildlife programme which is not based on scientific research is pretty valueless. The three Government biologists (Gordon Williams, Kaj Westerscov and Ron Balham – whom we did not meet because he has gone south with Ed Hillary) do not find it easy to make the Societies accept unpalatable truths, and the Societies have the final say on season lengths, bag limits and so on. Actually the season length is very short though different in each area. The longest is 4 weeks and shortest a fortnight. (All seasons include weekends at each end). The bag limit on ducks is 10. Black Swans and Canada Geese are unlimited.

In my view it is high time the Acclimatisation Societies became Wild Life Societies and cease to perpetuate in their titles the disastrous policies of introduction which have wrought such havoc with the native species.

We transferred to a new set of motors and went to Auckland by way of a lake with 1,500 Black Swans in sight and said to have 48,500 more 'round the corner'. Apparently we saw only 5–10% of the water, and there was said to be a greater concentration in some other part, so there might have been 20,000.

We went to another swamp where there were a dozen or so Grey Ducks and there had an excellent tea with beer. The driver of our car – a high official of the Society – said he had several Pukekos in his deep freeze and were they a kind of duck!

SUNDAY 13 JANUARY

We set off with Graham Turbott in a Department of the Interior car, to go to Waipu to see the Brown Ducks. We had a picnic lunch overlooking the Bay with the islands called the Hen and Chickens beyond. Below was the flat farmland through which the Brown Duck streams go winding. We arrived at the hotel just after lunch, to be met by a small party of whom the leader seemed to be an elderly gentleman called Prickett with an elderly wife. They had been working hard 'to find the ducks for us' and had set up a hide by the river quite close to the town. We went there first.

The fields were full of a grass called *Paspallum* the flowers of which are covered with a sticky substance consisting largely of ergot [a product of the fungus *Claviceps purpurea* sometimes used as a drug]. This is so bad for clothes that it was necessary to wear bathing shorts. We decided to put up a hide, and then for some of the party to try to drive Brown Ducks up towards us. Four of them had recently been seen down there. But they are crepuscular or nocturnal creatures and much given to hiding in the rushes or overhanging bushes by day, so that when Charles and I had been there for nearly an hour the drivers – including Phil – arrived having seen nothing.

So it was a case of 'Up sticks' and away to a place called, I think, Ryans where a pair of Brown Ducks had been seen sitting on a willow branch beside a bridge two days before. This seemed a pretty long shot, but 20 minutes later Phil and I were tip-toeing up to the bridge with Prickett just behind. Nothing was in view, but suddenly ripples came from under a thick tangle of willow scrub on the far bank. Surely it would be a Pukeko, but no! Out swam two little Brown Ducks. They were exactly the same, and though, no doubt a pair, I could see nothing in plumage to distinguish the sexes. The male, judged on behaviour and slightly larger size, had a split upper mandible at the tip. Almost at once the pair disappeared into cover again. They were only 10 yards away and made no attempt to fly. Prickett went quickly above them and they turned down and went under the bridge.

There was much to-ing and fro-ing before the little ducks were finally held in a state of equilibrium in a patch of willows on a little island. Charles and I then fixed up our cameras overlooking a small patch of sunlight and Phil most skilfully manoeuvred the birds into it, and took stills of them at the same time.

After half an hour they came to tell us that five birds had been located a little further down stream. The river was very thickly grown with willows and we walked in the brilliant evening sunshine through a hay field newly cut. Almost at once I caught a glimpse of a pair but it was far too fleeting and too dark for photography. Stationed in the centre of a sharp bend in the river under the dark trees we waited and in due course five Brown Ducks appeared. These were far more nervous than the first pair. The most important thing was that one of the males was in fairly bright colour, and a slanting white line on the sides of the tail forward of the black under tail coverts was quite conspicuous.

On the way back across the paddock Charles took some shots to establish the habitat. Then we piled into the cars, fairly well satisfied. As we drove back to town we passed over a river bridge not a quarter of

Anas chlorotis
Brown Duck.
Waipu
13th January 1957.

a mile from our hotel. Here the earlier cars had stopped, and at once we saw the reason. Out on the open river swam three Brown Ducks. To be sure they went off down stream when the crowd spewed out of the various cars, but Gibson, who had joined us, went down one side and Cavanagh went down the other. We saw a brief aggressive rush by the brightly coloured male against the third bird which thereafter disappeared. The pair, however, swam back up stream.

I crossed to the far bank to move them out into what was left of the setting sunlight. They were under a bush and I walked right up to it and could see them looking up at me with apparent nonchalance. There was an old landing net lying on the bank and I picked it up to persuade them to swim out. I could quite easily have caught at least one of them had I been so minded. As it was they swam quietly out and I had a grand view of them. The male's head was very dark with a green sheen, but what interested me most was a sharply defined jet black area on the back of the head, just where it is black in the drake Pintail. The whitish neckring (narrower than in the Mallard) is turned up at the back to what seems to be the beginning of a Pintail's white vertical neck streak. The bird looked in shape surprisingly like a Kerguelen Pintail.

Suddenly I felt that this was not at all the degenerate Mallard which we had supposed it to be, but a bird with many pintail characters. Thinking about it afterwards I am convinced that this is very near still to 'the original duck' – that is to say it is descended, and perhaps not very much altered by selective pressure, from a basic *Anas* which was a common ancestor to Mallard and Pintail. This seemed to me to be a moment of truth, and perhaps one of the most valuable conclusions to be drawn from the whole of our tour. To me what is most fascinating about the study of evolution is to be able, by looking at a branch, to judge just how high up the trunk it branched off in those far away times. So the Brown Duck is a primitive and not a degenerate. The Chestnut Teal has varied more, no doubt under heavier selective pressure in Australia.

So we filmed the pair of Brown Ducks in the evening light and found that they had kept an excellent dinner for us at the hotel. And on Tuesday it was goodbye to New Zealand and Australia.

New Zealand Brown Ducks.

Hood Marine Iguanas.
Amblyrhynchus cristatus
venustissimus.

Most brightly
Coloured males.

7. Mar. 1959

Average
rather
less
bright.

30"

Galapagos Dove

Nesopelia
galapagensis

⅓ hat size

CHAPTER 6

The Galápagos Islands

DIARIES 2 AND 3 1959

In the early 1950s I became deeply involved in the work of the International Union for Conservation of Nature and Natural Resources (IUCN), and was a member of its board when it decided to celebrate the centenary in 1959 of the publication of Charles Darwin's most famous book, *The Origin of Species**. This involved creating a Foundation to set up a Charles Darwin Research Station in the Galápagos Islands.

As a life-long admirer of the great naturalist I was also instrumental in persuading the BBC, in conjunction with IUCN, to mount a small filming expedition to the Galápagos as part of my series of *Look* programmes which had been running for four years and were to run for a further ten years. This was to be one of the programmes shown under the title *Faraway Look*; Philippa and I were to be accompanied by Tony Soper as cameraman. Our objective was to film as many animals, large and small, as we could find, and Phil was to take still photographs of them all as well.

We called in first at the British Virgin Islands, where we stayed for a few days with the Administrator, Geoffrey Allsebrook, at Government House. We swam on the reefs off Tortola, Bellamy Cay and Virgin Gorda recording the fishes we saw, and we rode up to the last remaining patch of original rain forest – only 80 acres of it – near the 1,700 ft summit of Sage Mountain, where we found species of *Peripatus* (primitive terrestrial arthropods), the strange evolutionary link between the worms and the arthropods – the great group which includes the insects, spiders and crustaceans. *Peripatus* looks like a velvet millipede. We caught large ground spiders and whip scorpions (also called Pedipalps). We filmed Free-tailed Bats and diving Brown Pelicans, and an Anolis Lizard with a forked tail.

From Tortola in the British Virgin Islands we went briefly to Antigua, where we snorkeled at Mill Reef, and thence onwards to Trinidad to stay with an old friend Dr Will Beebe who was then 82 years old, but just as good company as always. He was our host at Simla in the Arima Valley where David Snow was studying the birds –

Butterflies of the Family *Heliconiidae* being studied by Jocelyn Crane at Simla, January 1959.

*Charles Darwin spent from 15 September–20 October 1835 in the Galápagos Islands on his voyage in the *Beagle*. The zoological observations he made during this visit were seminal to the ideas expressed in the *Origin of Species*. As he says in his Diary of 1837 'In July opened first note book on "transmutation of species". Had been greatly struck from about month of previous March on character of S. American fossils and species on Galápagos Archipelago. These facts origin (especially latter) of all my views.'

Peripatus sp.

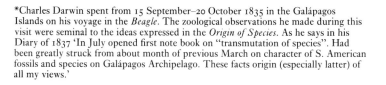

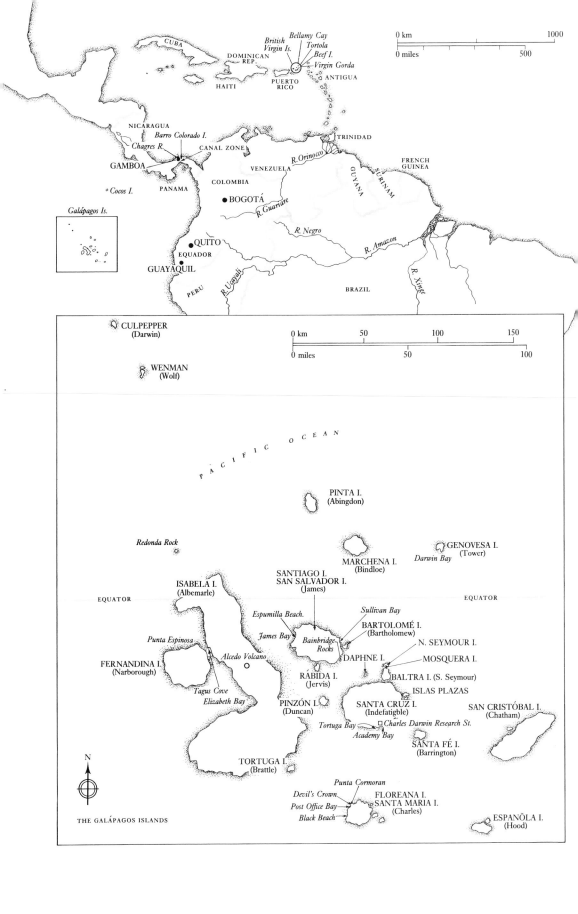

0 km _____ 1000
0 miles _____ 500

CUBA
DOMINICAN REP.
HAITI
PUERTO RICO
British Virgin Is.
Bellamy Cay
Tortola
Beef I.
Virgin Gorda
ANTIGUA

NICARAGUA
Barro Colorado I.
Chagres R.
CANAL ZONE
GAMBOA
COLOMBIA
TRINIDAD
VENEZUELA
R. Orinoco
GUYANA
SURINAM
FRENCH GUINEA
Cocos I.
PANAMA
● BOGOTÁ
R. Guaviare
R. Negro
R. Amazon
Galápagos Is.
● QUITO
EQUADOR
GUAYAQUIL
PERU
R. Ucayali
R. Xingú
BRAZIL

0 km _____ 50 _____ 100 _____ 150
0 miles _____ 50 _____ 100

CULPEPPER
(Darwin)

WENMAN
(Wolf)

P A C I F I C   O C E A N

PINTA I.
(Abingdon)

Redonda Rock

GENOVESA I.
(Tower)
Darwin Bay

MARCHENA I.
(Bindloe)

EQUATOR

SANTIAGO I.
SAN SALVADOR I.
(James)

ISABELA I.
(Albemarle)

EQUATOR

Espumilla Beach
Sullivan Bay

Punta Espinosa
James Bay
Bainbridge Rocks
BARTOLOMÉ I.
(Bartholomew)

N. SEYMOUR I.

Alcedo Volcano
DAPHNE I.
MOSQUERA I.

FERNANDINA I.
(Narborough)
Tagus Cove
Elizabeth Bay
RÁBIDA I.
(Jervis)
BALTRA I. (S. Seymour)
ISLAS PLAZAS

PINZÓN I.
(Duncan)
SANTA CRUZ I.
(Indefatigable)
SAN CRISTÓBAL I.
(Chatham)

Tortuga Bay
□ *Charles Darwin Research St.*
Academy Bay

SANTA FÉ I.
(Barrington)

TORTUGA I.
(Brattle)

N

Punta Cormoran
Devil's Crown
Post Office Bay
Black Beach
FLOREANA I.
SANTA MARIA I.
(Charles)

ESPAÑOLA I.
(Hood)

THE GALÁPAGOS ISLANDS

notably manakins – which have a fascinating pattern of courtship behaviour, and Oil Birds, which can fly in their nesting caves in total darkness using echo-location to guide themselves. In my diary I wrote this about our host:

Juvenile Blue Parrot Fish, *Scarus coeruleus*

William Beebe, at 82, is immediately recognisable as a great man: a visionary who is still as greatly moved by the wonder of animals as ever he has been in all his long and adventurous life.

He is tall and very thin – perfectly erect, though now rather frail looking. His desk is in one corner of the large room which is part-laboratory part-living room of the research station at Simla. One end of the room consists of huge folding doors drawn back in the day time so that the whole end of the room is filled with the superb vista of the upper valley, the slopes thickly forested and aflame with blossoming immortelle trees. The little terrace, down a few steps from this great open window, is planted with flowering shrubs especially to attract hummingbirds, of which two or three species are common, and 16 have been recorded.

Our projected trip to Galápagos raised great enthusiasm in him, and he told us in detail of his adventures there and about diving in shark waters with a cage into which he could climb if necessary – but when a shark did approach him he couldn't find the door! He told us in some detail about his bathysphere (an object used for deep-sea observation) and showed us pictures of the fishes he saw a quarter of a mile down.

On the last evening of our short 5 day stay we heard a piping noise in the forest. It was quite common and we had heard it every night. We asked Will what it was. 'Some hold it is an amphibian, some an owl – we have never been able to determine which – so far.'

The next staging post of our journey was the island of Barro Colorado in Panama. It became an island during the building of the Panama Canal, by the flooding of Lake Gatun. The research station on it had been created by Dr Frank Chapman of the American Museum of Natural History in New York, who was an old friend of my mother's and who had befriended me at the time of my first New York picture exhibition (1938). It was therefore a place I had heard a lot about and had long wanted to visit.

From the top:
Antillean Bananaquit or Honey-Creeper, *Coereba flaviola*; Antillean Crested Hummingbird, *Orthorhyncus cristatus*; Emerald-throated Hummingbird, *Sericotes holosericeus.*

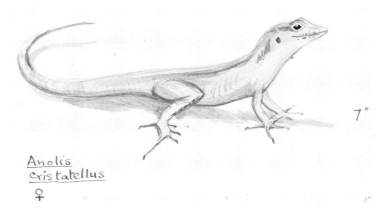

Anolis
cristatellus
♀

7"

Ground Spider. Natural Size

This species grows
considerably larger, & the
abdomen is often much
fatter. Larger ones are
rather darker in colour.

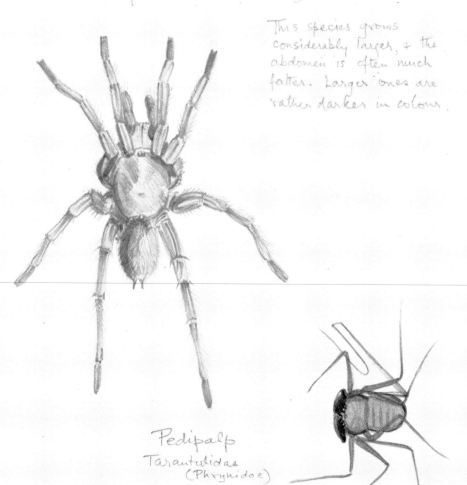

Pedipalp
Tarantulidae
　　(Phrynidae)

The first pair of
legs are developed
as antennae. These
pedipalps are reputed to
grow so large that their
'antenna' legs span almost
a foot, i.e. twice as big
as this one.

Tortola. Jan 1959

TUESDAY 27 JANUARY

Dr Martin Moynihan, Director of the station at Barro Colorado, met us in Panama City with a young Kinkajou on his shoulder. We all went by train to Friholes and by boat to the island.

We were woken by Howler Monkeys before dawn the next morning so we began our filming work early that day and the next.

FRIDAY 30 JANUARY

We set off from Barro Colorado in the dark with Martin Moynihan to Gamboa where dawn was breaking as we embarked in an aluminium boat. We buzzed up the Chagres River, past weed booms, to an area of weedy half-floating islands. There were many little black jaçanas with yellow-tipped red bills and yellow primary and secondary feathers. The immatures were white-breasted and surprisingly unlike the adults.

We crossed to a new area of pools carpeted with white waterlilies and water hyacinth and there, as the airthrust engine stopped, we looked at 5 little reddish brown birds swimming slowly away from us through the thick weed. We saw at once that they were Masked Ducks – the object of our day's excursion. There were two males and three females. Two of the five carried their tails up, the rest down. The heads were flat-topped, about half the length of the body. The tail was long, other-

Above: Jack, *Caranx latus*.
Below: Palometa,
Trachinotus goodei.

Longuemar's
Hermit Hummingbird,
Phaethornis l. longuemareus.

wise they looked rather like *Thalassornis*, the African White-backed Duck. The females' heads were most strikingly marked so that I though of young grebes or of the parrot fish *Scarus croicencis* – the Mudbelly. We watched them for 15–20 minutes and when we tried, rather ineptly, to get closer they flew up. We never saw them again although we hunted the marsh in the direction they took. We found a flock of 50 Lesser Scaups, and had lunch on a forest point which offered a dryshod landing, where I sat down in an ants' nest and was badly bitten. Then after further searches for the Masked Ducks I had a swim in a shallow pool. It was enchanting and the weed scenery was wonderful. One little fish nibbled in the small of my back, another my nipple. Most of the water here was out of my depth, yet the weeds came to the surface in many places. There were deep shadows under the floating weed and rhizomes of the half-floating island. The shadows were rather alarming. How many snapping turtles were hidden in the soft green weed below? It was hot where the water was trapped by the weed.

When my swim was over (Panama tummy prevented Phil and Tony from joining me) it was time to start home so, with the breeze behind us, we whizzed down the river again to Gamboa. And so back to Barro Colorado island.

From Panama we flew to Quito (Ecuador) and spent one day – 5 February – looking for torrent ducks on the San Pedro River.

FRIDAY 5 FEBRUARY

We travelled out from Quito in two cars, and our guide was Signor Ponce. We stopped the cars where the road and railway cross a large fast-flowing river by a natural bridge. The river was far below and on stones beside it was a pair of slate grey tyrant-flycatchers behaving exactly like wagtails. Signor Ponce said that the torrent ducks were to be seen on this stretch of the river in the early morning.

We began to work our way along the left bank of the river, going downstream. There were frequent sets of rapids, and fine vertical cliffs in many places, with a marvellous red flowered bromeliad growing on them. We had lunch on a slope overlooking the river and Signor Ponce said he thought that at this time of day the ducks were resting on some rocky ledge under the banks, and the best time of day to see them was 7 am. We finally decided to strike on towards a river junction some way further down.

The two young hunters moved off, and presently we heard them shout and saw them waving on the hillside a quarter of a mile away from which they could see down the next reach of the river. Signor Ponce went off at the double, then came back, at the double, for Tony's camera. We followed. Eventually, scratched and breathless, we reached the group overlooking the river and they pointed excitedly downstream. There, sure enough, was a female torrent duck fishing at the edge of the rapids.

She kept jumping up onto a stone, then into the torrent and diving at once. She stayed down for about 10 seconds and then emerged and hopped up onto the next stone, all the time working upstream. Then I saw another female nearer to us, and she fished up towards us until out of sight under the cliff below.

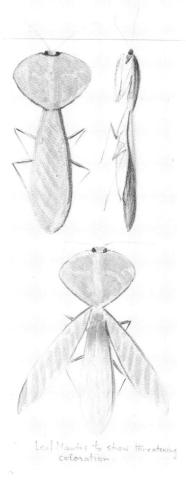

Leaf Mantis to show threatening coloration.

Masked Ducks in the Chagres River, Panama.
30th Jan 1959.

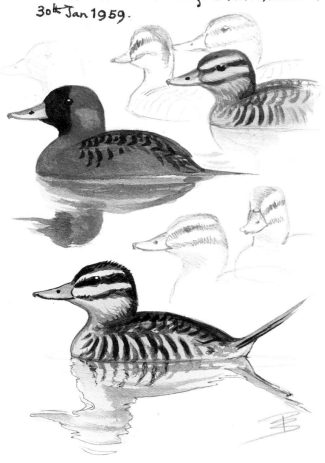

We were only a few hundred yards from the road when I spotted a torrent drake fishing in a set of rapids, and we watched the bird preening on a stone for 10 minutes or more. Then we stalked down through a field of maize, emerging about 30 yards from the rock where he was sleeping. Eventually he moved downstream, after which he was unwilling to move any further but remained on a ledge of the cliff two or three feet above the water, with his head to one side but not under his wing. We left him sitting there. During the preening he had frequently used his tail as a support. We had a very good look at his plumage. There was no suggestion of a dark neck ring as in the southern races, and this was, as far as I could tell from both male and female, a typical Colombian Torrent Duck.

And so back to Quito.

Merganetta armata colombiana
San Pedro River. Ecuador. 5 Feb.1959.

On Friday 6 February we left Quito and flew to Guayaquil, our taking off point for the Galapágos Islands.

SATURDAY 7 FEBRUARY

Took off from Guayaquil at 12 noon in a Curtis freighter – 12 passengers in a 48 passenger aircraft. This was a one–off trial excursion flight to test out the tourist potential for the islands. The pilot had never flown this route before. With us is a group of Ecuadorian tourists – including a poet and dramatist, a mother and a small baby returning to San Cristóbal, the Captain of the patrol boat which will be taking us round the islands, and us. The Captain of the aircraft is an American, Captain Dick Torrance, and the whole atmosphere is fairly informal.

We landed safely on Baltra after the radio beacon went off the air, but the islands had been apparent from the patch of high cloud above the 8/8 low cloud cover. This was definitely a relief as the Galápagos Islands are named by some as 'The Enchanted Isles' because they were supposed to sink into the sea at times. If a ship or aircraft were to miss them there is no land between here and Japan. We were met by Gusch Angermeyer and Chris Zuber of *Paris Match*.

Chris had already been in Galápagos several weeks taking film and stills for his magazine but he had not had a chance to travel from island to island. He had learnt that we would be taken around in a *patroullera* – a 50 ft patrol launch of the Ecuadorian Navy – and he came to meet us for the express purpose of hitching a lift. He was clad only in very brief bathing pants and opened with 'Would you like me to show you the islands?' We were a little doubtful, but in the end it was agreed that he should come with us.

It was a half hour walk to the quay where we found the patrol boat with Angermeyer's fishing boat lying outside it. Here we met Johnny Angermeyer (Gusch's son), 14, brown and longhaired and un-shy, he speaks English as his native tongue, and knows about animals.

We went looking for lizards and saw the red crabs on the lava rocks of the shore. There were pelicans and boobies and dusky gulls and the tracks of turtles up the beach. The lizards were tame but virtually uncatchable.

We slept in the open on the quay in sleeping bags on our air mattresses. It was cool but not cold and some mosquitoes turned up in the morning.

SUNDAY 8 FEBRUARY

We set off for San Cristóbal in the patrol boat which has a crew of 12.

Wreck Bay, San Cristóbal – capital of the Galápagos Islands.

The journey took four hours arriving at noon. Ashore we were received by the Naval Governor, who led us to his headquarters – an imposing stone building. Here, in about an hour, we worked out a plan to make two long trips in the patrol boat, the first to the northern islands, the second to Isabela and Fernandina. We saw lava lizards and black Darwin's finches and the Yellow Warbler (sometimes called the Mangrove Warbler), and 4 tame tortoises – 2 from Santa Cruz and 2 from Isabela. Not much difference between them that I could see.

Evening – drinks at the kiosk at the base of the pier, then supper at the Miramar Hotel – a tiny place where I am now writing to the tune of 3 guitars and the charming singing of Ecuadorian songs. The supper was good but the mosquitoes were bad round our ankles. And so to bed in the Naval Barracks.

MONDAY 9 FEBRUARY

To Santa Cruz in the *patroullera* – about 4 hours. We passed close to Santa Fé and saw goats. On arrival we saw our first marine iguanas on the cliff near where we anchored. We swam in murky water and Tony saw a large shark.

At Carl Angermeyer's (Gusch's brother) house we found the verandah covered with small marine iguanas, and one large male ran up to Carl to be scratched. The little ones – one was sitting in a geranium pot on the balustrade – ate banana. Curled up in a corner was a half grown sea lion, and over the edge of the balcony were quantities of the big red crabs. As well as all these native animals, free to come and go at will, was an alsatian and a small white cat.

We ate at Susan Castro's – food scanty, and slept comfortably in the Castro guest house after moving beds into the sitting room to get air without mosquitoes.

On Wednesday 11 February we made an early start in the *patroullera* for Tower (Genovesa) Island where we intended to stay for a couple of days. The sea was glass calm on the way over and we had a marvellous view at close quarters of a pod of five Sperm Whales. We spent two days filming the birds and beasts of Tower and we were all struck by the tameness of the animals. Indeed we liked the island so much that we decided to alter our schedule and stay an extra day.

FRIDAY 13 FEBRUARY

We climbed to the crater lake. Chris went on ahead after we had agreed to go in company, but it did not matter. All through the 10–20 ft high vegetation – bare trees without leaves – *Scalesia* (daisy trees) – there were nests of the Red-footed Booby and occasionally pairs of Great Frigate-birds.

When we finally reached the crest of the ridge we had a fine view of a lake about half a mile in diameter, with a belt of green algae in the shallow waters round the edge, a green wreath of mangroves making a striking contrast with the grey and purple lava of the 200 ft cliffs surrounding the crater.

The only birds on the water were Galápagos Pintails, swimming out from under the mangrove branches. We saw 20 or more but there were very likely 5 times as many under cover. The only other bird I saw on the water was a Red-footed Booby. But the trees and cliffs were covered

The Marine Iguana
Amblyrhynchus cristatus
Santa Cruz race.

with boobies and frigates. Most of the Red-footed Boobies have well-grown young about to lose their white down, but we have found two females sitting on eggs, on neatly built up nests on top of old ones. Thus we seem to be between two breeding seasons. The same seems to apply to the Blue-faced Boobies which have almost feathering young and the frigates which have feathered white-headed immatures still being fed as they sit about in the bushes. Only one female have we found with an egg, and courtship is in full swing.

The frigate-bird sequence seems to be as follows: The male takes up a territory and blows up his huge red throated balloon – the size of a good sized party balloon and in due course a female chooses him. When she does so she descends from above very close to him, so that their wings intertwine. Every time she leaves he watches for her return with pouch inflated, from time to time spreading his wings, throwing his

Drake Galapagos Pintail
Anas bahamensis galapagensis
James Bay. Santiago. 14 Feb 1959
"Patillo"

Great Frigate-birds,
Fregata minor ridgewayi,
and their courtship display.

head back and making a musical polysyllabic coo-ing – a very beautiful sound. As he does so the wings vibrate. An even higher degree of ecstatic intensity is reached in this display when the female arrives. The male then wags his head from side to side with a soft clicking sound.

The next stage seems to be that the female takes charge of the nest site and the male brings twigs for its construction, often robbing other males or Red-footed Boobies. When the male arrives with a twig there is a formal greeting ceremony and some intertwining of necks and bills and often of wings. When the nest is complete the female lays a single egg. We only saw one bird incubating and so we do not know whether the male also incubates.

The most striking thing about the frigate-bird, after the balloon-like scarlet pouch, is the great size of its wings – as if they belonged to a larger bird – so that the body goes up and down as they fly. The legs and feet are tiny. Combined, these make the bird extraordinarily clumsy when trying to perch among branches. In flight however it is very beautiful, and we saw large numbers – over a hundred – soaring together in thermals. The white- or cream-headed immature frigate-birds were dotted around the bushes in the colony, and many were also flying. We saw them being fed by regurgitation by males and females, to the accompaniment of a loud sad call almost like a human baby. Adult female frigate-birds have a white feathered throat patch in approximately the same area as the bare scarlet skin of the male.

The breeding period of the beautiful Fork-tailed Gull seems to be more flexible. Many had eggs; one of them was definitely laying while we were there. Two pairs had small young. Most of the young were well feathered, many trying their wings and a few on the wing. The young are also handsome, broadly barred in black and very pale grey on the back with a white head and dark patch round the eye, giving the impression of a very large eye. The adult gull is comparable with Sabine's Gull for sheer beauty. It is extremely handsome. The birds were not very aggressive either to us or to each other, although I saw, and filmed, a brief attack by a parent on a neighbour's feathered baby. The cry was very varied – a plaintive mewing at the intruder, beginning (in high intensity) with a crackling sound. Sometimes the crackling alone, and sometimes something very like a human laugh.

Galápagos Fork-tailed Gull,
Creagrus furcatus.

Hyles
~~*Deiops*~~ lineata florilega   Nat. Size.
?*D. livornica* ssp.?
Small Hawk Moth which flew to light on the
quarter deck of the Patrol Boat at 7.0 p.m. 14 Feb 1959
at James Bay, Santiago (James). Galápagos.

The next day we sailed to James (Santiago) Island early in the morning – but not as early as we should have, perhaps the excesses of last night's supper of lobster and potato soup followed by lobster and rice were catching up on us! We were still at James the following day.

Galápagos Flamingo.

SUNDAY 15 FEBRUARY

Cloudy all day, but exciting. The *patroullera* moved 2 miles to the south end of James Bay. Phil and Tony and I went on round the coast in one of the two fishing boats which had spent the night anchored near us. The objective was a colony of Galápagos Fur Seals described as large by Eibl Eibesfeldt [distinguished German zoologist] and said to be 'south of James Bay'. We had gone no more than 2 miles when the boat anchored and we were ferried ashore as this, it seemed, was the place.

To be sure there were a great many sea lions, but we were far from certain whether they were the Galápagos Sea Lion, *Zalophus wollebaeki*,

Lava beach on James Island.

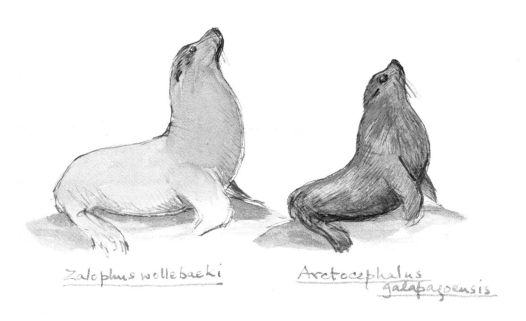

Zalophus wollebaeki *Arctocephalus galapagoensis*

or the much rarer Galápagos Fur Seal, *Arctocephalus galapagoensis*. There were many young ones in almost chestnut fur far up on the rocky shore. In the water there were big bulls and many quiet friendly cows. I filmed a bull as he came for me and only stepped aside when he filled the whole screen and I had to use my tripod to fend him off. It was a young male and at about 6 feet he slowed up, so that the merest nudge with the tripod leg caused him to stop, and then to withdraw. I found two sleeping babies who were all the time charming, even when fast asleep. Later Tony and I filmed 6 young ones in a hollow in the rocks, and I sat all in amongst them. Several times they came up to sniff my hand. Earlier Phil and I had thrown sticks to some young playing in a pool and they had seized them and dashed round the pool, playing delightfully. We must swim with the young ones later, but I can accept Eibesfeldt's statement that the adult males are really dangerous. They are huge animals.

I began to have terrible doubts about the identification of our seals. I decided to talk to the fisherman about it. Those we were looking at had only one '*pelo*' (hair), the other kind (Galápagos Fur Seal) had '*dos pelos*' and was smaller, but with a big head (a reference to the fur which is all the same length in the sea lions, but consists of longer 'guard' hairs with short soft hairs in between in the fur seals (*dos pelos*). If we would go with him he would show us. We went 200 yards along the shore and then out onto the cliff edge and he pointed to a small sea lion. '*Dos pelos*' he said and we looked carefully and he was right. It was a smaller seal, duller and darker in colour – with almost a hoary effect of the fur. The head was proportionately broader and the muzzle shorter. The nose was a small black dot no larger than my little finger-nail. The ears did not seem to be down curved as in the commoner species, and the hind legs and after end of the body were smaller in proportion to the heavy fore quarters. The largest we saw, of some 30 or 40 was not more than 5 ft long, whereas the bulls of the other species must have been quite twice as long.

The fur seals were if anything tamer than the sea lions, climbed vertical rock faces in the most agile manner, and had a roar much more like a lion than the 'troak-troak-troak' of the sea lions, so familiar from the Californian species seen in zoos.

Two things were surprising. First the comparatively similar appearances of the two species which could easily lead to confusion even among careful observers because of the great differences in colour between wet animals and dry ones, the considerable individual variation, and the apparently regular change of colours with age in the sea lions. The other extraordinary thing was that both species were able to live together on this same stretch of coast, apparently all mixed up. I had the impression that the fur seals were forced to use steep and difficult lava faces by the fact that all the easier rock slopes were territorially occupied by the larger and more aggressive species. It might well be that the pressure of the sea lion is more significant than the pressure of man in limiting the population of the fur seal.

We had used most of our film on the sea lions and I only had 40 ft of colour left out of 250 colour and 200 black and white when we discovered we were filming the wrong beast! We reminded ourselves of a certain affinity with Noel Coward's Mrs Wentworth Brewster (who discovered in the *nick* of time that life was for living).

During lunch, and after it as we sat in the patrol boat's wheelhouse writing up our notes it began to rain. At first Tony thought of washing his hair and his shirt. Then as shower followed shower we thought of filling waterbottles from the rain collecting on the awning aft. Finally as the rain became heavier we developed a technique of running it down our arms into buckets. From this stage a pipe was rigged from a funnel straight into the freshwater tank. As the dregs from this tank had looked like tea for the last couple of days we were glad to have this improved water situation. The collecting of it was attended with considerable hilarity. Everyone greatly enjoyed our makeshift arrangements. Afterwards we had bully beef for tea. An amusing if not a productive afternoon filmwise, and an enjoyable day.

On the following day progress was slow because we were towing a fishing boat to save its fuel. The wind was blowing onto the only landing beach at Daphne Island, so we could not land. Eventually the fishing boat was within his fuel range of San Cristóbal, so we slipped the tow and headed towards the Islas Plazas, where we anchored in the narrow channel between the two islands and went ashore on the southern one. Here we saw our first land iguanas.

MONDAY 16 FEBRUARY

At the top of the island I saw the tail of an iguana protruding from a hole. He blew himself up to his best size to prevent me from extracting him, but it was no good. He opened his mouth showing a curious little round pink tongue, but he was slow and could not turn on me so that there was no real risk of being bitten. Underneath he was quite yellow and even above he was yellower than any others we had seen. After filming him in close-up we put him back in his hole and walked to the east end of the island, passing a huge bull sea lion with a harem of about 30 cows – one with a very newly born calf. At the top of the cliff were a few of the shore crabs and a few marine iguanas. The young Captain

More than averagely brightly coloured male

Land Iguana of
Las Plazas Islands,
Conolophus subcristatus ssp.

View from Plazas Islands looking towards Santa Cruz.

joined us, and, to the sound of calling Fork-tailed Gulls and barking sea lions we came back to the beach at dusk.

That night there was so much dew that Phil decided to sleep in the wheelhouse, but I slept on the foredeck. It was not a good anchorage for a peaceful night, as the swell came through, and the tide was so strong that it drifted the boat broadside to the waves. Then there is the trouble here of getting the temperature right for sleeping. Lying on top of a sleeping bag (on an air mattress) is just too cold and inside it is just too hot! But we have not been troubled by mosquitoes at night on board. So I slept adequately under the moon with the constant cries of sea lions as the background music of my night.

TUESDAY 17 FEBRUARY

Still on South Plaza Island. A lovely, lovely day – in such a beautiful and exciting place. We started work early, and were ashore at 7.30 in bright low sun. At first we filmed cactus trees and ourselves walking through them. Then by chance a Galápagos Short-eared Owl came out of a bush and sat at my feet and got himself filmed. Also under the bush was a headless Audubon's Shearwater – the small species with fleshy-grey legs and feet – which the owl had obviously been eating.

Then on to film the land iguanas, more visible and numerous in the bright sun than they had been the night before. Very bright yellow ones were fairly rare, but there were a few beautiful ones, especially a half sized one which was orange on the back with yellow head, legs and feet. We singled out a very well marked male and spent half an hour (in our bathing shorts) getting scratched to pieces by the cactus chasing it about until finally he went down a hole under a bush and we caught him. This was all in aid of big close-ups of his head and crest.

We returned to Academy Bay, Santa Cruz Island later that day where we stayed in the Castros' 'spare house'. In the next few days we filmed and made preparations for our expedition into the interior in search of Giant Tortoises or 'Galápagos'.

FRIDAY 20 FEBRUARY

Our adventure began with a long hot walk up the path leading to a group of plantations in the interior of the island. Soon after leaving Puerto Ayora (or Academy Bay) we had to negotiate a path up the cliff or *barranco* that curves round the back of the village. The walk was supposed to take 2½ hours, but as we were taking it slowly, stopping to film on the way, and were carrying our rucksacks and all except food and bedding (to follow with Cesar Moncayo the same evening) the trip to the Hornemann's house, where Chris had arranged for us all to stay, took about 4 hours. The change in vegetation is striking from the arid leafless trees and cactus of the coast to a tropical rain forest, with bananas, coffee, orange and lemon trees. But the change is quite gradual. There is no tree line or anything like that. First of all the *Opuntia* trees get taller and taller – the highest almost 30 feet – a prickly pear atop a reddish tree trunk. More trees are in leaf, and the mosses and lichens are richer – until finally there are festoons of hanging moss, bromeliads and lianas.

A delightful feature as we neared the settled area was a long hedge of scarlet hibiscus in full bloom. Otherwise we thought it an unattractive landscape in which to live, for nowhere could one see more than 30 or 40 yards in any direction until we came suddenly upon a

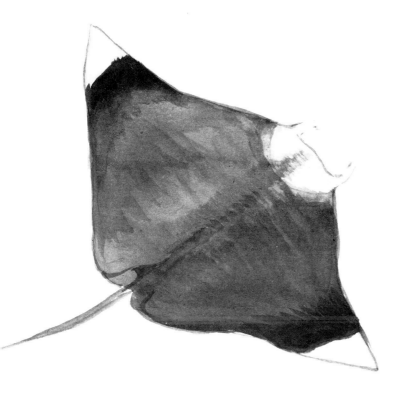

Manta ray, *Manta birostris*, seen off the east coast of Santa Cruz, north of the Islas Plazas, 16 February 1959 and again in the Fernandina Channel when the white tips were less sharply marked.

Orchid from the
hill country in Santa Cruz,
20 February 1959.

clearing with a football field. Soon after this the path to Hornemann's house became much wilder and more seldom used. We walked along a scarcely detectable track, through deep vegetation up to our knees, stepping over fallen tree trunks, until we were near to the house. Chris whistled. His whistle was answered exactly in the same pitch, and the reply was repeated. This was Sigvart Hornemann, the 13 year old son. As we approached the house which stands on a knoll, Chris went on ahead to warn Mrs Hornemann of the invasion which was about to descend on her.

We were greeted rather formally by Mr Hornemann, a tall bespectacled old gentleman with a grey beard. He is Norwegian, speaks some English, and spends his time reading philosophy, particularly Albert Schweitzer. He built his house 30 years ago – the first house in the interior when everyone told him it would be impossible because there was no running water.

Mrs Hornemann was dark, with spectacles, very charming and welcoming, speaking perfect English and excellent French. She is German.

She called to Sigvart who eventually arrived, an attractive blond child who does most of the chores of the household. Until 4 months ago his 17-year old sister was there to help, but then a yacht passed by and a young American fell in love with Friedl, and swept her away to a wedding in Panama a few days after her 18th birthday. Sigvart is a practical boy, who cuts the wood, tends the animals, deals with the farm and helps his mother in the house. He came up to shake hands without a trace of shyness, explaining that his hands were too dirty and offering his wrist. He spoke perfect English, very fluent French and prefers to speak Norwegian although German was presumably his native tongue. And of course he spoke Spanish as well – five languages at 13.

We cleaned the mud off our trousers and shoes under a tap, and later sat down to a magnificent meal of pork. It seems that a dog running loose from an Ecuadorian plantation nearby had savaged the small pig which had had to be destroyed. Their bad luck in this was good fortune for us, for the meal was memorable, and the company excellent. Afterwards we put on rain coats and went half a mile to the neighbouring plantation belonging to the Kastdalen family. Mr Kastdalen and his 30 year old son Alf came out in the heavy rain to meet us as we came up the path. Alf is a blond giant who knows more of the flora and fauna of the interior than anyone else. He had the scientific names of birds and trees at his fingertips, and straightened me out on Darwin's finches. He also had Bob Murphy's *Oceanic Birds of South America* and Swarth's list of Galápagos birds. Murphy confirmed my polymorphic diagnosis of the Red-footed Booby, and my little drawing earlier in this book confirmed that we had indeed been watching and filming *Fregata minor ridgewayi* at Tower.

I was very pleased with these confirmations and conclusions – but regretted not having much longer with Alf Kastdalen – a wonderful chap with the largest feet I have seen on a man (with the possible exception of Walai, the Fijian giant at Korolevu).

Alf came with us for part of the way in the pouring rain and we returned to the Hornemann's house in the dusk.

SATURDAY 21 FEBRUARY

We put on wet clothes and set off at 7.15 with Ghilberto Moncayo on the long trek into the Tortoise Country. We had 4 donkeys and a horse. We passed by the Moncayo house in the hills – a beautiful setting – and the day being clear, we could see Floreana (Charles) and Gardner rock lying to the east of it. They were more than 30 miles away. At Moncayo's house we found his little blond 10 year old step-son, Gunnar, and his father.

Ghilberto left his own horse at the house and we set off with the 4 donkeys and my horse. We shortly found that the 10 year old Gunnar was to accompany us and 3 large dogs. These were rather like reddish alsatians, and one of them was more or less brindled with stripes like a tiger.

The way was led by one pair of donkeys driven from behind. From time to time Moncayo headed them off in a new direction, so in this way we followed a very winding route which was the line of least resistance. We left the cultivated areas and crossed a large open tract of rolling country with tall grass and an ubiquitous convolvulus extensively eaten by some very numerous caterpillar which I could not find – probably a nocturnal feeder, and not, I think, a hawk-moth. Then we entered the forest again – a forest which frequently changed its character slightly, but remained essentially the same for the rest of the journey.

We had been walking for about 3 hours when we came to our first Galápagos, a tortoise about two feet long. He was dismissed as '*muy chico*' – very small – and we did not stop to film him. This was because we had agreed not to delay the outward journey by photography. Whether, in the light of events, this was a wise decision will always remain debatable. The weather was bright, intermittently sunny, and there was no sign of rain. On the other hand had we wasted much time in unpacking and repacking cameras we might have had too little time to reach the big tortoises. Who knows! Who knows!

An hour or so later we passed another 2–2½ foot tortoise – most beautifully marked, with a shiny black shell.

At about noon, when we had been walking for nearly 5 hours, I leading my horse, we came upon a much larger tortoise in a pool of water. Here we decided to unload our cameras. Chris thought that this was a psychological mistake, as if we appeared content with this animal Moncayo would make no effort to find us a bigger one. Chris wandered away and himself found first one and later a second much larger tortoise. Still, however, these were not the real giants.

Meanwhile there was some discussion about the plan, about food, and about who should film which tortoise first. The cry at this stage was '*más grande*' – bigger tortoises. Moncayo explained that the two bigger ones he had seen on his preliminary expedition two days before had been another 3 hours away. This seemed doubtfully worthwhile. So we decided to camp here, and spend the remaining hours of daylight searching the neighbourhood carefully. Moncayo took us to one rather large tortoise which Chris said he had filmed previously. Phil approached to within 4 or 5 feet before it withdrew its head. She then 'rode' on it, but it did not walk.

Afterwards the sun came out and Chris and I left our lunch and went back to this tortoise which was nearly 3 feet long. It had begun to move.

Juvenile giant tortoise or 'Galápagos'.

Chris dashed round it but strangely did not upset it much until it suddenly saw him and gave a loud trumpeting noise, not unlike an elephant. The tortoise went on walking again and I tried to get in front of it too. But it turned and in due course stopped. We wasted a good deal of time on this animal, waiting for it to start up again. Meanwhile Tony had made good films of the original smaller tortoise moving in the pool and feeding. He went off with Chris to film the shell of a slaughtered tortoise in a pool, and found a pair of teal beside it. Chris said the lower half of the shell still had meat on it. It is alarming the rate at which these great animals are being killed. Alf Kastdalen could not see how their extermination could be avoided except by breeding in semi-captivity in an enclosure. Obviously this requirement is now very urgent.

Presently Moncayo returned shouting that he had found a much larger tortoise. We followed him for three or four hundred yards and finally came upon a huge animal quietly feeding in front of us. I set up my camera quickly, in the hope of getting some film before the creature became aware of our presence, but then the others arrived. I implored Chris to wait until I had made my shot, as he had already filmed one tortoise without even showing us where it was, but in the most brash and thoughtless way he pushed past and went up on one side to get a clear view free from bushes. The tortoise saw him at once and stopped feeding. For a short period it went on, and I managed to get one indifferent shot, then it stopped altogether and sulked. Chris and Tony only shot a few feet each.

By now a dark cloud had come up, and we decided to leave the tortoise for the night. If we touched it, the story went, it would walk all night, but if we left it alone it would still be nearby next morning. Fortunately Chris was dissuaded from his plan of tying the animal up with a rope as Moncayo said he would break the rope. Chris said he would go back to camp and get his flashlight and take some stills. We hoped he would not go too close.

We started back to camp just as the rain began and were soaked through by the time we got there. We cut spreaders and sticks for the jungle hammocks with Moncayo's machete while he made a fire with the judicious use of a small jar of petrol which he had brought with him.

Then we set up the jungle hammocks. [These are hammocks with a kind of tent over them which is part of the structure.] When we had finished we were pretty cold but the rain eased and finally stopped in time for Tony and Moncayo to cook up some corned beef hash and beans and some coffee. Mrs Hornemann had packed some meat and fruit for us. Altogether we had a very respectable evening meal and, as the rain still held off, we were able to change into dry clothes before climbing into our jungle hammocks.

Sketches for the logo of the Charles Darwin Foundation for the Galápagos Islands.

SUNDAY 22 FEBRUARY

Once again we were lucky that it was not raining at breakfast time and I put on wet clothes again in order to try to dry them out. The light was not good enough to film the tortoise (all we needed was something to establish its scale), so we filmed the camp fire and the jungle hammocks in the murky darkness of the sodden trees. We had no sooner finished than the light got worse, but as it was already nearly 10.00, and 10.30

was the scheduled departure time, if we were to be back at Academy Bay that night, we went off, with little Gunnar as our guide, to find the big tortoise. He was not more than 15 yards from where he had been the night before. He was in a pool, completely inactive, and in a few moments it began to rain. We stood half under the trunks of trees waiting for the rain to stop, and in due course when it was no more than a drizzle we made the shot of Phil climbing onto the tortoise's back.

It was probably not so good as the ride she had made on the other and smaller tortoise the day before (which in spite of that had only walked 20 yards during the night). Gunnar climbed on afterwards and the tortoise walked a few yards so long as Chris kicked it rather hard. Chris was delighted at having discovered how to make the tortoise go, and could not understand why we should take a dim view of this kind of treatment.

Using Phil's hand measurement we reckoned that the length over the top of this tortoise's shell was $4\frac{1}{2}$ ft and using my eye, I reckoned that the shell was just over 3 ft from front to back. The other surprising thing about this tortoise was the bright yellow under the throat; if anything it seemed more intense on this big specimen than on the smaller ones. Maybe he was coming into breeding colour as they are said to move down towards the coast during the rains to breed.

By the time we had finished the photography it was nearly 11 am and we were another half hour loading up the donkeys. The rain was heavy and we were soaked to the skin. First we all walked and then I rode for a short while. All the time I was thinking that we had no film record of this cavalcade and eventually I began to wonder whether we could not somehow get some pictures in spite of the rain. At last we decided to stop, unload my little camera and while Chris held a plastic bag over it Tony would film the passage of the expedition. A little later when the rain stopped we did a second group of shots and finally a third. These were all in slightly different terrain, and together with a few shots of finches and red flycatchers and some of mosses and ferns, will help I think to get us to the tortoise country in the film.

A little further on we left the horse. The worst part of the walk now began as the road was very much worse than it had been on the way up. The mud was deep, and stepping from lava rock to lava rock in slithery muddy shoes was terribly tiring and painful. Our top halves had long since dried out and now became wet again with sweat. So we struggled back to Academy Bay at about 6 pm after six and a half hours of walking. We had probably not covered more than 20 or 25 miles all told, even less as the crow would fly, but we had had a tough three days, and it had been a memorable excursion.

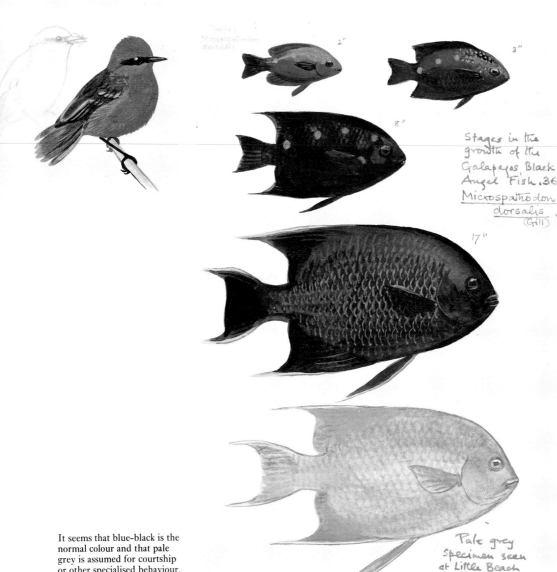

Vermilion Flycatcher.
Pyrocephalus nanus.
Santa Cruz.

We were stiff and full of aching pains after our exertions and so we spent the next day drying out and writing up the adventure. Later in the week we went over in the *patroullera* to Elizabeth Bay and then Tagus Cove on the island of Isabela (Albemarle).

FRIDAY 27 FEBRUARY

From Tagus Cove we decided to go over to Punta Espinosa on Fernandina (Narborough) Island and so after breakfast we weighed anchor and went across. The bay behind Punta Espinosa was open and a big swell was coming into it. At first we steamed on for a couple of miles to see if we could see any larger bird colonies, but nothing looked any better and it was evidently unlandable anywhere except in the little bay, so back we went, and nosed in.

Microspathodon dorsalis

2"

3"

8"

Stages in the growth of the Galapagos Black Angel Fish. 36. Microspathodon dorsalis (Gill)

17"

It seems that blue-black is the normal colour and that pale grey is assumed for courtship or other specialised behaviour.

Pale grey specimen seen at Little Beach Sta. Cruz. 24 Feb. Another at Hood 8. Mar.

Marine iguanas at Punta
Espinosa, Fernandina.

Marine iguana
swimming off Fernandina.

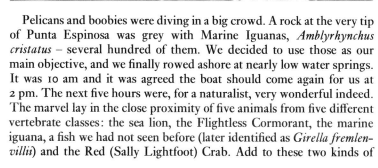

Pelicans and boobies were diving in a big crowd. A rock at the very tip of Punta Espinosa was grey with Marine Iguanas, *Amblyrhynchus cristatus* – several hundred of them. We decided to use those as our main objective, and we finally rowed ashore at nearly low water springs. It was 10 am and it was agreed the boat should come again for us at 2 pm. The next five hours were, for a naturalist, very wonderful indeed. The marvel lay in the close proximity of five animals from five different vertebrate classes: the sea lion, the Flightless Cormorant, the marine iguana, a fish we had not seen before (later identified as *Girella fremlenvillii*) and the Red (Sally Lightfoot) Crab. Add to these two kinds of

Galápagos
Flightless Cormorant,
Nannopterum harrisi.

Sea lions at
Punta Espinosa, Fernandina.

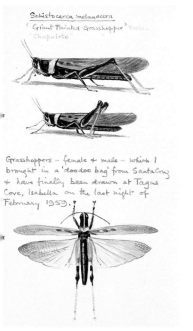

Schistocerca melanocera
('Giant Painted Grasshopper' **bache-** 'Chapulete'

Grasshoppers – female + male – which I brought in a 'doodoo bag' from Santa Cruz + have finally been drawn at Tagus Cove, Isabella on the last night of February 1959.

herons, the Galápagos Hawk, the Mangrove Warbler, some lava lizards, Hawksbill Turtles and the new species for our fish list – and you have the ingredients of a wonderful day. All these animals were set in a landscape of strange lava formations, grey sandy beaches and mangrove trees. It was strange to see the sea lions among the mangrove roots.

We all gravitated towards the big mass of iguanas on the point. There were certainly 300 and perhaps more, and all the time many were coming and going. At the same place there were 3 or 4 Flightless Cormorants and a pool with 6 or 7 sea lions. All these creatures kept the four of us busy photographing for more than two hours, and rarely getting in each other's way. I filmed iguanas feeding on brown weed at my feet, and being climbed over by crabs. Tony got a magnificent sequence of a young Flightless Cormorant begging food from its parent, and being fed by regurgitation in the white foam of the breaking waves.

The iguanas were also spectacular in the surf, diving just before a big wave arrived. As the tide rose they began to work back from the outlying skerries in numbers. In a crack in the lava below me as I filmed were some of our new fish which were surprisingly carp-like – olive brown, and from above very broad in the head.

In due course we all reckoned that we had sated ourselves with filming, and we gradually withdrew to the central mangrove tree where we had left our rucksack of food. Here, very satisfied with our morning, we had a splendid lunch – with a can of pork brawn in wine jelly which was excellent on Ryvita – and so was the strawberry jam, chocolate, raisins and lemon (or rather lime) in the waterbottles. A luncheon fit for kings.

Afterwards I went back through the mangroves to our landing place to meet the boat. I was worried about how it would get in as the seas were bigger. I found a Mangrove Warbler's nest – an extremely beautiful cup with many feathers. The female flew down from it. I did not disturb it. Maybe tomorrow we can see if it has eggs or young.

The tide was flowing into the tide pools, into one pool had swum a golden brown spotted turtle – a Hawksbill of which I obtained a tiny scrap of black and white film. He was in the very shallow water, and I wished I had tried to look at him with a mask and identify him for certain. We had seen him, or his brother (or perhaps they were sisters) in the channel through which we had entered the lagoon as we arrived.

So we re-embarked and after unloading gear at the ship and embarking the outboard motor, we set off to go round the south east side of the bay. Unfortunately the motor was stopped to go close to another marine iguana colony and never started again. The iguanas were filmed from the boat only moderately effectively.

Tomorrow I will count one of the iguana colonies, but I think there must be 2–3 hundred in each. No doubt in certain places there are bigger colonies in Fernandina. The animals are larger than most of those we have seen – much larger than the Tower ones. They are very dull coloured, even though the breeding season seems to be in full swing. There is no part of them which could not be described as dirty black, though some have a reddish tinge in patches. Many are sloughing (changing their skins). The males must be 4 ft long. In the colony at Punta Espinosa (on the Point itself) we saw only one small one, about 18″ long. Some of the digging females were quite small – barely 2′ 6″.

The lava lizards are the largest and darkest we have seen. They are less handsome than the big grey ones on Santa Cruz or the palish ones on Isabela that we saw at Tagus Cove last night.

We finally rowed (Tony and I) all the way back – half a mile – to the *patroullera* while the two engineers in the boat fruitlessly tugged at the string of the outboard. Thereafter we chugged over to Tagus Cove, where soon after our arrival it rained. We hope it will stay clear in the night so that we can sleep on deck.

We spent the next few days back at Punta Espinosa filming and searching for signs of an iguana's nest in the hope that we could film a female at her business.

MONDAY 2 MARCH

Our last day at Punta Espinosa and another wonderful one. For four days we have made our picnic camp under the same shady mangrove tree, with a Mangrove Warbler singing above and sea lions in the pool below, and a colony of *Amblyrhynchus* on the rock opposite.

Our morning of bright sun was fraught with indecision. We had two subjects to get – an iguana actually laying an egg as Chris had got – and some more iguanas under water. Chris says we can use his egg-laying sequence, but it is much easier and better if we have our own. There was a chance of it clouding over later in the day and we needed sun for the underwater. On the other hand the tide would be getting lower the later we left it. We decided to start with the iguana eggs, so we went along to the beach at the end, which seems to be the best. There were only about 3 females who looked as if they meant business.

Female hawk-moth,
Manduca rustica calapagensis,
which flew on board
at dusk on 1 March 1959
at Tagus Cove, Isabela Island.

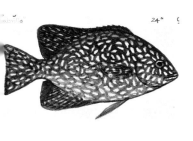

'Cabrillo', *Oplegnathus insigne.*

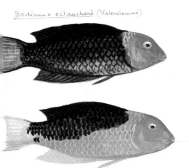

'Golden Parrot Fish',
Bodianus eclancheri.
Four males and one female.

The colour was superbly tropical – the essence of an equatorial beach – the green mangrove with white stems, the grey beach and the curling lazy green waves bursting and splashing high on the lava reef behind. I dug some sham holes to encourage the good ladies to get on with their laying, and in a few minutes three of my four holes had been taken over by iguanas. But meanwhile the clouds were building up. I had the feeling that Tony would rather be getting the underwater shots and so we decided to leave the females to their burrows and rig the camera in its underwater case.

We walked all the way out to yesterday's reefs only to find that the south east breeze had already whipped up a little chop, and we thought we should do better on the north side of the point opposite our picnic camp.

Here Tony and I launched ourselves for a wonderful hour in rather cold water. I was no sooner in the water than I met a small turtle. It was a Hawksbill Turtle, *Eretmochelys imbricata*, as I had a good view of the overlapping plates of the shell and the broad tail plate – as opposed to the narrow plate in the Green Turtle (*Chelonia virgata*).

The first iguana we found underwater was filmed and snapped and finally came to the top for air just like a huge newt, and down again. We found a part of the reef rich in the so called 'Golden Parrot Fish' – marvellous creatures about 18″ to 2 feet long, and infinitely variable in orange and white and black. (These were Golden Hogfish, *Bodianus eclancheri.*) We also met again our spotted fish of yesterday which I am still at a loss to place – a fine creature of dark brown with greenish yellow spots in irregular shapes like some obscure Italian pasta – or chopped spaghetti (*Oplegnathus insigne*, locally called 'Cabrillo').

Picnic lunch was varied this time with hot corned beef and baked beans and bananas to follow, which were very good dipped in naranjilla jam. We decided after lunch to make one last despairing effort to snatch victory from defeat. We had two hours before we must leave. We would go back and try to film an iguana laying an egg.

So back we trudged to the beach at the point, and sure enough two neighbouring holes had females sitting inside them head outwards. At once we started to dig down to the tail-end of one of them. We found it only just in time. The animal heaved and the first egg was layed before we had properly laid bare the area of operations. The head end of the iguana was still in the burrow. We made one shot as the egg moved down into the hollow we had dug. Then with Chris's information that the second egg would follow in 8 minutes time, Tony waited while I dug down to the second female. Sure enough, in 8 minutes out popped the second egg. Meanwhile I had found the burrow of the other female. But she laid her second egg as I was digging. Nevertheless Tony got a shot of her a few seconds after it was laid. Then back to the first female to watch her emerge and cover up the hole. While this was going on a very amusing fight took place between a female who had just laid and another who intended to use the same hole. After much head shaking and mouth opening, they met head on in a short butting match, as described for courting males by Eibl Eibesfeldt. Then one head slipped under the other and slid forward under the belly of what turned out to be the vanquished animal, which was lifted clear off the ground and thereafter departed. There is evidently a great density of eggs in these beaches because when digging down to the second laying female I passed a hole with two hardened eggs in it.

The day had been triumphantly successful. We returned to the *patroullera* very well satisfied. We sped away down the Fernandina channel towards the anchorage in Elizabeth Bay. On the way we passed the big school of a hundred or more dolphins which we had met between Tagus Cove and Punta Espinosa in the early morning. Then the water had been glassy calm and there had been dolphins every-where, and sea lions with them, and a few sharks' fins. We had slowed down and circled a couple of times to film them in the low morning sunshine. Once a mother and calf had jumped side by side simul-taneously.

It was a calm night as we anchored behind the two little islands in Elizabeth Bay. I awoke at about 4 am on the foredeck and the sea lions and penguins and Blue-footed Boobies were making quite a lot of noise. At 5.25 the ship began to come to life and someone started the generator. The noise and bustle seemed to affect the animals on the island. Tony went ashore in the little panga with the recorder, and I got the generator switched off again, but had the greatest difficulty in keeping the crew quiet. Tony returned with good sound of a baby sea lion, but not much of penguin, and I wished I had woken him an hour earlier.

TUESDAY 3 MARCH

We steamed for almost 12 hours through rain and confused seas to Academy Bay (Santa Cruz) arriving at 6 pm – a fairly hellish passage with no food, and poor Phil's leg very bad (this was an infected mos-quito bite which became an abscess and was very painful). Chris was sea-sick much of the time, but we could not muster much sympathy for him.

Phil went to the naval station when we got ashore and the chap there – evidently trained in some medical proficiency injected her efficiently with the penicillin we had brought with us. Afterwards we returned to the Castro house where we live, and had a desperate time in the semi-darkness of a dying torch and a feeble lamp, trying to open a bottle of Coca-Cola. After supper with the Castros we slept ashore.

Phil was given another penicillin injection before we set off for San Cristóbal (Chatham) Island the following morning. The doctor at the Naval Base at San Cristóbal persuaded Phil to have an incision made in the abscess and although this was very painful and unpleasant for her, and she suffered some nausea from the new antibiotic she was given, she was at least well enough to be able to come on the expedition to Hood (Española) Island in the *patroullera* on Saturday.

SATURDAY 7 MARCH

Phil had her last dressing at 7.30 with the removal of the last of the infection. She is better and brighter. It is a very great relief. We said our farewells to the Governor who has really done us very well, even if the water was short in his barracks. At 8 am we sailed for Hood and arrived at 11.30. It is a low island, about 7 miles long, green since the recent rains.

After some difficulty we persuaded the Captain to stop opposite a little bay near Punta Caballos, where the Galápagos Albatross is said

Hood Island.

to breed. Eibl Eibesfeldt found 14 adults and 5 well grown young on 24 September 1957, and describes in some detail exactly where to find them. He thought that September was the end of one breeding season and the beginning of the next.

We saw quantities of turtles as we went in towards the shore in the skimmer (now invariably used as a row-boat). The others, Tony, Chris and an old fisherman who was supposed to know the island, set out to find a track across country, but I felt sure the shore would be easier and quicker, so I set out along the shore saying I would meet them on the south side of the Punta peninsula.

I soon began to see exciting things. The male iguanas are extremely bright in colour by comparison with any others we have seen. A line down the back, including the crest, and the fore-arms are light bluish-green, like copper on a roof. The rest of the body is a bright crimson-pink blotched irregularly with brownish black. Striking rather than handsome. The lava lizards are much larger and brighter than those we have seen elsewhere. They have broad vertical dark bars and much red on the male's body, while the female's head is bright orange-red. Some females were sluggish because of imminent egg-laying.

I walked along a jeep track from which the lava rocks had been removed. The grass grew sparsely but quite green, and everywhere were the little doves not quite as tame as we had been led to believe, but nevertheless engagingly unafraid. They are pretty birds with blue skin around the eyes and red legs. The plumage is predominantly reddish brown with black and white spotted flanks. On a beach which I passed were a lot of cow and calf sea lions, but no bull that I could see. Soon after I came to the colony of Blue-faced Boobies and frigate-birds. Here, according to Eibl there should have been albatrosses, but there were none. I looked critically at all the frigates. Although some males had practically uniform black plumage and blackish feet, there were intermediate ones with pink-tinged black feet, and the majority had pink feet and were therefore *F. minor ridgewayi*. I do not think it possible that the two species could be nesting together in close company like that. I wonder if *magnificens* is a good species, and if so whether it really breeds in Galápagos – or perhaps it occurs as a straggler. (On a later trip we visited a colony of *magnificens* on N. Seymour Island.)

I decided to make some more colour films of the frigates, and had been filming them for an hour when, from the opposite end of the colony, came three blood-stained mud-covered figures who had been fighting their way through rough going ever since we had parted. Apparently Chris had asserted that he knew the way. Poor Tony was exhausted and exasperated. However they set to filming at once. We found a marvellous place where iguanas and gulls and gannets were all silhouetted first against black cliffs and then suddenly against the white water and spray of the huge breakers which boomed against the rocks below. The contrast was dramatic and should make wonderful pictures. We made slow motion shots of the frigates soaring along the cliff front, and Tony got a shot of a Fork-tailed Gull walking on an iguana. This is now a famous ploy, for Chris got such a shot at Tower, and keeps talking about it as an example of his patience and the good fortune which attends him who waits. He pronounced 'gull' as 'girl' and the first time he told us, we wondered what girl he had filmed standing on an iguana. Tony now has his 'girl' not only standing but *walking* on an iguana.

We had lunch in the sun because there was no shade to be had, and it was very hot indeed. The butter in the can was suitable for dipping asparagus, but we had no asparagus!

After lunch we explored a cliff to which we had seen tropic birds flying. After filming them in flight we climbed down, and found one on a ledge and about to enter a hole in the rocks. On the rocks they can hardly get along, and have to use their wings to help. They have a harsh loud call. We picked up a tail feather. Chris coveted it, but later showed us a bigger and better one (probably plucked from a bird!) and told us he had found young and would show us.

Great Frigate-bird.

We filmed doves on the way home, and I snorkelled for about a quarter of a mile, seeing many turtles and two sharks, one rather larger than I have seen before underwater. I also saw a very large parrot fish and some even larger Diabolo (Ladyfish – *Elops*) about 3 feet long and looking not unlike Tarpon.

We filmed doves on the way home, and I snorkelled for about a quarter The turtles were curious about us and swam round looking at us. At one time I could see five together. So close did they come that we could easily check their scales. From the head plates we established them as Green Turtles, *Chelonia virgata*.

After the weekend we left Hood and cruised back to Santa Cruz for a couple of days' rest. On our last day we visited Tortuga Bay where the Darwin Research Station may be based.

We returned to Academy Bay that evening to find that at the Castros' house all our belongings had been unceremoniously removed from one of our rooms and piled into a heap in the bedroom to make way for a gaggle of American tourists. Tempers ran high that evening, not only because of this one high-handed action, but also because our leaving these Enchanted Isles seemed to be in jeopardy. I noted in my diary that evening: 'By the time we got to sleep the

plans were like a comic opera with a bad plot'. But in fact we need not have been so worried because Saturday 14 March remained the day of our departure.

SATURDAY 14 MARCH

Phil did a morning of packing and I painted 3 hawk-moth caterpillars, then went along to see Tony at Chris's house, where I found little Sigvart Hornemann, and entertained Alf Kastdalen to Coca Cola during which I tried to persuade him to record his knowledge of natural history, and find out some more about the hawk-moths. I had a guilt feeling about all these things which left Phil with so much of the packing to do – and I rather exasperated her at the end by going on painting my third caterpillar until the very last moment. Somehow I can never see why it is upsetting to go on doing things till the last moment. But I know that it is so, yet I was so very keen to get the pattern of that last caterpillar onto paper before we left and it seemed the only important thing at the time. Phil says it is simple – I should have started earlier. She is quite right.

Mike and Sue Castro charged us fantastically little for board and lodging. For 5 weeks with two periods of 10 days away – but our things in the rooms all the time – the bill was 280 sucres – just over £5. We finally paid another 200 sucres for the room while we were away, but we had to insist on doing so.

So with a final farewell to Chris, who was in good form and very friendly, (so that we quite forgot how maddening he can be!) we chugged out of Academy Bay in Carl's boat with Gusch and Johnny just in front carrying Dick Torrance and his friend – a Mr Appleton.

On the way out of the bay we passed over a big manta ray. I reckon these fish are probably about 7 or 8 feet from wingtip to wingtip. We had a good view of it, and although the wingtips were all black on top there was a suggestion of the pale patches on either side of the head, so these colour patterns which we have seen and William Beebe reported may well be no more than individual variation in this particular species, or race, or population of manta. I wonder how much is known about colour variation tendencies in fishes.

Carl's boat was very slow against a head sea. Later we set the sails and it went better. We left at 1.15 pm and arrived at the Plazas Islands at 6. It was not a comfortable night as quite a sea was running in the anchorage between the two islands, but we slept out under the stars – for our last night in Galápagos and it was delightful to hear the barking of the sea lions.

We weighed anchor at 5.0 am the next morning and sailed the last few miles to Baltra and the airstrip. That afternoon we flew to Guayaquil on the Ecuadorian mainland. We had been in Galápagos for five weeks.

① Sphingid larva   Lycium Hawk Moth
feeding on grey green shrub, similar to Bougainvillia.
Tortuga Bay. Sta Cruz & Academy Bay. Sta Cruz.
13 Mar. 1959.
There is a
phase of this
larva which
has less black
on it.

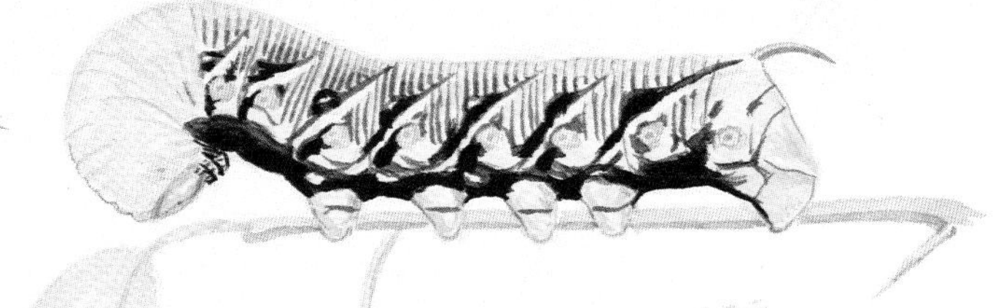

?still
unidentified

Flower of
shrub on which
No① was feeding.
Lycium sp.

② Muyuyo Hawk Moth
Sphingid larva
feeding on
__Cordia lutea__

("Muyuyo")

Tortuga Bay. Sta Cruz
13. Mar. 1959
Young larva
has black horn.

Somewhere between
Privet & Poplar Hawk Moths.

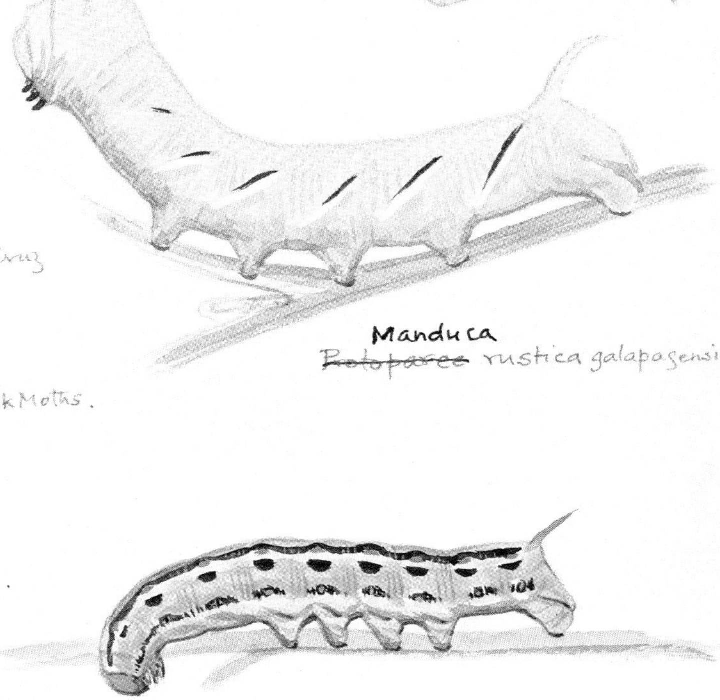

__Manduca__
~~Protoparce~~ rustica galapagensis

③ Sphingid larva
feeding on
Common Purslane
__Portulacca oleracea__

Academy Bay 14 Mar. 1959

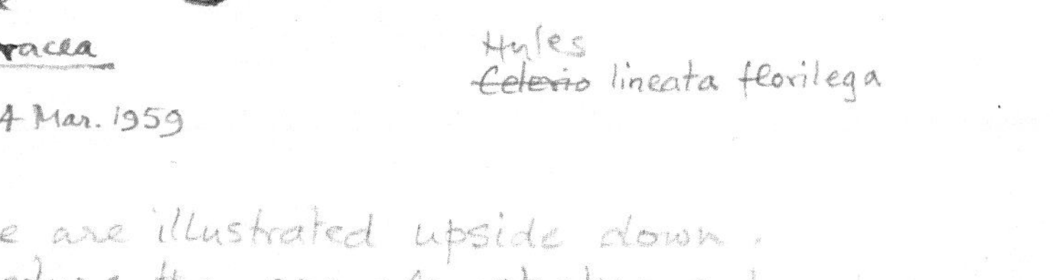

Hyles
~~Celerio~~ lineata florilega

Note:
These Larvae are illustrated upside down.
     In nature they are almost always __hanging__
       from the stem of the food plant.

CHAPTER 7

Galápagos Revisited

DIARY 5   1961

In September after attending the Arusha Wildlife Conference (in Tanzania), I was invited to go to Quito to assist Professor V van Straelen, President of the Charles Darwin Foundation for the Galápagos (of which I am an Executive Committee Member) in his negotiations with the Government of Ecuador.

There were a few days of meetings including a courtesy visit to the University of Quito, to bring greetings from the University of Aberdeen [of which I was then Rector] and an audience with HE José Maria Velasco Ibarra, President of the Republic of Ecuador, who arranged for an Air Force DC3 to take our Mission to the Galápagos Islands on the following day.

The party included the Ecuadorian Under-Secretary of the Ministry of Education; a scientist from the Quito Observatory; Robert Stretton – British Chargé d'Affaires in Quito; and Raymond Leveque – the Swiss zoologist engaged by UNESCO to build the Charles Darwin Research Station on the island of Santa Cruz.

We started from Quito soon after dawn, refuelled at Guayaquil, and came down through the low cloud some 5 hours later to see, (with some relief) the island of San Cristóbal on our port side. There is no radio beacon in the Galápagos Archipelago, but by skilful dead-reckoning we were exactly on track.

We flew to Santa Cruz, and along the south shore to Academy Bay where we circled twice before heading back north-east to the airfield on Baltra. From the air we were able to see the progress of the new laboratory and other buildings and we saw the people who had come out of their houses to wave at so unusual an event as the arrival of a plane – many of them my friends of our previous visit $2\frac{1}{2}$ years before.

Out in the bay lay half a dozen great manta rays, 10 feet or more across their 'wings'. Along the shore we saw a school of big sharks lying near the surface, and some sea lions in the surf; and inland among the dry leafless thorn bushes and the tree-cactus we saw some donkeys and a great many goats, their paths showing plainly as a network through the bush. Goats – one of the world's most destructive animals – were introduced deliberately into these islands to provide food for shipwrecked mariners, now providing food for the settlers, but depriving the giant tortoises of their basic food supplies. What is not eaten by goats is devoured by donkeys and cattle. Wild pigs eat the tortoise eggs and wild dogs eat the newly hatched young. As a result these unique and marvellous reptiles are on the verge of extinction. Most of what remain are on the islands of Isabela and Santa Cruz where recently 780 have been marked by Ghilberto Moncayo, who led us in to see the tortoises in 1959. Now he finds few unmarked ones, and also very few young ones. It will be touch and go if these superb animals can survive in the Galápagos conditions of today.

As we swept round to land on the wartime runway at Baltra we saw a converted landing-craft at anchor in the bay, waiting to take us round the coast to our destination. We taxied to the far end of the runway where a party of about 20 Ecuadorian sailors were lined up beside a truck.

The sailors were quick and helpful and we were soon spinning down the road to the quay which was so familiar from our previous visit. Within $\frac{3}{4}$ of an hour we were chugging out in *El Buzo* (the *Diver*), the converted landing craft, bound for Academy Bay. El Buzo was not designed for passenger transport in rough weather. She had come to the islands as part of the abortive American attempt to set up a lobster fishing industry in San Cristóbal. Of the 100 people who joined the scheme only one family and one other man – Ed Niles – still remained in the islands. Ed was the owner of *El Buzo*.

Raymond suggested that we should turn right outside the bay at Baltra so as to see some interesting animals in the straits between Baltra and North Seymour. We passed close over the dark backs of two big mantas, and along the cliffs of North Seymour we saw Blue-footed Boobies, and Magnificent Frigate-birds. These, in a breeding colony, were quite different from the Great Frigate-birds with which we had become familiar on our previous visit. There were big young, but still all white in their down, in most of the nests. The extent of the white on the females is different from *Fregata minor* and the chin is black.

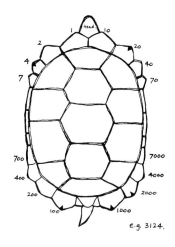

Tortoise marking protocol:

e.g. 3124.

Sea lions on Mosquera.

A single fur seal lumbered down the rocks and then disappeared into a hole. The Little Shearwaters were going in and out of their holes in the cliff and so were Lesser Noddy Terns. And all the way along were my favourite Galápagos seabirds, the Fork-tailed Gulls. Two young came along, in white plumage with only slightly speckled backs and huge eyes. Raymond confirmed my belief that they must be largely nocturnal or crepuscular.

The little island of yellow sand beaches (Mosquera) in the strait between Baltra and North Seymour was covered with sea lions – perhaps 200. As soon as we came round it we found ourselves heading into steep seas and *El Buzo* was reduced to about 4 knots. At this rate it was going to be a long plug, wet and cold and miserable. To relieve the gloom we sighted three Galápagos Albatrosses, working their way singly across wind by dynamic soaring. The wings were surprisingly bent at the wrist. They were dark sooty-brown with white heads. It was exciting to know that our fears for their survival were unfounded, and that although last time we had seen not a single one on Hood, at the right season they still apparently teem there. Raymond has marked 1,500 adults and believes there are between 2,000 and 3,000 pairs. He wonders whether the goats have not been advantageous to the species in clearing spaces in the thick bush which did not formerly exist and which give greater opportunities for nesting to the albatrosses.

We saw the bigger of the two shearwaters (the Sooty – *Puffinus griseus*), which nests on the moorlands at the tops of the islands and later we saw one coming out from inland over Academy Bay, and diving down to the sea. It is a much bigger bird than Audubon's, with a longer more pointed tail. In shape it is clearly built for speed and high performance. It is certainly the most graceful shearwater I have ever seen. In February and March 1959 we had seen only very few and those only in the distance. To add to the range of Galápagos tube-nosed birds, we saw the little Storm Petrel, *Oceanodroma tethys*, a 'House-Martin' hovering over the waves like a butterfly.

Before reaching the Plazas Islands we were joined by a great school of dolphins – a hundred or more which played around us. One did three great leaps, in the last of which he appeared to loop the loop.

It became dark and the wind became lighter. We turned the corner under a bright moon, and after another two hours we came into Academy Bay. The tide was low, but in spite of that there was just enough water to creep in past the pier into the inner harbour, and alongside Ed's house at the foot of the *barranco* – the fault in the lava which creates a cliff and forms the anchorage of Academy Bay (so named by the California Academy of Sciences 30 years ago), or Puerto Ayora.

We had scarcely made fast when a white outboard motorboat arrived driven by Forrest Nelson. He is a smallish active man, with a rather high pitched quick voice, crewcut grey hair, and, as I afterwards discovered, very bright blue eyes. It was at once clear that he was a man of considerable efficiency. With all our baggage we were whipped back across the bay in the motorboat to a new dock built by Forrest at Eden, and installed in two brand new, well built cottages – the Professor in one, Robert Stretton and I in another. A few minutes later we were walking back along the path to the house where Forrest is now living, pending the completion of the new house at Eden. At

Sandy's we were greeted by Forrest Nelson's young wife who is a sister of Sigvart Hornemann. She is a blonde gazelle who speaks as many languages as her brother and has a composure and serenity which is utterly impressive. She is even more unusual than her strange little brother whom we had met in 1959. She had a delightful French greeting for the Professor, and an excellent dinner for us all.

On the morning of 21 September I staggered precariously down the slippery rocks to renew my acquaintance with the Galápagos fishes. With me on the shore were Small Ground Finches, *Geospiza fuliginosa*, Mangrove Warblers, turnstones and red crabs. Under water, which was cold, but not prohibitive, I was again in wonderland. There were 3 species of sea urchins, two of starfish, and a profusion of small reef fish dominated by the two very similar (but entirely distinct) species of

Galápagos damsel fish.
From the top:
Beebe's *Eupomacentrus beebei*,
Beebe's *Microspathodon*,
Eupomacentrus leucorus,
Eupomacentrus arcifrons,
(*Pomacentrus*) *Nexilosus latifrons*.

pomacentrids, one brown with yellow tail and blue eyes (*Eupomacentrus arcifrons*) and the other with a white-striped tail and yellow eyes (*E. leucorus*) – and in either case deliciously aggressive, the clowns of the rock pools. *Abudefduf saxatilis* the Sergeant Major, blennies, small green groupers (*Epinephelus labriformis*) and many more of my old friends of 1959 were there in the pools off Eden. In my mask I took a 30-armed starfish to show Professor van Straelen at breakfast.

In the morning we inspected Forrest Nelson's half finished house at Eden, and the two buildings under construction on the site to the east. They are advancing extraordinarily well. No buildings in Santa Cruz can compare with the sound construction methods and the simple but efficient architecture which in another six months will be the Charles Darwin Research Station and Mr Nelson's adjoining hotel. We inspected the road which has been made, the half-finished dock, the workshops, laboratory and dormitory block (still only in its earliest stages). In intermittent drizzle we showed the Professor Santa Cruz Lava Lizards, Lava Gulls, Darwin's finches, Yellow Warblers and Santa Cruz Marine Iguanas. Two young ones were caught showing well developed transverse stripes. With these we carried out Darwin's famous experiment of throwing first a young iguana, then a full grown one, out to sea.

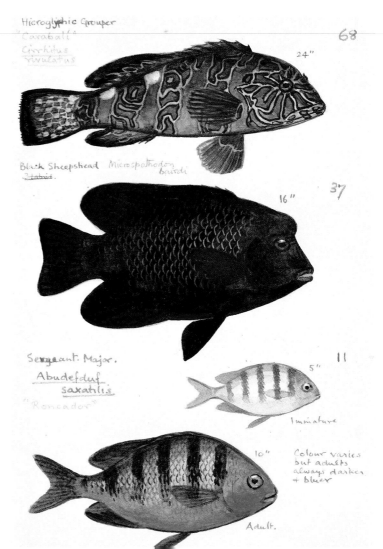

Hieroglyphic Grouper
"Carabali"
Cirrhitus rivulatus

68

24"

Black Sheepshead *Microspathodon bairdi*
Labrid.

37

16"

Sergeant Major.
Abudefduf saxatilis
"Roncador"

11

5"

Immature

10"

Colour varies but adults always darker + bluer

Adult.

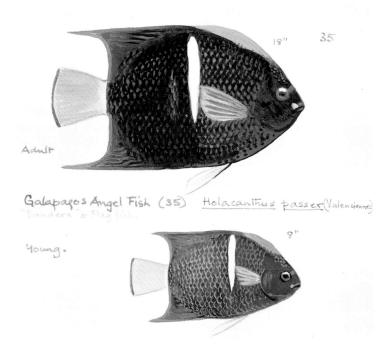

Galapagos Angel Fish (35) Holacanthus passer (Valenciennes)
'Bandera' = Flag fish.

In both cases the animals at once swam ashore again. Darwin suggested danger from sharks as the reason for this behaviour, but it seems that water temperature may be the real cause.

After a mighty lunch, Forrest took us across to Little Beach in the motorboat. The sea was rough and great waves were breaking on the point outside the beach, but in spite of that I decided to swim out and look at the fishes. At first the big waves in the narrow cleft of lava were rather awe-inspiring, but eventually I plucked up courage to swim out, and found no great danger. I saw my friends the Yellow-tailed Surgeon Fish (*Prionurus laticlavius*), the blue and orange Galápagos Angel Fish (*Holocanthus passer*), the big black damsels with blue streamers (*Microspathodon dorsalis*), the old black sheepshead (*M. bairdi*), the big blennies, and the blue jewel fish (which are the young of *dorsalis*). It was too cold to stay in long.

Later I went up to see Susan Castro. She took me a few hundred yards up the main road to the hills to the house where an old Ecuadorean woman was caring for our Galápagos tortoise, rescued from the valise of a tourist at Baltra in 1959. The tortoise had grown huge and un-recognisable. In $2\frac{1}{2}$ years it had doubled its length and must have increased its weight by 5 or 6 times. I re-established that the animal belongs to the Charles Darwin Station. Sue Castro was very cordial and friendly, sending messages to Phil.

I walked back to Pelican Bay through the village, and past the new store jointly owned by Schiess and Bud Divine. It was dusk when I went into the Ghilberto Moncayos' new concrete house. Gloria greeted me on the doorstep, and was equally friendly . . .

My diary ends there rather abruptly.

CHAPTER 8

The Lindblad Explorer
in Galápagos

DIARY 20 1974
DIARY 24 1976

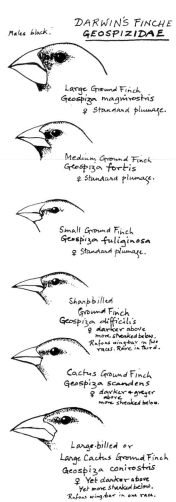

DARWIN'S FINCHE
GEOSPIZIDAE

Males black.

Large Ground Finch
Geospiza magnirostris
♀ Standard plumage.

Medium Ground Finch
Geospiza fortis
♀ Standard plumage.

Small Ground Finch
Geospiza fuliginosa
♀ Standard plumage.

Sharp-billed
Ground Finch
Geospiza difficilis
♀ darker above
more streaked below.
Rufous wing-bar in two
races. Rare in third.

Cactus Ground Finch
Geospiza scandens
♀ darker & greyer
above
more streaked below.

Large-billed or
Large Cactus Ground Finch
Geospiza conirostris
♀ Yet darker above
Yet more streaked below.
Rufous wing-bar in one race.

In 1967 my friend Guy Mountfort suggested to Lars Eric Lindblad, the creator of a highly-successful travel enterprise, that he might invite me to lead one of his tours to the Antarctic (described in Chapter 15). The invitation, which included Philippa, duly came, and this was the beginning of a long and happy association with a most inventive, dynamic and delightful man.

We have now taken part in twenty four Lindblad expeditions, mostly in the *Lindblad Explorer* (LE) a wonderful 2500 ton passenger ship which spends her time going to places where passenger ships do not normally go.

In 1974 we revisited Galápagos twice in the *Lindblad Explorer* once more taking a rather indirect route to the islands. We left Slimbridge in the middle of March to fly to Toronto where there was a WWF [World Wildlife Fund] (Canada) meeting which I was to attend. During our week there we were continually on the move and I had a streaming cold. Nor was comfort to be found at our hotel – the static electricity was so fierce that blue sparks flew from the door key and one got a shock from every door handle, light switch, elevator button and even when Phil and I kissed!

We left Toronto at the end of March and flew to New York and then down to Bogotá, Columbia, and so on April Fool's Day:

MONDAY I APRIL

Flew on from Bogotá to Quito. We called in at the British Embassy which is directly across the road from the Hotel Quito. The Ambassador, Peter Meynell, took us to lunch at his house. He had been a colleague of Wayland's [my half-brother] in the Foreign Office.

The afternoon was devoted to the new WWF coin scheme in which we hope Ecuador will participate*. I stayed at the hotel but had time to look at the birds in the hotel garden. Phil went on the sight-seeing tour with the rest of the party. Later Cristóbal Bonifaz Jijon [old friend,

*Briefly, the Conservation Coin Collection (CCC) was an international programme sponsored by WWF and IUCN. Its aim was to find a number of countries willing to issue legal tender coins, one gold and two silver, carrying wildlife designs relevant to the country. Proof and uncirculated versions of the coins were put on sale to collectors worldwide by Spink & Son of London. Revenue from these sales accrued to the WWF and IUCN, as well as to the coin-issuing countries which were also encouraged to use their funds for conservation. 24 countries issued conservation coins between 1974–1980 although, in the end, Ecuador was not one of them. The programme raised from US $5 million for wildlife conservation.

member of the Board of the Charles Darwin Foundation and ex-Ecuadorian Ambassador in Paris] came to see me, and together we went over the road to the Embassy to explain Bonifaz's plan. This was that the personal letter from Prince Bernhard to the President on the coin scheme would be left with the Ambassador, who with the Minister of Agriculture, and perhaps the Minister of Finance, would seek a Presidential audience to deliver it. The suggestion that some of the Government's face-value share should go to the National Parks was thought by Cristóbal to be very timely and appropriate. It was planned that at the end of the first trip (the LE was making two trips out to the islands), the Ambassador, who had to be in Guayaquil that day, would come on board the LE to report Conservation Coin Collection progress (which he subsequently did).

We boarded the *Explorer* the next day at Guayaquil and sailed down the Guayas River coming out into the open sea on Wednesday 3 April. The map shows the routes of the two trips each consisting of ten days in the archipelago. As I was on duty as the 'resident naturalist' on these expeditions I had little time to write up my diary, beyond making notes.

These record that on the following day we had several sightings of whales, some breaching with huge white splashes. I saw Sperm Whales for certain in one pod. Some observers averred that their whales had pointed snouts. Many that I saw spouted diagonally and were therefore certainly Sperms. I also saw a Killer Whale – its white pattern being characteristic but the dark part was surprisingly brown. We had about a hundred dolphins swimming ahead of the ship for nearly 5 miles (possible *Tursiops*). There were some very small babies. Also, out in the open ocean, we saw some Red-necked Phalaropes.

On 4 April we arrived at San Cristóbal, formerly called Chatham Island, and went to look at the Darwin statue which is a fine bust on a vertical column, San Cristóbal Lava Lizards were all around and on it. On a walk up the hill, with good views of the Medium and Small Finches and the Small Tree Finch, as well as the San Cristóbal Mocking Bird, I found many full-grown larvae of the Muyuyo Hawk-moth, *Manduca rustica calapagensis*. Its food plant 'Muyuyo' is *Cordia lutea*. Many of the passengers were intensely interested in Darwin's finches, the *Geospizidae*, and I made in my diary a quick identification key.

At South Plaza Island the highlights were: swimming with the sea lions, watching the Swallow-tailed Gulls [the new name for Fork-tailed Gulls], fishwatching from the cliff top – seeing many big Yellow-tailed Mullet and quite a number of sharks – and the tameness of the land iguanas. My notebook records that they were much tamer than 15 years ago.

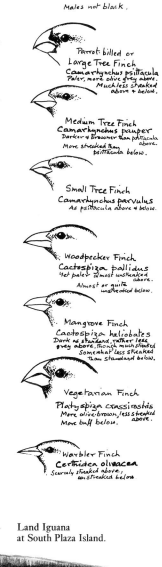

Males not black.

Parrot-billed or Large Tree Finch
Camarhynchus psittacula
Paler, more olive grey above.
Much less streaked above & below.

Medium Tree Finch
Camarhynchus pauper
Darker & browner than psittacula above.
More streaked than psittacula below.

Small Tree Finch
Camarhynchus parvulus
As psittacula above & below.

Woodpecker Finch
Cactospiza pallidus
Yet paler almost unstreaked above.
Almost or quite unstreaked below.

Mangrove Finch
Cactospiza heliobates
Dark as standard, rather less grey above, though much streaked. Somewhat less streaked than standard below.

Vegetarian Finch
Platyspiza crassirostris
More olive-brown, less streaked above.
More buff below.

Warbler Finch
Certhidea olivacea
Scarcely streaked above, unstreaked below

Land Iguana
at South Plaza Island.

Galápagos Fur Seal. .

At Genovesa Island (more often called Tower), which is the rim of a large crater forming Darwin Bay, my diary records that we had a delightful swim with Galápagos Fur Seals. They waved one, two or occasionally three flippers in the air, and went to sleep at the surface with their heads hanging downwards. They were no less tame than the sea lions, but perhaps a little less playful. If one turned to swim away, they almost always followed. The reason for lying asleep with their flippers above water is obscure, but possibly has to do with temperature control – perhaps as a cooling mechanism. The Tower Marine Iguanas are a rather small sub-species and totally black.

On 7 April we were at Jervis Island (Rábida). We found 19 flamingoes on the lagoon behind the beach, which finally flew out to sea and sat on quite choppy waves about a mile from shore. Swimming again with the sea lions was the highspot of that afternoon, and also of the next when we were at Sombrero Chino, a very small island belonging to the Bainbridge Rocks group. It was on one of them, which has a crater with a small crater lake, that we found 18 flamingoes. We landed from four Zodiacs (inflatable rubber dinghies), climbed 20 feet up the rocks and peeped over into the crater lake, which was about 300 yards in diameter and surrounded by green vegetation, mostly *Bursera graveolens*, with a belt of sedges at the water's edge. When our heads appeared above the rim, the flamingoes on the very far side ran together. I noticed they had one half-grown chick with them, and later, with binoculars, saw four nest mounds with an egg on one of them. When we first appeared, the flamingoes were nowhere near the nests, though they walked back to them under the influence of the disturbance, which led me to the conclusion that the egg was probably addled. (At our next visit two weeks later the egg was in the water, which confirmed my diagnosis.)

On 9 April the ship anchored off the west coast of Isabela (Albemarle) Island, so that we could climb the 3,700 ft Alcedo Volcano. Thirty-two people climbed to the rim of the caldera, including Phil. From the ship to the top and back, the walk was about 13 miles. Whilst they were climbing, the ship went across the Espumilla beach and lagoon on the west end of Santiago Island, where there were at least 30 Galápagos Pintails – one family had five ducklings – but on this occasion no flamingoes, although there were said to be 21 up in the Salt Lake Crater on the same island. When we got back to the Isabela shore to collect the returning climbers, I found a group of 16 Galápagos Penguins quite near the landing beach, and watched them, and a manta ray jumping close offshore.

I walked up to meet the returning Alcedo party. I went about two miles up, seeing very few birds but lots of brown Viceroy Butterflies and several *Myiarchus* flycatchers. I missed the first walkers, but crossed to their returning line in time to intercept Phil with Gina Dieterin. They had seen about twenty tortoises. The oldest climber to reach the top on that day was 73.

A few days later, on 12 April, we were at Hood Island, alternatively called Española, which is the only known breeding place for the Galápagos or Waved Albatross, *Diomedea irrorata*. On our first visit

Galápagos Large-billed Flycatcher, *Myiarchus magnirostris.*

fifteen years before, the albatrosses had not been nesting, but now there were a number at their nest sites, several sitting down having possibly laid their single egg. The earliest recorded laying date appears to be 9 April. My diary notes that, although in 1962 the population of the Waved Albatross was estimated at 6,000 to 7,000, a more recent and complete census indicates that in 1974 there were 13,000 pairs, i.e. 26,000 adults, plus, say four years' worth of young at, say, 6,000 first-year birds, 4,000 second-year birds, 3,000 third-year birds. All this adds up to 39,000 individuals (another later calculation produced about 48,000 individuals). Most albatross species are believed not to breed until they are seven years old.

Hood is one of the three most wonderful islands in the archipelago (the others being Fernandina and Tower). The seabird colonies and especially the albatrosses are the main features, but the profusion of the Galápagos Dove, the huge Hood Lava Lizards (the largest), the pink and green Hood Marine Iguanas (the brightest), the long-billed Hood Mockingbird (the longest), the very tame sea lions (?the tamest), and all of them with a background of spectacular cliffs, huge waves and a blow hole, add up to a day which I think everyone on board agreed was altogether fascinating. Snorkelling that day produced 32 species of fish.

SATURDAY 13 APRIL
Floreana (Charles) Island.
The star feature of the day for Phil and me was swimming in and around the Devil's Crown which is a submerged crater. Before going underwater we had walked along the edge of the flamingo lagoon at Punta Cormoran. In the lagoon were 25 flamingoes, more than 50 pintails, a number of waders including Black-winged Stilt, Whimbrel, Semi-palmated Plover, Grey Plover, Sanderling, Least Sandpiper,

The Devil's Crown, Floreana.

Wandering Tattler and Grey Heron. We had watched Brown Pelicans fishing and observed a curious behaviour of Noddy Terns. When the pelican has dived and caught a beakful of small fish it returns to the surface and some of the fish – usually in a damaged condition – escape from its pouch through the edges of the beak. In order to exploit this source of food the Noddy Tern sits waiting on the head of the pelican, jumping into the water as soon as a titbit appears.

On the edge of the lagoon we had also seen Galápagos Penguins, and flying overhead were Magnificent Frigate-birds. There were Yellow Warblers, Small Ground Finches, and Thick-billed Flycatchers in the bushes.

However, the most exciting part of our day was to swim inside and outside this tiny crater called the Devil's Crown. The water inside was less than 100 yards across and only 4 feet or 5 feet deep, with some small coral heads. Outside it fell steeply away as a lava cliff to the sand about

Galápagos Penguin,
Spheniscus mendiculus.

Part of a school of
35 hammerhead sharks,
probably *Sphyrna lewini*,
seen at the Devil's Crown,
Floreana Island, 13 April 1974.

30 feet down. Opposite one of the half-dozen entrances to the crater – the easterly one – we looked down to see a school of 35 hammerhead sharks, about 25 feet below us. Most of them were from 6 to 7 feet long, but bringing up the rear of this amazing procession were half-a-dozen bigger ones, the largest certainly 8 to 9 feet long. They paid no attention to us, swimming with a leisurely waggling tail which produced a side-to-side 'wagging' of the head. We looked carefully at the outline of the front of the 'hammer' and thought they were most probably the Bronze Hammerhead, *Sphyrna lewini*. We went back to the place half-an-hour later and saw a whole lot more. Altogether that morning we reckoned there must have been not less than 70 hammerheads in this amazing school.

On Sunday 14 April, we spent the whole day on the island of Santa Cruz (Indefatigable) where at Academy Bay (Puerto Ayora) the Charles Darwin Foundation for the Galápagos Islands has its Charles Darwin Research Station.

SUNDAY 14 APRIL

The new Director of the Station on this visit was Dr Craig Macfarland, who gave us a lecture in the new Tortoise House. We walked to the tortoise pens in great heat. (One lady of 80+ fainted away and had to be taken back to the ship by stretcher, where she duly recovered.) The rest of the morning was spent with Dr Jerry Wellington, a Peace Corps biologist making a basic collection of specimens including fish. He had copies of the relevant literature and we were able to work out many problems and find many names. Rod Salm joined me in the lab. It was very hot and a towel was required for brow-mopping. Back to the ship for lunch and afterwards to call on Carl Angermeyer, who now has his marine iguanas at the back (landward side) of the house – sixty or more came when he called and fed them on bananas on his verandah.

By 17 April we were back at Guayaquil, where we embarked a further load of passengers in the *Lindblad Explorer* and forthwith set out again for the second circuit of the Galápagos Islands. It was especially interesting to see how much the breeding season had advanced since our visit two weeks earlier. At Tower Island the

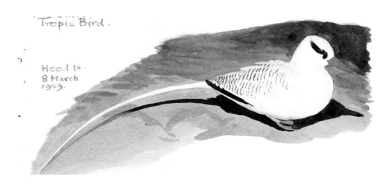

Tropic Bird.

Hood Is.
8 March
1959.

nesting frigate-birds were almost, but not quite, as numerous as they had been 15 years ago. The Red-footed Boobies were definitely less numerous. We saw no pintails at Tower either time, but the Yellow-crowned Night Herons and the Swallow-tailed Gulls are evidently doing very well there. In a bay to the south-west of the landing beach there is a warm lagoon with many damsel fish. Swimming out into the choppy water outside the bay, I came across a very large hammerhead shark, perhaps 12 or 13 feet long, with three inquisitive jacks, (*Caranx ignobilis?*).

Black-finned Crevalle (Jack),
Caranx ignobilis.

TUESDAY 23 APRIL
Morning – Sullivan Bay and Bartolomé. We walked up the hill in the early morning. It is a harsh volcanic scene, but there is a very fine view from the top – where a male lava lizard had a territory on the topmost rock. The secret of coming down was to keep on the soft sand of the

Butterfly fish (above)
and aberrant Coachman.

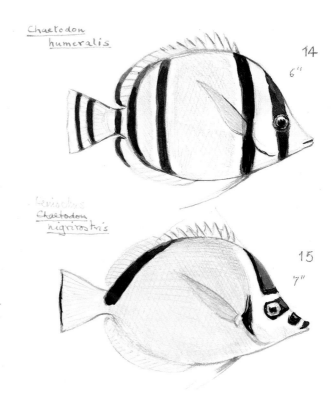

Chaetodon
humeralis

14

6"

Chaetodon
nigrirostris

15

'7"

path. If everyone does it, though, the sand will all soon be at the bottom of the steep slopes.

Afternoon – Sombrero Chino. Bainbridge Rocks. Swam in the lagoon with Phil. Lots of *Chaetodon humeralis*. Swam close up to a group of eight penguins. A few Golden Hogfish, *Bodianus eclancheri*, one of which was being bothered by a false cleaner-fish that was biting it. Later we went over to the beach, where the young sea lions played with the Zodiac's ropes enchantingly.

WEDNESDAY 24 APRIL

Morning – Jervis (Rábida). The flamingoes were less tame than on the previous visit and had soon flown out to sea. They did not land on the sea, which was much calmer than last time, as before. Snorkelling eastwards from the beach was marvellous. Clear water and lots of fish. A large dusky apogonid (cardinal fish) was entirely new to me. Pelagic fish were passing – Rainbow Runner, *Elegatis bipinnulatus*, a kingfish, *Seriola*, and schools of big yellow mullet, some of which were tame and evidently curious. The Zodiac was anchored near the favourite cave of two White-tip Sharks which caused some hilarity.

As we were leaving from the beach there was an extra bag without an owner. It belonged to Byrd Stevenson – a passenger. Back aboard sure enough her tag was missing from the board. A first search was made by Sven Lindblad to the eastward. When he came back to the ship I joined him and we searched westward where we had been snorkelling. There had been a current sweeping out from the point and it was already an hour since we had missed her. Far on beyond our furthest snorkelling point, round the corners into a bay, we found her sitting on a rock, slightly cut about the ankles but otherwise unperturbed. She was expecting to find a Zodiac round each succeeding corner.

Afternoon – James Bay. Cruised round Buccaneer Cove. Saw four goats. Landed at the old settlement beach where a hawk sat in a window of one of the buildings. Walked southwest along a path for three-quarters of a mile to the fur seal grottos. Here the fur seals were delightfully tame. After most people had taken their pix we swam round the point seeing a large Galápagos Shark, and into the grottos which required a dive under the lava bridge at that state of the tide.

Inside it was utterly beautiful and delightful. Some sea lions were there as well. A rainstorm came up but barely reached us as we walked back with Francisco along the path. The nearby volcano looked *marvellous* in the shadow of the rain cloud. Walking out we found in the path two last instar [last larval stage before pupation] Striped Hawk-moth larvae. I could not identify the slim 'weed' they were on (and presumably eating).

Altogether a good day.

There was an expedition to the Alcedo Volcano at Isabela the next day. A few days later we were at Floreana.

SUNDAY 28 APRIL

Floreana.

A Blue-footed Booby which took fish scraps from the stern of the *Lindblad Explorer* was savaged by five pelicans, and had to be rescued from drowning. This had been done the night before and it had been kept in an aquarium overnight. In the morning it was released, flew directly down to land on the sea, bathed copiously for several minutes, and then flew off strongly, leaving two feather lice in my hair.

That day we saw a Golden Plover, which was only the second record for Galápagos. In the lagoon there were thirty-five flamingoes and sixty Galápagos Pintails. In the Devil's Crown there were fewer hammerhead sharks than last time, but it is by far the best snorkelling we have had in Galápagos. Visibility 50 to 60 feet, 25.5°C water and 47 species of fish.

I saw an intermediate fish between *Pimelometopon darwini* and *Halichoeres nicholsi*, seeming to confirm my earlier suspicion that *darwini* is the adult male (or 'terminal phase') of *nicholsi*. The fish had the gold spot on the opercle and the vertical dark smudge, but still retained the horizontal dark median line. The most beautiful sight was a mixed shoal of Yellow-tailed Surgeons and White-banded Angels – perhaps 200 with a slight preponderence of surgeons. The eastern entrance is the best and the total biomass of fish is staggering. I cannot remember where I have ever seen larger numbers.

I didn't go ashore at Post Office Bay, but went to the bun-fight at Black Beach in order to make my number with Mrs Witmer. Whimbrels in the paddocks by the house. Her sister lived 30 years in England with the Duke-Elders (Royal Eye Specialist).

Saddle Wrasse,
Halichoeres nicholsi.

TUESDAY 30 APRIL
Santa Cruz.

Greeted at the Charles Darwin Research Station by Nellie – the Great Blue Heron. Nearly an hour's work with Jerry Wellington and Rod (Salm) on fishes.

We went to Carl Angermeyer's (wife Marge) to see his iguanas. There were 65, the most he has counted there is 85. Then on to see brother Gusch and his grotto. He talks continuously and rather wildly. 'No one owns anything' but in the next breath 'The Angermeyers own Galápagos.' During lunch we sailed to Barrington/Santa Fé.

Afternoon – Barrington. Many turtles and Eagle Rays in the bay as we came in. Two sea lion beaches, 50 on one and 80 on the other. Galápagos Hawk.

Climbed the high *barranco* to find Barrington Land Iguanas. Found the first right at the top of the climb, *Conolophus pallidus* – paler, pink under its arms, with a more smiling mouth, moderately tame. There was also a Warbler Finch and a pair of *Myiarchus* flycatchers. Phil went on with the rest, led by Tjitte de Vries, to find more iguanas, but I started back to get some last snorkelling in. I helped the descent of Mrs Olson down the steepest part of the path, and then went on to the beach.

The goats have been eliminated from Barrington by the National Park authorities, and already the vegetation has regenerated remarkably. *Scalesia* (daisy trees) were reproducing well. The snorkelling was a little disappointing – though there was a marvellous shoal of mixed surgeons and angels (*Prionurus* and *Holocanthus*) with a group of mullets (*Xenomugil thorburni*) passing above them, just in front of me in the evening light. (A Striped Marlin was seen jumping.)

LAND IGUANA

Conolophus pallidus. Barrington (Santa Fé) only.

Conolophus subcristatus. Fernandina, Isabela, Plaza
and Santa Cruz, formerly Baltra & Santiago.

Two years later in 1976 we made two more circuits of the Galápagos Archipelago in the *Lindblad Explorer* – the fourth time we had been to the Enchanted Isles.

WEDNESDAY 31 MARCH

Our old friend, Keith Shackleton, had been on the last cruise in the ship, so we went to the airport in Guayaquil to see him off, but he had not yet arrived. Eventually he came with a blonde girl who had been a SCUBA instructor on board. Her exit card had been filled in wrong and Keith had gone to the passport office with her to help clear up the mistake. As neither of them could speak Spanish, a hilarious misunderstanding developed in which it was believed by the authorities that they wished to be married, and arrangements were all lined up. Finally the misunderstanding was corrected, bigamy was avoided, their seats in the plane were confirmed and we wished them *bon voyage*.

We taxied back to the hotel in time for the guided tour of the city which was not anything very special. Upon our return to the Continental Hotel, however, there was something *very* special. John Brooke had been walking early that morning in the small public park immediately opposite to the Continental Hotel, where he had seen six or seven iguanas in the trees and down on the grass. He offered to show us the place before lunch. At first we could only find one, high in a tree, but later we discovered more, some again down on the ground or on lower tree trunks. They were *Iguana iguana*, and up to 3 feet long. In a quite low tree about 9 feet above a park seat was a Two-toed Sloth. It and the iguanas must have been liberated in the park, one would suppose. What was so encouraging was to find they were allowed to survive. We were told there were terrapins in the little artificial pond, though we didn't see them.

After an endless lunch, we embussed for the docks and came to the *Lindblad Explorer* where we found Eric Shipton [mountaineer] and Phyllis Wint whose son William is one of Dafila's Oxford friends.

And so off to Galápagos with a ship full of 1001 Members* (actually *not* quite full – barely 60 passengers) including many old friends: Nancy Legendre with daughter Janet and grand-daughter Marina, Robin and Jane Cole, John Brooke, Bob and Emmabel Egbert, Charles de Haes, with the Argentinian naturalist Francisco Erize as Expedition Leader Hasse Nilsson – the Captain – has his red-headed wife Ami (Ann-Marie) on board as Purser. And there is an understudy Captain Kjell Smitterberg (pronounced Tshell).

This was to be the first of two more circuits of the Galápagos Archipelago, and one of the most agreeable features of it was that we were now getting to know the animals we might see and the more intimate details of the islands we visited. On this first circuit came a very special adventure for me. Two years earlier Phil had climbed Alcedo, and I had been most of the way without going to the top. It was a situation which had to be rectified and so on Wednesday 7 April I made the ascent. The diary for that day reads as follows:

*1001 is a group of World Wildlife Fund benefactors who were invited by its then International President, the Prince of the Netherlands (Prince Bernhard) to subscribe $10,000 each to a capital fund. It took 2 years to fill the 1,000 places (Prince Bernhard was the '1'), but since then it has remained full, with a waiting list.

WEDNESDAY 7 APRIL

Alcedo Volcano, to see the tortoises. Starting at dawn I went to the top in 5 hours and 20 minutes up and 2 hours 45 minutes back to the beach. The view over the crater (caldera) was spectacular. About 20 people went to the summit. I was the last of the first batch. Then Eric Shipton took four more up to a different part of the ridge. Phil did not come to the top this time having done it during the trip in 1974.

We did not find tortoises so low down as we had done in 1974 – in fact the first one was high up where we had found them copulating at the luncheon point on my previous climb – the point from which I turned back.

I started the ascent of the steep slope to the rim just before 11.00 with 'Kix' Kixmiller and Robin Cole. Their rate of climb was considerably higher than mine. I got quite out of breath trying to keep up with them, so decided to take it much more slowly. It was very hot indeed, in spite of a slight breeze blowing up the hill. Small cumulus clouds were forming for a while but they came to nothing, and soon it was almost clear again. I found myself stopping for every thirty feet or so of height gained, turning to look back and face the wind until my respiration rate improved. Looking back I could see a large tortoise walking across the open.

The inside of the Alcedo Volcano, Isabela – prime habitat of the giant tortoises, part of the Ecuadorian national park which now covers most of the land surface of the Galápagos Islands.

I wasn't feeling very strong and suddenly I realised that I needed food. I had had half a cup of water before the first *Pisonia* tree. Eventually I found a partial shadow from a grass tussock, ate some chicken and a hardboiled egg, followed by an orange, and felt much better. I had probably lost 15–20 minutes, and Robin and Kix had disappeared over the ridge.

The ship was a tiny toy $8\frac{1}{2}$ kms away. I plodded endlessly on and suddenly I was there. There was a group of crew members under the rather taller bushes on the rim. I looked out over the caldera unable to see the steam crater. But the view was very beautiful. The only cool place to sit was on the outside of the rim, where I ate the rest of my packed lunch in the breeze. It was 12 noon. 'Mad dogs and Englishmen . . .' There was a medium-sized tortoise quite close and five within the general vicinity.

In due course we set off downward in twos and threes. I found that my downhill pace was rather faster than some of the others and eventually I found myself alone, ahead of some of the crew, who had stayed up longer. It seemed easier to follow the tortoise and donkey paths further to the left than where we had climbed up. Near the foot of the steep bit I heard a loud hiss under a bush and there was the biggest tortoise I have ever seen. Or so he seemed. He was huge. (His shell must have been nearly 4 ft long.)

The painful part of this early descent was in the thigh muscles above my knees and on the soles of my feet, and all the way down I was slightly troubled by these pains. I had carried a spare pair of shoes and socks, and when almost back to the coast I decided to change into the new shoes – but after a short distance in them I regretted it, and changed back. I reached the beach 15 minutes earlier than my estimated 3 hours for the descent, and was pleased to be back. It took me a longish time to change for swimming. It might have been better to walk straight on into the sea.

The sand of the beach was very hot and there were complications between where one could safely leave shoes – and flip flops – and where one could put on flippers. When I was finally in the sea it was bliss, even though I could only swim with my arms. There were a lot of very large Streamer Hogfish, *Bodianus diplotaenia*, and great shoals of *Prionurus* (the surgeon fish). I do not think I need ever again climb Alcedo!

The other feature of these later visits to the Galápagos Archipelago was my greatly improved knowledge of the fish fauna. For example, at Tower Island, on the day after my Alcedo climb, I was able to identify a new fish species, *Stethojulis axillaris*, a Dancer Wrasse, which was the first record for Galápagos.

My diary has two other notes in it. The first is 'fur seals effervescing', and refers to a delightful underwater observation of a fur seal which had dived off a cliff where it had dried out, and for some minutes was seen exuding bubbles, like an Alka Seltzer tablet!

The other adventure deserves a more detailed description because it was immensely exciting. At one point the cliff round Darwin Bay (Tower) casts a shadow over the deep water at its foot. As we went by in a Zodiac, we could see, not far below the surface, a school of large, bright yellow rays swimming in a tight bunch. I was very anxious to get into the water with them, and finally went over the side of the Zodiac, just in time to see them disappearing along the foot of the cliff. Visibility was about 60 ft that day.

Before long I suddenly realised that they were turning back and called to Phil and Soames Summerhays to come into the water quickly, which they did. The rays were about 2 feet from the surface, and there were 72 of them in the school, the largest almost 3 feet across, the smallest about 2 feet. They swam directly towards me as I lay on the surface ahead of them and they passed no more than 3 feet directly beneath me. They went straight on towards the others, who were waiting for them. We all followed them for a bit, but then in a few moments we saw that they had once more turned and were coming directly back towards us.

We realised then that they were feeding on plankton which was evidently richer in the shade of the cliff. From end to end the shade fell on the sea for a length of about 100 yards, and each time they got to the end they went out into the sun and turned almost in formation, looking fantastically beautiful, before swimming back into the shade towards and directly underneath us as we watched. This went on for about half-an-hour, and was an utterly memorable sight. I painted them twice, once in the diary and later as an oil painting, now in the possession of Ron and Valerie Taylor.

Golden Rays,
Rhinoptera steindachneri.

Rhinoptera steindachneri. Tower Island. 8.4.76.

A male Green Turtle was cruising in the shallowish water at the head of Tagus Cove. The shoal of grunts (one of them is shown below) was using the head and carapace for scraping off ectoparasites. The turtle was not disturbed by this or by me, 20 April 1976.

During this trip Eric Shipton and Phyllis Wint became our great friends and Phil often walked and climbed with Eric when I was busy fishwatching.

Our visit this time to the Devil's Crown off Floreana was specially exciting. When we first reached the hammerhead shark place, there were lots of them quite near the surface. We counted about 28 but, as soon as we got close to them, they went down to 25 feet. Phil took a photograph of one hammerhead moving away from her and, when it was developed, we found the head of another one coming into the picture much closer. But these hammerheads never gave any of us any trouble at all, and there were often up to a dozen of us in the water at the same time.

On the second of our trips that year, Kjell Smitterberg was Captain, and it was no less enjoyable than the one before. There were some special new experiences which I recorded, rather laconically, in my diary:

Angel fish, surgeon fish and a Scalloped Hammerhead (with some other fish species) at the Devil's Crown when the tide was turning.

WEDNESDAY 21 APRIL

Santiago (San Salvador, James).

James Bay – morning. Butterflies everywhere and Giant Painted Grasshoppers. Eric's party to top of Sugar Loaf. I counted 32 hawks (in the binoculars from the fur seal grottos) circling the climbers at the summit. Many more fur seals in the grotto than 2 weeks ago. About 30–35. We managed to stop the swimmers from driving them out of the inner pool, and everyone saw them underwater who wanted to. Also two female sea lions. Fishes quite good. *Trachinotus stilbe* juveniles in foam. I was stung on the shoulder, possibly by the coelenterate which I saw yesterday. Cruise round Buccaneer Cove during lunch.

Afternoon – Marvellous snorkelling around some rocky islets 500 yards from the north end of Espumilla Beach. The five foot White-tip Sharks were there as before, lying on the bottom. We had two Spotted Eagle Rays which swam below us for some time. One was 5 feet across the wings, the other much smaller.

Found a small golden fish. (Phil had seen one of them in Fernandina Channel.) It seemed to be a juvenile pomacentrid, though at first sight I thought it was *Naucrates ductor*.

Spent some time drawing the wrasse below, which I subsequently saw in Sullivan Bay next day.

Fur seals in the grotto, Santiago (James Island).

Marbled wrasse seen off Espumilla Beach and later in Sullivan Bay.

THURSDAY 22 APRIL

Bartholemew. Sullivan Bay.

SCUBA with Soames Summerhays off the lava flow of Santiago. My first bubbling for a couple of years. A delightful morning. Highlights: *Epinephelus panamensis*, *Rypticus bicolor*, *Canthigaster amboinensis*, *Lythrypus gilberti*. The shore party saw the White-tipped Sharks on the far beach, also the courting eagle rays. Janet Heiligmann had a special relationship with a young male sea lion which climbed onto her knee and examined her face with his whiskers.

FRIDAY 23 APRIL

Morning – Mosquera and North Seymour.

Starving baby sea lions. Sanderlings still in winter plumage – 50+ turnstones, oystercatchers, Great Blue Heron.

Afternoon – Academy Bay, Santa Cruz.

Afternoon at the Charles Darwin Station on Santa Cruz. Arrangements rather poorly organised. No special treatment for this prestigious group who could help the finances so much. I should have organised a tour of the labs etc, instead of which they were kept waiting – shown only the tortoise-rearing house and the adult tortoises (without expert commentary except in the house) and were disappointed.

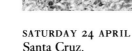

SATURDAY 24 APRIL
Santa Cruz.

Early morning expedition to the tortoise country. Started in darkness. 51 people in single file. I saw 9 tortoises. Others saw 12 and Francisco, who got lost in the process, saw 16. While we were in the Rain Forest it rained! Many introduced plants. Ubiquitous cucumber vine. Beautiful views of *Platyspiza crassirostris*, the Vegetarian Finch (male) and a pair of *Camarhynchus* (*Cactospiza*) *pallidus*, the Woodpecker Finch. Courtship feeding of female by male. Also masses of *Certhidea olivacea*, the Warbler Finch. Vermilion Flycatchers and one Large-billed Flycatcher. Total walk 13–14 kms.

SUNDAY 25 APRIL
Darwin Bay, Tower (Genovesa).

Morning – Prince Philip's steps – a fifty foot cliff climb with a permanent rope to help climbers. Red-footed Boobies with well-grown young. Great Frigate-birds still courting and one egg laid, and broken. Darwin's finches – *Geospiza conirostris* and *Geospiza magnirostris*

Above:
Vermilion Flycatcher,
Pyrocephalus rubinus.
Below:
Woodpecker Finch,
Camarhynchus pallidus,
Santa Cruz Tortoise Reserve,
20 April 1976.

Band-rumped Storm Petrel,
Oceanodroma castro. Came on
board at night near Tower
Island. Released following day,
with another. Both headed
along the ship's wake, gaining
height for orientation on their
nearly 200 mile return flight.

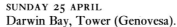

(singing 'Peeterer' – quite tuneful – Phil found a nest – domed like a sparrow's nest). Also *Geospiza fuliginosa* and *Certhidea olivacea*. About 3,000 *Oceanodroma tethys*, Galápagos Storm Petrels, flying over their breeding area. This was a very striking spectacle. Over an open area of jumbled lava rocks about three quarters of a mile long and a quarter of a mile wide were hundreds upon hundreds of little storm petrels all within about ten feet of the ground wheeling this way and that over what was evidently a massive breeding colony, all the nests being hidden deep in crevices. One Galápagos Short-eared Owl.

Swam at foot of steps. Moorish idols. White-tip Shark.

Afternoon – Snorkelling on west side of Darwin Bay. Very murky. Interesting *Caesio*-like school of fishes. Quick trip to beach then back to coral bay. Two interesting fishes: *Stethojulis* sp. again, and an excellent view of a wrasse once seen in the Devil's Crown. Perhaps related to *Thalassoma lunare* or *T. lutescens*.

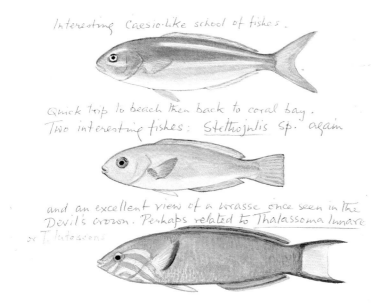

The end of this expedition was to be at Panama, and I had conceived the idea that we might stop briefly at Cocos Island on the way. We would only have a couple of hours and would almost certainly be unable to land, but this time it was real exploration.

TUESDAY 27 APRIL

Cocos Island (belonging to Costa Rica). It is 4 miles × 2 miles. It was difficult to persuade Francisco Erize and Kjell Smitterberg (Cruise Director and Captain) that a morning at Cocos Island would be more exciting than a second morning at Tower. But eventually the penny dropped. And so at 5 am we were close to the island and waiting for the dawn. In the ship's lights white birds flew past. I thought they were tropic birds, but with daylight we found that they were Fairy Terns (*Gygis alba*). The part of the coast we were opposite was precipitous and luxuriantly wooded. When the sun rose the green was brilliantly

Magnificent Frigate-birds, *Fregata magnificens*, from above and below, immature far right. Compare with the slightly smaller Great Frigate-birds, *Fregata minor*, on page 135 in which the throat is white, the sheen on the crown is green instead of purple, and the pale brown markings on the upper side of the wings are much more prominent.

rich. Red-footed Boobies were flying past the ship, and so were Brown Boobies (which we had not seen in Galápagos). High overhead were Magnificent Frigate-birds. We only had four serviceable Zodiacs, so two cruises were arranged. On the first cruise along the cliffs we found the 14th Darwin's finch with its black long-billed males (13 of the 14 species of *Geospizidae* (Darwin's finches) occur in Galápagos, the 14th is found only on Cocos Island).

We also found that the Noddy Terns were whiter on the crown than those in Galápagos, and we saw an egret, though the species was not determinable.

The second cruise began with a visit to the cliffs and only the last 20 minutes was spent snorkelling. We anchored in about 40–50 feet of water on the north east side of the southernmost islet on the south east coast, about 20 yards from the cliff face where many Noddies were sitting. Soames went in first and immediately gave vent to a kind of 'view hulloo' which he reserves for the very most exciting underwater discoveries.

The water was very clear (80 feet visibility) and teeming with fish. There were half-a-dozen very large *Caranx* – brilliant blue and golden green, there were huge shoals of Black Trigger Fish, *Melichthys ringens*, with a few *M. vidua* amongst them. The *vidua* with black-edged hyaline swimming fins (dorsal and anal), pink tail and white peduncle, were quite spectacular among the black *ringens*. I tried to write down all I saw but I could not decide which was most interesting – those common to Cocos and Galápagos or the new species not seen in Galápagos. As it turned out, the vast majority were common to both (12 out of 27). Interestingly, at this site, *Acanthurus glaucopareius* was *far* more numerous than the surgeon fish *Prionurus laticlavius* – an opposite situation to Galápagos. It was terrible having to come out of the water after 20 minutes in order to be back at the ship by 9 am. But clearly this was an enormous bonus to most of the passengers, and a great improvement over an extra morning at Tower.

As we sailed on along the coast on course for Panama, we came to a bay sheltered from the south east swell where landings might have been possible. We had deliberately not gone to Chatham Bay, where, according to 'the Pilot', the easiest landing could be made because we did not have permission from Costa Rica to land, and we thought there might well be a military garrison there. Although no passengers had landed, the Captain had asked the Tongans (two crew members) to go ashore and get some fresh coconuts. This they had achieved by swimming ashore from a Zodiac and climbing the palms. The mission was successfully accomplished.

As we headed away from Cocos several fins of marlin were sighted and two dolphins came in to the ship's bows. We were doing $14\frac{1}{2}$ knots. After 4 or 5 minutes, one of them raced ahead and jumped clear of the water, then went off to the side and later reappeared riding the stern wave. The other remained for another 6 or 7 minutes immediately ahead of the ship weaving across the sharp bows. They were *Tursiops*.

WEDNESDAY 28 APRIL

At sea. And so to a day of lectures – Eric Shipton on Everest history and the Yeti (he pronounces it Yayti) – later an excellent piece by Canadian David Lank (who has a very attractive wife Ellen) on conservation, called 'The America that vanished' and illustrated entirely with paintings – mainly Audubon. In the evening we showed the Wildfowl Trust slides of Phil's. I began with a story followed by a passage about Eric, just so that the people on the cruise should recognise the quality of this astonishing and modest man.

It was also a day of packing for Phil and my last access to Soames's fish photographs, which are very good. (His photos of invertebrates are also outstanding, and he lectures very well about them. He is really a most engaging person.)

The packing tired Phil a lot and I didn't help as much as I should have done because of painting fish. Francisco had a party for the staff in his cabin, attended by the Captain, Soames Summerhays, Francois Gohier, Geoff King, Edouardo Shaw, Ruth Zimmerman (Hostess), Ami Nilsson (Purser – Hasse's red-headed wife), Eric and Phyllis, Roy Sexton and Ruth, and us.

It was a good party, and a nice farewell to the ship, I have come to hate farewells – shymaking things and somehow endless on the *Lindblad Explorer*, because you never know when will really be the last time you will ever see them.

Red-billed Tropic Bird, *Phaeton aethereus*.

CHAPTER 9

Africa: Uganda and Kenya

DIARY 4   1961

As a boy I had spent a holiday at El Djemm in southern Tunisia, where I learnt to ride a camel, but my first visit to Africa south of the Sahara was in 1956 at the invitation of Ralph Dreschfield, Attorney General of Uganda and Chairman of its National Parks. My task was to perform the opening ceremony for the newly built safari lodge at Paraa on the Victoria Nile below the Murchison Falls, and Philippa was with me.

We returned to Uganda at the beginning of 1961:

MONDAY 23 JANUARY

We were met by Alec Haddow, of the Virus Research Institute, who was to put us up, and John Blower, of the Game Department, with whom we had tried to catch ducks back in 1956.

After breakfast with the Haddows I had a brief look at the garden birds, Red-throated Sunbirds everywhere, also a Grey-headed Sparrow, a bulbul, swallows, a woodpecker with red head and rump, a Woodland Kingfisher, a *Streptopelia* dove, and two Horned Owls high in a tree looking down at us with fluffy horns.

That evening, after signing the Governor's book, there was a party at the Haddow house to which came David Masawa – African zoologist from Makerere College who is to accompany Gerald Watterson on his East African tour – Stage 1 of IUCN's (International Union for Conservation of Nature and Natural Resources) African Special Project, which will set up guide lines for basic conservation in East Africa.

TUESDAY 24 JANUARY

By car to Murchison Falls Park. On the way we stopped to get pix of pelicans nesting in a big tree. The young were fully grown and almost fledged. One placed its whole head and neck inside its parent's throat.

And so by the ferry to Paraa, and the Safari Lodge which I had opened five years before.

John Savidge was delightfully welcoming. He is now Warden of the Park. We had originally recommended him for a Parks job. Frank Poppleton, who was here on our previous visit, is now really a part of the Queen Elizabeth Park but is here for a while helping John.

We were installed in the bedroom built for the Queen Mother's visit. Below the terrace came an elephant (it is called the Lord Mayor), and two other herds were just across the river, together with waterbuck, Fish Eagles, Sacred, Hadada and Glossy Ibis, Egyptian Geese, Lily-trotters and crocodiles.

It is a superb place – every bit as good as we remembered it.

Carmine Bee-eater.
Merops nubicus.

WEDNESDAY 25 JANUARY

A day with John Savidge at Buligi – and *what* a day! Elephants, rhinos, and Carmine Bee-eaters, and never a dull moment.

We set off in the de luxe Land Rover on the road to Buligi and the shores of Lake Albert. The first stop was to watch a white hawk in a tree-top. It had red eyes and eyelids and a short tail which wagged up and down incessantly and comically. It was a very pretty bird – a Black-shouldered Kite.

Next stop was for a Side-necked Terrapin seen crossing the road in a very dry area. We took him on with us to the next water we came to – a very small pond where we photographed him again, and also took pix of a moth with a white line down its wing to represent grass with a node.

There were plenty of Oribi – difficult to photograph as they move the moment the car stops, and Uganda Kob – and in some areas Jackson's Hartebeeste in larger numbers than we remembered from our previous visit; though this time visibility was extended because the grass fires were more advanced than last time, and although the effect is a little bare and desolate, it means you can really establish what large mammals are on the ground.

So down to the West Nile (Albert Nile) where there was a profusion of dragonflies with velvet black bars across their wings. They were concentrated in the shade under a tree in which we saw the display of the Striped Kingfisher.

We photographed elephants and then came to the first tree-full of Carmine Bee-eaters. Later we came upon more and yet more. At one point they were hawking round a group of elephants. We lunched under a bush near the first tree, and subsequently photographed 'orange tip' butterflies of two probably unrelated species. At Buligi where the road bends south we found Madagascar Bee-eaters mixed with Carmines and Phil took many pix. We saw some Reedbuck – black nose and short forward curving horns, and a Bushbuck, with a conspicuous pattern of white spots.

We took a critical look at some yellow wagtails. There seemed to be two subspecies – one typical Blue-headed and one with longer legs and a larger bill and all black head. There were also immatures which might have been yet other yellow wagtail forms.

We circled a small sized bustard which was very confiding. Later along the edge of the bay, or lagoon, by which hundreds of Sand Martins were migrating, we saw the beautiful Cinnamon-crested Bee-eater, a small green one with a blue bar across the upper breast and reddish below it.

We returned to Paraa (seeing 2 Martial Eagles) at about 7. I have not described more than 10% of the bird species seen, and no mention of the waterbuck and the Warthogs. It was a wonderful and memorable day, packed with interest and enjoyment.

Next day we visited the incredible Falls where the Victoria Nile passes through a cleft in the rock just 27 feet wide, and then on Friday we decided to go fishing for Nile Perch just below the Falls. Ever since the war I had lost interest in killing animals, but having been since my early years a keen fisherman I could not refuse the offer. I still clung to my youthful enthusiasm for a sport which, like other

Madagascar Bee-eater.

*Merops superciliosus
Common at Lake Baringo
Sept 1969.
Several by our camp.*

blood sports, I subsequently concluded was something I no longer needed nor wanted to engage in. But I was writing at a time when this conclusion had not yet crystallised in my mind.

FRIDAY 27 JANUARY

It was a much hotter day than its predecessor, and the sky was very clear. I had been shirtless for two hours on the way up the river, but now I had put it on though its short sleeves left my wrists and forearms getting steadily redder and redder. We had lunch under the rock opposite the Experts Pool and then went back – Phil to fish from the Claw and I from the bottom end of the same pool. After half an hour Phil foul-hooked an *Elestes* of about 2 lbs. I went round to the top of the pool, standing on a wall of rock on the very edge of the thundering falls. It was an exciting place to fish from, but I touched no fish.

We decided to have one last despairing shot at the Claw – which I had not yet fished. I tried one normal cast, and at the second I threw a plug (which floated) out into the fast water and let it go down stream taking an extra 20 or 30 yards of line. When I came to reel in, the wire guide failed to flip back into position. With a big jerk I got it back, but the handle had no effect, and the whole drum of the reel began to ride up and off the spindle. Frank came down onto the rock to help me.

'The reel's had it,' he said. 'The only thing to do is to wind it on by hand.' There was 40–50 yards of line out and to wind it on like cotton onto a cotton-reel was going to be a long job. 'I'll pull it in', said Frank, 'if you wind on.' 'No' said I, '*I'll* pull it in, if you wind on', and I began to pull in. Frank's attempts to repair the reel – tightening up a nut and pushing it all back on again and having a second and a third try, meant that the 50 yards of line had now been out in the pool for perhaps 5 minutes, and not surprisingly it seemed to have snagged up. Then suddenly the line tightened and whatever was at the other end was clearly alive and had every intention of going in the opposite direction.

I had no idea how big the fish was but he was on about 25 yards of line and I was in no position to give him any more. The line took a turn round the wire guide on the reel and then went direct to Frank who was holding the drum. Frank and I agreed that we had virtually no chance of landing the fish and the only thing was to pull him as hard as I could and hope to get him close enough to be gaffed, before he broke us.

At that moment he got his head out into the current and I had to yield. I was holding the line in my left hand, the run burnt a little furrow in the skin of my finger. Then I learned that the right way was to hold the line against the cork handle of the rod. Just before the run the fish had shown himself, momentarily looking to Frank like a 15–20 pounder, and the next time its great head surfaced I asked Frank despairingly whether it was further away than before. We had to admit that it was.

After that he swam up our way and I got him in to about 10 yards and then held firmly during his next determined effort to get out into the fast water. The breaking strain of the line was 23 lbs, and I must have been pulling at least 22 of them.

Frank had dropped the drum of the reel into the crack between the detached rock on which I had been fishing and the mainland and it sank out of sight into the pool. The only way to retrieve it was by pulling in the line wound round it as fast as possible. By an almost superhuman

White-headed Plover
Xiphidipterus albiceps

Hitherto unrecorded in Murchison Falls Park.

Murchison Falls.

effort Frank, with excited assistance from two African rangers, recovered the reel and I still had the fish on the other end of the line.
Gradually I had worked it in till Frank went forward to gaff it.

Unbelievably the great Nile Perch was hauled out onto the rock. He
was well hooked on both sides of his mouth. Frank's conservative
estimate of his weight now appeared to be an underestimate but we
continued to play for safety. 'Must be 25', 'Might be a little more', etc.
I tried to think of big salmon I had seen as casts – at that rate this ought
to have been over 40 lbs.

So home and champagne for dinner to celebrate the fish which turned
out to weigh 42¾ lbs! Looking through the Fishing Book at the lodge
we found that Keith Shackleton's best had been 40 lbs – though he
caught two of that weight. But he had a reel to play them on. My fish
only took about ¼ hour to land. If I had had a reel I should most certainly have taken twice as long, and should never have dared to pull
him so hard. I still do not quite know how the line held.

We left the Lodge the following day, arriving in Entebbe after the
six hour drive, ingrained with red dust. After the weekend we flew
to Nairobi [Kenya].

TUESDAY 31 JANUARY
Morning with lions, mid-day at the Coryndon [now the National]
Museum and afternoon till dusk in the Nairobi Park.

Mervyn [Cowie, then Director of the National Parks, Kenya] and
his wife Val took us into the Park after an early breakfast and we found
a pride of ten lions. This consisted of two adult lions known as 'the

Hot, bored Lion. (one of the spivs)
Nairobi Park

spivs', two young lions and six young lionesses. We spent an hour within about ten yards of them and Phil should have some wonderful pix. On the way to the lions we saw a pair of Silver-backed Jackals.

At the Coryndon Museum I was taken round by Dr Louis Leakey – the Director and archaeologist – seeing some good dioramas, Joy Adamson's paintings in watercolour of flowers and portraits of native tribesmen in their tribal dress, a new technique of casting snakes on branches which produced remarkably lifelike models, bird, fish and insect galleries, and reproductions on artificial cave walls of wonderful cave paintings. Most impressive to me was his infectious enthusiasm. My attention was riveted to what he was telling me all the time I was with him.

Previously he had shown me the new Snake Park, in the charge of his son, with live snakes, chamaeleons, frogs etc. I handled a rock python which was rather wild, a small green tree snake, and a larger brown snake with down turned nose. They told me there were 39 kinds of chamaeleons in Kenya alone and I saw two half grown specimens of the largest. It grows to three feet long, but these were only about 2 ft long – though none-the-less impressive animals.

Louis Leakey, who described how we met in about 1930 with Donald McInnes pigeon shooting at Childerly (or somewhere else near Cambridge), had an extraordinary manner and a rather trying nervous laugh. But his discoveries in archaeology and palaeontology are of first importance.

He took me up to the Bird Room, there to meet John Williams – the distinguished curator of birds – who was also vastly impressive and very charming. He began by presenting me with a Tule Goose skin collected by Jim Moffitt in 1940 in Solano County, California, which he said we ought to have. It was a delightful gesture.

Dr Robert Carcasson showed me some hawk-moths and just before lunch Dr Leakey showed me 'the most marvellous example of mimicry in the museum'. Mimicry was misused in this sense perhaps – as the hemipterid bugs he showed me were pretending to be flowers. They existed as a colony of about 20–30, and were bright yellow. They clustered at the top of an herbaceous plant which bent over with their weight and hung down. But most remarkable of all – every colony contained a few individual bugs – from one to five which were green instead of yellow and these green ones were always at the end of the plant representing buds. If the colony (family) was disturbed within half an hour the green ones would be in the 'bud' positions again. How do they know? There is a similar white species, but it has no buds.

After lunch at the Lobster Pot in Nairobi with Mervyn Cowie, Leakey drove me down past my mother's statue of Lord Delamere, which is really rather fine, though the head is a trifle too large (he is seated, dressed in a cardigan).

WEDNESDAY 1 FEBRUARY
With Mervyn in the Land Rover to Tsavo Park West, to lunch with the warden, Tuffy Marshall, and his wife Viola.

The most marvellous example of mimicry – hemipterid bugs pretending to be flowers.

'Black-eyed Susie'
Chamaeleo bitaeniatus hoeneli

The local Agamas are brightly coloured. The male has an orange yellow head but the rest of the animal is very bright blue. The females are cryptic brown with some bright brick red spots on the back.

We motored 25 miles to Mzima Springs through quite pretty country but entirely devoid of mammalian life. It was extraordinary that there were no great herds of antelopes, as the grass looked lush enough. It seems that available water holes were too few, bore holes and water troughs are being installed to try to bring back the herds which were poached out many years ago.

Mzima Springs, with rather tame Vervet Monkeys – one with a toto [baby] – were very lush and green and the clear water gushed out of the lava rock. There were raffia palms and papyrus, and great blue chub-like fishes (*Barbus* species).

Further down, we watched half a dozen hippos in a clear pool from an observation tower with a covered approach. A cormorant was fishing underwater.

Further down still was a very cleverly designed submerged tank with windows through which a shoal of about 100 *Barbus* (largest about 5 lbs) could be seen at very close quarters. There were also a few large 'sucker fish' – mormyrids (?), some tiny *Tilapia* and some small eleotrids (loach-like).

We dug out and photographed some ant-lions at the bottom of their comical traps – and also found a wingless wasp mimicking an ant, caught in one of them.

After dark the return road was full of nightjars – one of which flew into the car and killed itself, so we brought it back and I drew it (opposite). Its eggs and nest are undescribed, and it is evidently very local.

A hare (smaller than the European) ran in front of the car. Later near the Warden's house, where we were staying, the headlights showed an elephant and a herd of 40 Impala.

THURSDAY 2 FEBRUARY

Photographs of lizards and moths before breakfast – then away to Tsavo Park East, where we were met by Peter Jenkins, Assistant Warden. We drove about 20 miles through the park to a camp specially set up for us on an island in the river. On the way we saw several groups of elephants – covered in the local red soil and looking almost chestnut-coloured. I saw a single Eland, and we passed many Impala, waterbuck, a lioness and two cubs, an Egyptian Goose with three full grown young, Lilac-breasted and European Rollers etc. The Athi River was dry but the Tsavo (fed by Mzima springs) was still running and there were certainly many more animals concentrated by it than we had seen in Tsavo West.

The camp, on an island in the Galana River, was in a most romantic setting under Doum Palms and we crossed a shallow sandy river bed to the island. Beyond was a cleft in the escarpment of the Yatta – the longest lava flow in the world. Through this pass was a well worn track from the waterless plain beyond to the river, and the site was selected for this reason.

At camp was the Warden of Tsavo East – David Sheldrick, his wife Daphne (sister of Peter Jenkins) and their little girl Jill, aged 6.

The camp was set up in luxurious style and we had iced drinks

Binary Fission' type growth of Doum Palm.

Donaldson-Smith's Nightjar
Caprimulgus donaldsoni.   Red phase ♂

Young Eland bull,
Taurotragus oryx pattersonianus.

Opposite:
Above: Tsavo elephants – red
from their dust baths of Tsavo
earth (before they crossed the
river).
Below: elephants drinking at
the Galana River, near our
camp, Tsavo East Park.

followed by a slap-up lunch. A character of special appeal was the
Sheldricks' young banded mongoose, which was absolutely and
deliciously tame and whistled almost perpetually.

After lunch and some pix of the mongoose breaking an egg by
throwing it backwards between its hind legs against a box, there was a
cry of elephants approaching. They were still up in the pass but
coming fast towards the river evidently intent on a drink. We took up a
position on the bank in the shade of a bush – seven of us including six
year old Jill – and waited for the elephants to arrive. Eventually they
came to the far bank of the river just below us and only fifty yards away.
At once they began to drink and splash water over themselves, occasionally lifting their trunks to sniff the wind, on which perhaps some evidence of our camp and ourselves may have eddied out towards them.
These elephants were a delightful reddish colour, because of the red
soil. There were 9 of them including a fairly small toto.

One of the elephants crossed the river to our island, and the rest
followed. Evidently they contemplated spending the afternoon in the
shade of the Doum Palms. They turned a little towards us along the
bank. We began to withdraw and the oldest cow saw us. We all began
to run, and David Sheldrick and Peter Jenkins turned and pelted them
with Doum nuts. This had little effect and the elephants headed on
towards the tents. About 20 yards short of them they turned and
skirted round one end of the camp as David Sheldrick started up a
Land Rover and rushed them, to speed them on their way. I do not
really know how dangerous the situation was – if at all – but it was
certainly very exciting for a couple of minutes.

David Sheldrick dug down a scorpion hole (completed by a ranger)
and found two scorpions. We photographed one in a soup plate, the
middle of which he spanned.

174

Impala.

Later we crossed with the Land Rover to the east side of the river and went up the shore track, seeing Impala, waterbuck, the lioness with her two cubs, all very thin, a fleeting glimpse of a rhino with calf, a herd of buffaloes, some Hammerkops, Woolly-necked Storks, Marabous, a fleeting glimpse of two Lesser Kudu females, and more distant elephants. But the most interesting feature of the drive was the variety of small birds. Doves, including a pretty pintailed Namaqua Dove with red brown wings, a sand grouse with black wings, a new green bee-eater (said to be the Madagascar), three species of small hornbills – red bill, white bill and particoloured bill (with black-billed female), Golden-breasted Glossy Starlings with long tails (*Cosmopsarus regius*), two rollers, drongos, shrikes, flycatchers. On the way home we saw a seven foot crocodile in the river.

We were back in camp before dusk, and Phil and I had a warm shower from a drum specially rigged and equipped for the purpose. Then, after a drink, we went 50 yards to the edge of the river to see the animals which had come in to drink. There were 18 elephants stretched across the silver track of the full moon which had just risen above the Yatta escarpment; and standing by the waterside was a rhino. All these animals were within 60–70 yards, silhouetted against the moonlight. It was inexpressibly lovely and romantic.

FRIDAY 3 FEBRUARY

I found a very large ground-spider in my trousers and one of the rangers brought in a delightful small grey dormouse with black lines through its eyes – very handsome. Its name – *Claviglis murinus*.

After breakfast and pix of the spider, Phil and I embarked in a Land Rover with Peter Jenkins for the 180 miles journey to Malindi on the coast via Mombasa.

SATURDAY 4 FEBRUARY

Rainy skies. Peter took us out four miles to see Archie Ritchie and wife Queenie. He is 74 and crippled with arthritis, but was the first Kenya Game Warden. They had a tame Lilac-breasted Roller sitting on the rung under a chair and catching grasshoppers thrown to it.

Rain or no rain – Queenie (who is quite splendid) led us to the reef. Peter and I set off to the outer edge with her, seeing Turnstones, Whimbrels and perhaps Curlew Sandpipers (there had been Sanderling and Grey Plover on the beach in front of the hotel).

In the pools near the shore were several *Pterois volitans* which is so beautiful and so poisonous. In one place there were 6. It was so dark

Lilac-breasted Roller,
Coracias caudata.

and overcast that they were more out in the open than usual. Queenie had brought bread for the Sergeant Major – *Abudefduf saxatilis*. Then Peter and I swam for an hour round the coral-heads. We must have seen 100 species. I found that I could basically classify most of them.

SUNDAY 5 FEBRUARY

Out to the coral gardens in the Ritchies' boat. Phil's first view of the fishes of the Indian Ocean. She agrees that they are as good as Fiji. Water superbly clear and fairly warm. I swam for $2\frac{1}{2}$–3 hours all told. Many species I had not seen yesterday. A great profusion of species and of fishes. The coral perhaps not so colourful as in Fiji or the Barrier Reef.

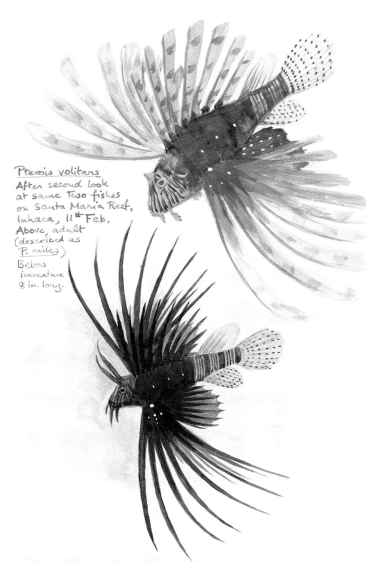

Pterois volitans
After second look
at same two fishes
on Santa Maria Reef,
Inhaca, 11th Feb.
Above, adult
(described as
P. miles)
Below
immature
8 in. long.

Pterois volitans which has many vernacular names: Lion Fish, Turkey Fish, Butterfly Cod (in Australia) and sometimes, incorrectly, Scorpion Fish. I think the most appropriate name is Fireworks Fish.

Above: Scissortail Sergeant, *Abudefduf sexfasciatus* (*coelestinus*).

Below: Sergeant Major, *Abudefduf saxatilis*.

Pig-Snout Trigger Fish,
Rhinecanthus aculeatus.

Foxface Surgeon Fish,
Acanthurus leucosternon.

The most colourful fish are a beautiful surgeon fish – *Acanthurus leucosternon* – which is violet blue with bright yellow dorsal fin, and a dark head outlined in white behind the eye and round the operculum. It is a very handsome fish by any standards. No less brilliant are the tiny blue and orange abudefdufs, and the Moorish Idol and chaetodons follow closely for colour. But a close look at some of the parrot fish, and particularly some of the smaller wrasse, shows wonderful colours and patterns. *Coris gaimard* – both young and adult (quite different) is a gorgeous fish. At least four new chaetodons, and on the way home – making my day – a Pig-Snout Trigger Fish (just one and very shy) *Rhinacanthus aculeatus*, the Humu-humu nuku-nuku apu-aa-aa of Hawaii – the first tropical sea fish that Phil ever saw, on Green Island on the Barrier Reef on Christmas Day 1956.

FRIDAY 10 FEBRUARY

Looking back on Malindi it was a lovely week. The first three nights were spent at the Blue Marlin Hotel – comfortable and excellent food; the last four in the Ritchies' cottage by the shore – 20 yards from the waves. It used to be their home until the encroaching sea persuaded them to build 50 yards further inland. There they live with the black dachshund Futsak or Footie and their Lilac-breasted Roller 'Chirpie'. ('Good bird – very good bird!' said Archie and threw it a legless grasshopper.)

For 2 days we fish watched. On the home reef I had a delightful meeting with *Dactyloptera orientalis*, the Flying Gurnard. It was about 6 feet below me on a patch of broken sand with dead coral rocks. It was only moderately cryptic and did not keep still but always turned slowly away so as to swim off. But it did not swim fast and could be followed. It looked rather like a nightjar. When swimming slowly the first few rays of the pectorals were stretched forward and the rest trailed behind. When speeding up the trailing wing was held in tightly. But when I got too close it would spread its great pectoral fins like wings, disclosing blue webs obviously intended to surprise and frighten off an attacker. I was able to drive it into shallower water so that it was only 3 or 4 feet below. As it passed over darker parts of the bottom its colour changed instantaneously, the spots – enclosed in a black outline – going from buff to almost black. I followed it for ten minutes but lost it just before Phil arrived.

Coming home alone from an excursion to the deeper water (big surgeon fish and a huge 30 lb parrot fish) I was in only 2 feet of water when I found my neighbour was a Black-tipped Shark about 3 feet long.

Dactylopiera orientalis
Flying Gurnard.

Cephalocanthydae
(?) (orybre family)

The doodoos [small animals] on land were quite good. We arrived with an eight inch millipede and found a second more attractive millipede with red legs in the hotel garden – the longest of this species that we saw was barely 6 inches. There was an enchanting diurnal gecko in the garden (?*Spherodactylus*) living on the trees – maximum length 5 inches.

On the night after the rain there was a considerable hatch of insects, including some sausage flies – the termites which emerge with wings for one night after which the wings fall off.

Next night there were Rhinoceros Beetles (also with arachnid parasites), a male with a horn, and a female without. They were difficult to photograph as they would not keep still. The garden spiders were big and impressive.

At a cocktail party with a Mrs Echlin (who keeps a lending library in the back of her car) we saw fruit bats and arranged to photograph them on a later morning, which we did quite successfully using a mirror to light them as they hung under the great leaves of the Wild Almond, *Terminalia catappa*.

On the last day we went out again in the Ritchie boat and tried several new places. There was a fresh wind (in which Phil and I had previously been for a sail in a Jumpahead Catamaran belonging to an old Swede called Fjalstad) which made the water choppy and a little murky. The tide was not so low as formerly and the sun was not so bright. But still it was *very* good. Two new chaetodons – one covered with dark spots. Phil went back by boat and I swam in. Two excitements on the way in. First four squids who were intensely curious about me. They swam rather faster backwards than forwards, but did a good deal of both – backwards for 2 or 3 yards, then forwards and slightly upwards for 2 or 3 feet, then backwards again. They had green spots. They approached me to within about 6 feet – sometimes backwards, sometimes forwards. They did not stay very close together, but always knew where the others were.

Squid about 8" long

The second excitement was a bunch of red filaments with white transverse markings which at first I took to be the head of a tube worm, but then I saw that it was a small *Pterois* – a poisonous dragon fish which seemed to be different from the large ones we had seen and photographed in the home pool (and nowhere else). Either this was another species, or the juveniles of *P. volitans* are strikingly different from the adults. The body markings were similar to *volitans* but the colour was brighter red. The 'antennae' were very long, barred with red and white and forked into a 'lightning conductor' trident at the tip. The spines (?) of the pectorals were immensely long and thin and white with red dots, and the filaments from the tail were similarly marked. Alas I did not notice whether there were filaments from the posterior dorsal. I think it may have been *Pterois antennata*.

And so our lovely coral week ended. We left early on the following morning. (Archie kissed Phil, so I kissed Queenie – who was somewhat taken aback!)

Mervyn met us in Nairobi after the flight from Mombasa in a Dakota – passing over the site of our lovely camp on the island in the Galana River.

On our way back to the Cowies' home we went through the Nairobi Park in the evening light and came suddenly on a lioness with three cubs (one male and two females) and two or three cars watching them. The pride was all in amongst the cars. The cubs played delightfully, rolling over each other (they were full grown). Finally the lioness left her cubs sitting near a small dam and began to stalk some wildebeest. We backed down the road and watched the stalk, which became very exciting. Eventually, crouching in tallish grass, and only just visible to us, the lioness seemed to be within 50 yards of her quarry and Mervyn thought she would make her dash at any moment. But the wildebeest would not turn their backs on her. They fed diagonally across her front and eventually they were 150 yards away. The opportunity had gone. The lioness raised her head. Mervyn lit her with his spot light. She paid no attention whatever.

SATURDAY 11 FEBRUARY

With Mervyn in his Land Rover to Nyeri. On the way we stopped in Nairobi to buy chinese white [paint] for this book and for me to re-record the short piece for the radio which I had bungled at the airport the night before. Miss Wendy Barnes met me at the new KBS broadcasting building and it was all over in 15 minutes.

So to the Outspan Hotel, Nyeri, where Lord Baden Powell spent the last years of his life. It is run, in conjunction with Treetops, by Major Eric Sherbrooke Walker whose guests we were to be. He and David Sheldrick's father started Treetops.

To lunch with them in their home on the slopes of Mount Kenya came Cecil Webb and his wife. 'How do you find chamaeleons, Cecil?' 'You just look in a bush', which tickled Mervyn.

After lunch Major Sherbrooke Walker drove us to Treetops. The last quarter of a mile must be walked. We were part of a 'full house' party of twenty-two, and walked up with the last five or six accompanied by old Sherbrooke Walker with a loaded rifle. There were stockades and ladders into trees in case we should meet an elephant.

The new hotel, which replaces the original one burnt down by the Mau-Mau six years ago (the one in which the Queen was staying on the night of her accession), stands on stilts overlooking the same round 'water-hole' but on the opposite side to the burned out tree trunk. It is supported not by a single tree but by a group of tree trunks planted in

Egretta garzetta
flattened for
fishing.

Ibis ibis
with trap set
for fishing

concrete. As we approached it from behind we could see a number of water birds on the round muddy pond – Marabou, Wood Ibis (*Ibis ibis*), white heron and grey, Red-billed Pintails and waders – and on the far side a family of Warthogs.

During the afternoon we sat on the lower of two balconies, in ex-aircraft chairs, watching the birds on the pool (including four species of ducks – Yellowbills, Redbills, a single female Pintail and a single drake Garganey), Bushbuck, the females red spotted with white and the males sooty, and Defassa Waterbuck. There were perhaps a dozen Bushbuck and two dozen waterbuck, two families of Warthogs, twenty

Kenya Defassa Waterbuck.
Kobus defassa raineyi
Drinking at Treetops

Bushbuck, *Tragelaphus scriptus delamerei*.
The rams are dark, the ewes chestnut.

baboons, which were quite tame and climbed all over the building. At tea time we repaired to the open roof, where the baboons took bread and cake from people's hands. Phil is not fond of baboons and was incensed by one which took a piece of cake out of her mouth. There were also a few Sykes's Monkeys, pretty grey green animals with yellowish markings.

I spent the afternoon sketching the Bushbuck and waterbuck. Just before dusk came a family of Giant Forest Hog, great black Giles animals. It was still light enough to see them quite well. Altogether a possible 9 Forest Hogs came, though some may have been repeats. They only came to drink, but 34 buffaloes were evidently also attracted by the patches of pink salt (renewed daily) which are laid down immediately below the balconies. Two flood lights, one above the other, are permanently shining from dusk onwards, and in their light animals even on the far shore of the pool more than 150 yards away can be seen. Those coming to the salt are, of course, brilliantly lit.

After a very good dinner during which we totted up species of birds with the young white hunter – Geoffrey Mason Smith – I peeped on the balcony and saw the disappearing shapes of two rhinos. They did not return until we had just gone to bed. We re-emerged to watch a cow rhino and her calf, which was, surprisingly, much more nervous than its mother. They were licking up salt within 20 yards of us, as the buffalo had been a short while before.

I discovered that by drawing back the curtain at the head of my bed, I could see most of the salt lick, and from here I watched mama rhino seeing off a group of buffalo who came within 3 or 4 yards of her. She moved aggressively towards them and they yielded at once. Later from my bed I saw another and rather smaller who stayed only a short while at the salt lick. At dawn I got up to take photographs for Phil of Mount Kenya, its jagged peak visible to us for the first time.

SUNDAY 12 FEBRUARY

Breakfast at the Outspan Hotel and then a drive over the Aberdares National Park with the Warden Bill Woodley and his charming new wife of a couple of months – Ruth. Bill, who had a striking record during the Mau-Mau emergency, was previously married to Daphne Jenkins, now the wife of David Sheldrick, Warden of Tsavo East, whose father started Treetops which is in a salient of the Aberdares National Park.

The road over the Aberdares led us across beautiful moorland, with two stops for waterfalls, the first at Magura Falls, the second where two rivers fall a thousand feet with first step falls of 3 or 4 hundred feet each. To see one of them we leaned over a precipice while our arms were held and photographed them lying on our tummies with our legs held. Phil took one looking straight down the falls (Gura falls).

We picnicked at 10,500 feet overlooking the Rift Valley, and then motored on to Naivasha down in the Valley. Here we had to decide whether to turn left to Nairobi or right to Nakuru and the gliding club which I had promised to visit. Although it meant 100 miles of extra driving in the Land Rover, we turned right and went to the gliding club at Lanet. It had been soarable all day until our arrival when it promptly clamped. The club fleet consists of T31, Grunau Baby and Cadet. The T21 was virtually written off a year or so ago when the pilot lost a leg and an eye, and his 'day member' passenger lost both her feet. Naturally this terrible accident has been a serious setback to gliding in Kenya.

Mike Garrod (lately of Dunstable) gave me a check circuit in the T31 (last time in such a glider was in New Zealand) and then I did a circuit in the Grunau. Entry for my flying log:

12.2.61 T31. P2. Autotow. 3 minutes circuit.
„ Grunau Baby. P1. Autotow to 1,050 feet.
„ 3 minutes circuit.

MONDAY 13 FEBRUARY

A day of hard work in Nairobi. A meeting with John Owen, Director of National Parks of Tanganyika [Tanzania] – evidently an able fellow and very keen. He persuaded me to sign an appeal (jointly with Bernard Grzimek [zoologist and conservationist] and some American judge).

Next a meeting with the Trustees of the Kenya Parks. They listened politely, but how to get more big donation money was the only thing that really interested them. Sir Charles Markham Bart, was in the chair. He was very pessimistic about the whole thing and did not seem to me to be seeing the wood for the trees.

After my piece I sat in while 'the man from the Ministry' (Webster) made a statement about the new National Reserves which are to be run by the Masai. They are very anxious for the Reserves to be accepted by UN as National Parks. This seems to be the only ace we hold, and could win a trick for conservation.

Next a broadcast interview to the Forces, in which I selected *A Bar at the Piccolo Marina* as my piece of music. I was not allowed anything serious, but afterwards they played me the last 3 minutes of *Rosenkavalier* which I would have selected. Having been starved of music for several weeks, I was greatly moved by this glorious passage, and could not see to do the little drawings in the autograph books which had been put in front of me.

After lunch I made a short introduction to a bird film to be sponsored by East African Airways and to be shot by John Pearson. He had brought a tame kestrel, a Woodford's Owl and a duiker, though we only used the kestrel in the film. They had only a very slender idea of how to shoot film in the studio which they had built for the purpose in a hangar at the airport. It was very hot under the lights and I had to be script writer, director, continuity man, the lot!

When we finally got back to the Cowie home, Phil, who had had a quiet day, had caught a beautiful three-horned Jackson's Chamaeleon. We took photos of it instead of going out into the Nairobi Park with the warden which had been arranged. It was really a lovely chamaeleon and Phil had found it in the garden by Cecil Webb's method – just looking in a bush!

TUESDAY 14 FEBRUARY

Mervyn drove us to Nakuru in his big Buick, with Val and John Williams of the Coryndon Museum who told us about the birds on the way.

We were rather late arriving but nevertheless they took us down to the edge of the lake where the ceremony of opening the National Park was to be held in the evening. There were hundreds of thousands of flamingoes all over the shallow soda lake (this salt lake is now far below

Rift Valley shrikes.

Above: Grey-headed Bush Shrike singing at the top of an *Acacia exanthophloea* after heavy rain.

Below: Black Cuckoo Shrike, *Campephaga sulphurata*.

its normal level). The strong north east wind was whipping up clouds of white soda and as we stood beside the platform being set up for the ceremony it was like a smoke screen in a war film. The dust was pungent and horrible. And I was in my best dark blue suit!

Lesser Flamingoes,
Phoeniconaias minor,
at Lake Nakuru.

Back to lunch at the Stag's Head Hotel. Its proprietor, Norman Jarman, is one of the prime movers in establishing the National Park and was in charge of all the arrangements.

After lunch Phil and I went off to a school to give a lecture with slides – Wildfowl Trust, Galápagos and our fishes from Malindi. It was a useful opportunity to get to know the order of the slides.

Then back to the hotel for tea and down to the lakeside for the opening ceremony of the Lake Nakuru National Park. The wind had eased and the soda dust was not too bad. The Governor – Sir Patrick Renison – arrived with the Mayor of Nakuru and the Chairman of the County Council. We all mounted the rostrum and the speeches began. All were short and the standard quite high. The Mayor read his and so did HE (the Governor). I did mine without notes, and tried to make it forceful. It seemed to go over fairly well, and Mervyn did a witty vote of thanks.

Then I was invited to join HE in his brand new Rolls for a drive down the lake side.

We passed many thousands of Lesser Flamingoes scattered rather loosely along the shore, with occasional Ruffs and Little Stints. But apart from the great numbers and the beauty of the flamingoes' shape and colouring, there was no greater interest in one stretch of shoreline over any other.

WEDNESDAY 15 FEBRUARY

A Flamingo Day

Before sunrise we were driven out by Norman Jarman and Tony Dando to a spring at the edge of the lake. Coming down towards it we passed a big herd of nearly 100 Impala, some guinea fowl and a single waterbuck. In the spring surrounded by thick vegetation we were shown 6 of the 12 hippo living on Lake Nakuru. They are in some danger as two have recently been shot, and the spring is half a mile outside the new National Park.

We waded nearly up to the top of borrowed wellingtons through soft mud and a bed of tall Reed Mace till we emerged at the edge into a hessian 'hide' of primitive design and construction. From its large 'windows' was a sight of incredible beauty and interest. The sun had not yet topped the hill behind us. The far shore of the lake was already sunlit but the uncountable masses of flamingoes, which stretched from the far distance to within twenty yards of us, glowed pink in the blue shadow.

On our extreme right where the stream debouched from the reeds was a group of half a dozen Hottentot Teal, but they had seen us arriving and they were soon away. There were also Marabou Storks which flapped away and cleared the immediate area of flamingoes, though before long they were walking back towards the hide.

As the sun rose from behind the hill the colour became more and more brilliant. Streams of flamingoes came in from far out on the lake, a triangular patch of bright scarlet under their wings lit by the low sunlight. There can be no more remarkable ornithological spectacle in the world.

We stayed in the hide for $2\frac{1}{2}$ hours, and Phil took many pix. In the foreground there were sometimes Black-winged Stilts, often Ruffs and most of the time Little Stints. There was also a female shoveler which sometimes swam almost amongst the flamingoes' legs.

Left:
Greater Flamingo,
Phoenicopterus ruber roseus.
Right:
Lesser Flamingo,
Phoeniconaias minor.

Lesser Flamingo.
Phoeniconaias minor.

Nakuru. 15 February 1961.

'Tikki', the Grey Bush Duiker, *Sylvicapra grimmia hindei.*

Silver-spotted Blue Butterfly, *Aphnaeus hutchinsonii drucei,* a lycaenid butterfly which was feeding on the flowers of a poincettia in John William's garden at Amboseli, 22 February 1961. The larva is taken and fed by ants which milk it of a secretion from the 6th segment.

FRIDAY 17 FEBRUARY

A meeting in Mervyn's office in Nairobi with Gerald Watterson (Sec. Gen. of IUCN) and Ian Grimwood (head of the Game Dept.). Also met Lee Talbot (American scientist studying wildlife at Serengeti) and his wife. After lunch John Pearson took us out to his home to photograph some of his tame animals. The duiker 'Tikki' was the most appealing. He has had it for four years and it is completely and charmingly tame and exquisitely beautiful. She is a female and about the size of a Labrador Retriever. The Pearsons also have a long coated Golden Retriever which often shares a kennel with Tikki. Most of Tikki's tameness is based on carrots and millet seed, and she was difficult to photograph in the shade dappled garden enclosed by a bamboo fence. Inside some bamboo aviaries Phil took pix of an eagle owl, a Woodford's Owl (called Woodford and borrowed from some friends) and finally, in the open she photographed 'Charlie' the adult female African Kestrel, in a big close up against the sky while it sat on John's gloved fist, controlled by jesses.

That evening we had a lecture in the Town Hall. About 700 people came including the Governor, and Sir Alfred Vincent (Chairman of Trustees of Royal National Parks) was in the chair. We showed slides of the flamingoes and us watching them, followed by Trust, Galápagos, and Malindi fishes. Phil operated the lantern and went on to the next slide without any signal. It worked extraordinarily well. The whole thing was quite a success and there was tremendous applause when Phil came up onto the platform at the end.

SATURDAY 18 FEBRUARY

A morning in the Nairobi National Park. The concentrations of animals were astonishing. In two places we saw seven mammal species in company, once at a salt lick, once at a dam. On the first occasion there must have been 200–300 animals: zebra, wildebeest, Kongoni, Impala, Grant's Gazelle, waterbuck and ostrich. At the Dam were zebra, wildebeest, Kongoni, Grants, Tommies (Thompson's Gazelles), giraffe and Warthog.

A ram Impala with 15 ewes was especially cooperative in photography as he and his wives stood in the shade of a tree. Mervyn said he had an exceptionally good head. They must be the most beautiful of all the antelopes.

Across a valley we saw an ostrich running, pursued by a small four-legged creature. We could not think what it could be; perhaps a hyaena, or a jackal. We converged on its course and found it to be a day old wildebeest which had mistaken the bird for mamma. The ostrich, embarrassed, had trotted away and the tragic little chase had begun. By driving the Land Rover between them (they were only 10 yards apart) we managed to separate them, but there seemed no way to get the little gnu to go back to where it came from', and anyway its mother may well have been dead or dying. The park was littered with corpses due to the drought and lack of food.

On the way back we saw an extraordinary concentration round a still flowing river of about 300 vultures sitting in tight groups on the ground.

In a Land Rover, which had known better suspension, we set off – six of us – on an excursion to the Ngong hills where the game has been pushed back and back by Kikuyu settlement. Eventually we found

Grant's Gazelle
Gazella granti.

Thomson's Gazelle
Gazella thomsoni

herds of buffalo, Eland and waterbuck high on the slopes above us. Later and nearer to the road were zebras, Kong'oni, Grant's, Eland, a giraffe and a Reedbuck – the first we had seen since Murchison Falls Park.

We motored across country and got fairly close to some Elands against the skyline. Then on to the highest point of the Magadi Road – more Kongoni and zebras – and a superb view across the Rift Valley with many giraffes far below us.

On the way back through the Masai reserve there were big herds of wildebeest, a few Eland, quantities of zebras, an adorable lone baby Tommy, and a herd of about 50 half grown ostriches accompanied by two adult females. One of the young was much smaller than any of the others.

So back to the Cowie home at dusk – much shaken up!

CHAPTER 10

Tanzania

DIARY 5   1961

Later in the same year I visited Tanzania (then still Tanganyika) to attend a rather important conference at Arusha. It was called the CCTA*/IUCN* Symposium on the Conservation of Nature and Natural Resources in Modern African States, and was organised in collaboration with FAO* and UNESCO*, from 5–12 September 1961.

On the afternoon of 3 September I drove to London Airport with my darling Phil, who came to see me off. In the BOAC lounge we were joined by Julian Huxley [biologist] and Juliette seeing him off and Max Nicholson [Director General of the Nature Conservancy 1956–1966].

4 SEPTEMBER

Arrived Nairobi. It had recently been raining – the third day of it – but the first significant rain for months (for 3 years said Julian).

We were met by the Minister for Tourism – Howard Williams – at least I was met by him, and at first had difficulty persuading him we must go back to meet Julian and Max.

Then we all set off by car to Arusha through the Nairobi Park. On my finger was 'Jackson', the Three-horned Chamaeleon which we have had in England throughout the summer.

On the way to the park we saw a giraffe and some zebra – and once in the park we were soon among the spectacular marvels of the African fauna – Grant's and Tommies, wildebeest and Kongoni, zebra, giraffes, Impala, Warthogs, a jackal. There were a dozen or more Kori Bustards in ones and twos, Wood Ibis, Great White Heron, Hadada Ibis, Marabou, a Bateleur Eagle, Lappet-faced Vulture, White-backed and Griffon Vultures, Crowned Plovers and a Grey-backed Pelican.

We let Jackson go on an acacia bush on the edge of a gully about 2–3 miles short of the Athi River Gate of the park. Julian H took still pictures of his release and then wanted to take a close-up of Jackson who had by this time gone so cryptic that Julian couldn't find him although he was only 3 feet from his eye. It was all very suitable for a chamaeleon who has taken a blowfly from Prince Charles' fingertip.

And so the conference began next day. Lots of people I knew. We met in a cheerful school building with a pleasant cloistered lawn to which we all repaired for the tea breaks.

Jackson's Chamaeleon,
Chamaeleo jacksoni.

*CCTA Commission pour la coopération technique en Afrique (Commission for technical co-operation in Africa south of the Sahara)
IUCN International Union for Conservation of Nature and Natural Resources
FAO Food and Agricultural Organization of the United Nations
UNESCO United Nations Educational, Scientific and Cultural Organization

The opening speech by the Governor, Sir Richard Turnbull, was a *tour de force*. For nearly an hour he spoke authoritatively on land-use, water conservation, forests, wildlife and ecology, quoting from the submitted papers at length. He had well and truly done his homework and it was a remarkable performance setting a high standard for the conference.

In addition to the main conference I got involved in meetings of the Ngorongoro Conservation Area Advisory Board, to which (with Julian Huxley, Professor W H Pearsall, Frank Fraser Darling [Vice President of the USA Conservation Foundation 1959–72], David Wasawo, Barton Worthington [Deputy Director-General of the Nature Conservancy 1957–65] and Bernard Grzimek) I was invited as an observer, and outside adviser. This led to some cloak and dagger work later, in a bold last minute attempt to save the Ngorongoro Crater from ruin.

My diary contains speech notes for the conference and the text of a radio broadcast I made:

'The Arusha conference which has just ended has gone more directly to the heart of the matter than I think any of us ever expected it could, and as a result, I believe it will be a turning point for Africa's threatened wildlife and perhaps even a turning point in Africa's whole future, because land and land use is at the root of nearly all of Africa's problems . . .

The conference soon made it clear that this was no 'animals against man' conflict. Conservation, they said quite firmly, is for man – for the long term benefit of mankind – his spirit as well as his belly.

In its wildlife, Africa has something unique which is the envy of the world. How to save it from destruction? Well, it's not just a technical problem of game management; it is a sociological, an educational, a political problem, and one of great urgency into the bargain. And the wildlife itself isn't only an aesthetic asset, or a cultural heritage – it isn't only a question of prestige, a sort of status symbol for an emerging nation. It can have substantial economic importance – as the basis, for example, of an increasingly valuable tourist industry – and as a source of protein in a protein hungry community. We heard how wild animals, being much better adapted than domestic cattle to the climate and conditions in tropical Africa, yield much more protein per acre than domestic animals do, and how they can do this without damaging and ultimately destroying the range, as cattle so often do.

We heard time and again the African delegates undertaking the responsibility for protecting their wildlife – asking for technical help and financial help for the conservation of the animals, and, more important, the wild areas in which they live – the habitat – that subtle relationship of soil, water, plants, animals, and man which make up the science of ecology. No habitat, no wildlife.

Well now, you know, this call for help from the Africans is going to have to be answered. I think there's new hope for the survival of at least a proportion of the former wonderful profusion of wild animals in Africa – and more than that I believe we shall find that the Arusha conference has given a new impetus to conservation all over the world which may yet save a significant part of the world's wildlife, even now at the 11th hour.'

I also visited the Ngorongoro Crater, by invitation, as part of a study group of seven charged with making a report to the Governor. The other six were Julian Huxley, Professor W H Pearsall, Max Nicholson, Barton Worthington, Frank Fraser Darling and Bernard Grzimek.

Next day I wrote an account of our early morning arrival inside the great caldera (which, as the volcanologists tell us, it should properly be called). It was intended as an article for a newspaper, but it was never finished.

Dawn in the Ngorongoro Crater

The narrow track ran steeply downwards through the cloud in the darkness of the dawn; tortuously it followed the mountain-side and we bounced down it in four-wheel-drive. It was cold and the wind was wet. We could see no more than twenty yards through the grey mist. It was hard to believe we were only 200 miles from the Equator.

Suddenly the mist began to clear below us as we came down to cloud-base, and we could see the steep slope gradually flattening out. In a few moments in the grey morning light we could see the whole floor of the Ngorongoro Crater stretching before us, eleven miles to its farther side where the land rose again and disappeared into the flat bottom of the dark grey clouds.

Below us on the colourless slope was a tightly packed herd of multi-coloured Masai cattle just emerging from the 'boma' or circle of thorns which had protected them from lions during the night. Spread out across the flattening hillside were a couple of hundred zebras and away to our right the plain was darkly spotted with hundreds of wildebeest.

Close to the road was a Silver-backed Jackal suckling five tiny cubs at the entrance to their earth. She moved away a little as we stopped to watch, and the cubs romped and tumbled delightfully no more than thirty yards away.

Over to the north-east the sun was beginning to break through the clouds and the blanket began to lift from the crater's rim. Soon the ring of mountains was visible all round and it was broad bright daylight. A herd of elegant Grant's Gazelles was moving down to drink from the last remnant of a swamp, for this was the height of the worst drought the crater had suffered in the memory of the Masai tribesmen who lived there.

We had come early to the crater in order to see the animals while they were still moving about, and before the heat of the day made them seek shelter in the scanty shade of the acacias and the dried up rushes of the swamp. We passed groups of beautiful little Thompson's Gazelles – smaller than Grant's with almost the same smart pattern of black on their sides, but less white on their rumps. The Tommies have longer tails which they flick incessantly from side to side.

Above the swamp is a remnant patch of acacia forest, showing signs of damage from elephants. Three species of vultures and four hyaenas were sitting about in a glade among the trees, evidently having recently finished the remains of a kill.

There was a profusion of unfamiliar birds, among them a hoopoe, and we stopped to watch a pair of tiny dik-dik, the smallest of the antelopes. The doe was playing 'hard to get' and the buck followed her round and round and round a small thicket, first one way and then the other.

Ngorongoro Crater.

Out on the close-cropped dry dead grass of the plain were some flocks of Helmeted Guinea-fowl, and two Bat-eared Foxes sat watching us as we came towards them, their huge grey ears framing their tiny fox-faces.

We circled back towards the swamp and stopped for breakfast close to a narrow waterway which was all that was left of what is apparently a wide pool in normal times.

That was as far as I got with the proposed article which I drafted in my diary, but there was one other entry for the Ngorongoro Crater – the first draft of the report of the inspection group to the Governor:

1. Having been invited to inspect the Ngorongoro Crater and parts of the adjoining Forest Reserve on 9 September 1961 and to consider future management policy in that area, and recognising that we saw it under conditions of severe drought, we believe
(i) that the role of the Crater Highlands in the conservation of water calls for the creation of new Forest Reserves and the effective protection of the existing Forest Reserve from further damage
(ii) that the spectacular scenery and outstanding opportunities for viewing wildlife in the Ngorongoro Crater combined with the evidence of very serious overgrazing, calls for the establishment of a strict wild-life sanctuary, and
(iii) that in order to overcome the difficulties facing the Masai which are brought about by water shortage and by over-grazing and other forms of bad land-use, an increased rate of pasture development in Masailand is urgently needed.
2. We are further of the opinion that the executive authority of the Conservation area should be based on a newly created District Commissioner, with the officers actually responsible for water, forest, wild-life, pasture and veterinary development, the representative of the Masai Federal Council and 3 other local representatives (because there are other water-users besides the Masai).

I did not return to England immediately after this conference but instead flew to the Galápagos Islands at the invitation of the President of the Charles Darwin Foundation, Professor Victor van Straelen – a journey described in Chapter 7.

CHAPTER 11

South Africa, Tanzania
and Sudan

DIARY 6 1962

In the winter of 1962 Phil and I went on a holiday to South Africa, Tanzania and the Sudan. While in South Africa I hoped to make a 500 km glider flight to complete the third qualification for my Diamond Badge (the other two, which I had already attained in England, being a flight of 300 kms to a pre-selected goal and a climb of more than 5,000 metres).

TUESDAY 16 JANUARY

Arrived Johannesburg by Comet with Phil at 3.0 pm. Met by Everard and Patsy Read [whose Pieter Wenning Galleries were handling my paintings], Mel Gilfillan (Chairman of the Wildlife Preservation Society), Boet Domisse and Pat Beatty (from the Gliding Club).

Planned glider flight for following morning. Installed chez Reads.

WEDNESDAY 17 JANUARY

Collected by Pat Beatty, wife and twin 5 year old boys at 8.30 and driven 10 miles to Baragwanath Aerodrome.

Looked at Pat's home-made glider (BJ 2) in which he became South African Champion 2 weeks ago at Kimberley. It is nicely finished with upswept tips, good flaps, no airbrakes and a startling performance. We rigged Boet's Skylark IIIb ready for an aerotow at 11.0.

There was much rushed briefing and 'task selection' for my 500 km goal flight (diamond flight), which was additionally confused by a Press interview and photographer.

We planned a dog-leg – 175 miles south west to Bloemhof, then 145 miles back east to Lindley. The wind was moderate north-easterly, but was expected to back to westerly during the day (though in fact it didn't).

For those who read this book, and don't already know, this is how cross-country gliding is done. In suitable weather the sun warms some areas of the ground more than others and from time to time large invisible 'bubbles' of hot air detach themselves and rise through the cooler surrounding air. As the bubble, which may be several hundred yards in diameter, rises into progressively colder air its upward speed increases, and in good gliding conditions it may be going up at more than 10 miles an hour. This is the process of convection. By definition a glider is always coming down through the air, but if its pilot can find air that is going up faster than the glider is sinking, he will climb. The bubble of warm air, which becomes a column of rising air, is called a 'thermal' and, by circling, a skilful pilot can remain 'centred' in the thermal if he correctly reads the instrument which tells him how fast he is climbing. It is called a variometer and most gliders have two of them.

When the top of the thermal reaches the pressure level at which

Skylark IIIb.

water vapour condenses, a cloud is formed. That level is called cloud base and as the process of condensation slightly raises the temperature, the 'strength' of the thermal (its upward speed) increases. So each of the white clouds that fill a summer sky are the outward and visible sign of a thermal and if the pilot flies under the cloud he will usually find (lift). Part of his skill involves distinguishing which clouds are young with hot air still rising under them, and which are spent, when he will waste his time looking for lift that has died out. For a glider flight using thermals the glider must be launched to a height at which the pilot can search for and find his first thermal. Launching can be by aero-tow, by auto-tow or by winch, the last two using the principle of the kite. Thereafter the glider proceeds in a series of spiral climbs in each thermal and a downhill dash to the next one. On some days of strong wind a sheltered slope facing the sun may generate thermals regularly every 20–30 minutes. When these get up to cloud base they blow down wind like bubbles in a stream to form a row of clouds called a 'cloud street' and if this lies in the direction of the flight task, progress may be very fast, merely slowing down in the lift to regain height under each cloud without the necessity to stop and circle.

Sometimes the clouds cut the sun off from the ground which is creating the thermals. The sky is then said to have over-convected. Towards evening the thermals are usually fewer and harder to find and they have died out altogether by dusk.

(This flight took place about $1\frac{1}{2}$ years before I won the British Gliding Championship at Lasham in Hampshire in May 1963.)

I was finally launched with an aerotow by Tim Biggs at 11.30 and released about 1,500 ft above ground (7,200 above sea level). I then couldn't find the thermal I thought I had released in, but finally found something rather weak – and staggered up to cloud base under a small watery little puff of cumulus at about 8,500 ft.

Everything felt very strange and I was pretty dithery. The tow rope had been jammed into the wrong part of the Ottfur hook and had not released at first attempt during the cockpit check. It was fully half an inch in diameter and the hook on the tug had no release. We had gone up at a bare 50 mph, which in this fairly rarefied atmosphere had meant a good deal of wallowing and this was only my third flight in a Skylark III. I was talking to Boet on the radio, and trying to read two variometers showing rate of climb (a Crossfell and a Horn), one, as I was reminded by Boet, calibrated in feet per second and the other in metres per second! Mostly, at this stage, the Crossfell stood at 3 fps up.

I set off at once and was soon pretty lost, having great difficulty in reading Boet's E2 compass and having no idea yet of the scale of my map. At this stage my chances of making a diamond flight seemed extremely slender.

After about half an hour the lift improved and I began to spin along down the 10–15 knot breeze under something like a cloud street. Pat had marked the map with hours to get me to my goal by 7 pm. I was half an hour early at the mark for 1 pm and nearly an hour early at the mark for 2 pm.

Navigation became easier when the Vaal River became big enough to follow. I kept reporting back by radio until Orkney – about 130 miles out, though I had had no reply since about 25 miles out. Apparently they heard me up to about 60 miles out, and were satisfied with my progress.

Soon after Orkney the sky over-convected ahead of me, with some trailing rain, but there was sunshine beyond. I decided to try to push through, keeping to the left of the falling rain, but it moved to the left too and I flew through hail. Fortunately many parts of the grey mass were still lifting and I was pushing along at 70 mph.

Bloemhof – the turning point – came up about $1\frac{1}{4}$ hours early, and I went over to the west side of it to find a thermal in which to take my photographs. I was down to 7,000 ft (3,000 above ground) having been operating between 9,000 and 11,000 for most of the way. By now the best thermals were 800 feet per minute but the average still only about 350–400 fpm.

I took 10 photos of Bloemhof, concentrating on the bridge over the river which has a weir immediately upstream of it. By the time I had climbed the overcast had drifted across my new track back to the east. I had to make quite an extensive detour to the south getting down to 7,000 ft again.

Finally I decided to work the leading edge of the overcast patch, which had lift, but not very strong.

Navigation was now much more difficult, with long spells without any identifiable feature in sight. With the unfavourable wind, the next towns and railways were always longer coming up than I expected, and I had some rather anxious times. My problem now, with the clouds becoming sparser, and having disintegrated almost invariably by the time I got to them, was whether I could get to my goal before dusk.

This worry was unduly pessimistic. I followed a small river from Kroonstadt up towards its source, got low and was swept back by the north east wind across a railway, used a cloud street at 60° to my course, spotted a town which I took to be Lindley and wasn't, corrected my error and found myself approaching my goal at last, soon after 6.0 pm. There was still good lift as I approached with 3,000 ft in hand and flew round confirming that I was at the right place and prospecting the airstrip. I failed to see a wind sock, but saw some smoke and ripples on a farm dam, and landed without difficulty on the deserted grass runway.

The time was 6.24 pm. The course time was 6 hrs 46 minutes (flying time 6 hrs 54 mins). I was glad to be on the ground as Boet's glider has no plumbing and the polythene bags he gave me were not watertight.

In due course a car came up the main road from the village and a young man, a woman and three children came over towards me. The woman turned out to be the wife of Lindley's magistrate. We parked the glider 'out of wind' and off the runway, then went to the hotel in the little town. It was the Clarendon Hotel and rather primitive. I telephoned from a call box, watching a swarm of kestrels – 100 or more – milling round the church tower.

Pat Beatty answered the telephone and there was an agreeable amount of surprise and much delight that I had reached the goal. Boet arranged that we should retrieve the glider by aerotow the following morning.

After supper the young man and his girlfriend took me by car back to the airfield, and we took off one wing-tip by moonlight. The night seemed calm.

I went to bed at 9.00 but was awoken by a loud noise of wind in the trees round the hotel. I put my hand up to the dangling switch over the bed to see what time it was, and got a violent electric shock which bounced me out of bed, and gave me cramp in one toe! However I was not burned.

It was 11.30 by the church clock and the wind was quite fresh. I was worried lest the tail of the Skylark might blow round and damage the wing-tip which we had put in the lee of the fuselage, so I walked out to the glider, built a small cairn of stones from the white airfield marker patches, against the tail skid and returned to the hotel at 1.0 am. All through my walk lightning had been flickering among some cloud which seemed to be advancing from the Basutoland hills to the south. Walking along the road towards the glider I had heard galloping hooves and was met by two runaway horses, which I circumvented on the way back so as not to drive them into town.

At 6.00 next morning, instead of 9.00 as arranged by telephone, Boet buzzed the hotel, and I got the manager out of bed to give me a lift out to the airfield. All was well with the glider. Boet announced that Don Ord would shortly be arriving too in a Beechcraft Bonanza with Phil. Boet had brought Chick (I never discovered his full name) to steer the glider on aerotow so that I could go back at high speed with Don in the Bonanza. In due course all this came to pass and by 9.30 I was back at Baragwanath. Was there ever a more luxurious retrieve?

We now wait to see that the photographs are OK.

And they are so it seems that I am the 7th British pilot to hold three Diamonds. The others are: Nick Goodhart, Tony Goodhart, Philip Wills, Ann Burns, Denis Burns and John Williamson.

We spent a part of the next day going to the picture gallery in Johannesburg – seeing their marvellous little El Greco, and Shannon's portrait of my mother. The gallery was established by Lady Phillips whose husband was Phil's godfather, after whom she was named.

We motored 60 miles out past Hartebeestepoort to Lady Oppenheimer's farm for the afternoon and evening. On a dam there we saw our first wild Black Ducks (*Anas sparsa*).

I spent part of the week-end painting some pictures for Ev's Wildlife Exhibition at the Pieter Wenning Galleries.

Ev lent us a car so that we could make a pilgrimage to Phil's old home – Beauchamp – at Westminster in the Orange Free State.

WEDNESDAY 24 JANUARY

A day of sheer delight, revisiting Phil's old and much loved home which she last saw when she was 12 years old. Although in 31 years much had changed, and Phil knew that it had been through a bad period when it had fallen into sad disrepair and the garden had been utterly neglected, it was now in the hands of an Afrikaans Doctor called Dupreez and his English wife who met us as we drew up in the shade of some fir trees.

Of all the houses I have seen in Africa this Beauchamp is the most beautiful. It looks out towards the mountain of Thaba Patchua 10 miles away across rolling farmlands. It is surrounded by fine trees and has a beautifully kept garden – though substantially different from the one planned by Phil's father.

The house had been altered inside, but Phil still found the cupboard

Beauchamp from the Kopje, with Thaba Patchua in the background.

from which she and her brother had clandestinely tried out their first gin! We wandered round the house, taking many photographs. My Phil was enjoying herself very much, for as she had hated her trips to England she had correspondingly loved Beauchamp very greatly.

We found the place among the thick fir trees which had been a special 'hide-out' for Evelyn and her. It was still a secret place and I was glad to be allowed there. It was called Adelaide. It was a happy place and we savoured it with our own enjoyment.

In the afternoon we returned to the house again and motored round the farm, then climbed to the top of the Kopje under which the house nestles. It was a glorious clear evening, and the view was stupendous. It is really one of the lovely places in the world.

THURSDAY 25 JANUARY

We went to Basutoland to see the scenery and the bushman paintings, accompanied by Michael Thatcher, with whose mother we had been staying, and John Plyman a local administrative officer who had been 23 years in Basutoland.

There was a 2 mile walk to the caves in a river gorge, where there are some prehistoric paintings. We photographed them after they had been damped by patting them with a soaked rag to bring out the colours.

The paintings are wonderful – superb Elands in polychrome (red and white), masses of figures – even in one place representing armies. There was a marvellously drawn leopard, and some exquisite birds, especially a guinea fowl of incredible sensitivity and beauty and an eagle in flight, also of great imagination. There is not a doubt that the early artist or artists were of immense calibre. Later drawings in yellow ochre were sometimes superimposed and of a vastly inferior quality.

I am horrified by the treatment these paintings are getting. In another 10 years or so they will have gone altogether. They *must* be preserved as soon as possible perhaps with some sort of plastic varnish, guarded by a warden and copied in their entirety before they deteriorate further.

No doubt this should be done at other bushman painting sites. I am determined to try to do something about it.

198

FRIDAY 26 JANUARY

In the morning we went to One Tree on the opposite side of the Kopje from Beauchamp, then climbed among the summer wildflowers to the top of the ridge, to look down once more on Beauchamp itself – its red roofs among the trees, the farm lands spreading away, a scene of special beauty.

Phil's tears were, as she said, the ones she had not dared to shed at the age of 12.

Then we walked down again to the car and away back to Westminster and Green's store, where we bought a tie for Evelyn and a shirt for me, and set off for Johannesburg at 12 noon, by way of Welkom where there is a great concentration of water birds on some pans of salt water pumped out of the new gold mines. Among them were 500 Greater Flamingoes.

We took some time to find the pans in the new and featureless town, with its scattered mine shafts, but eventually we were directed to the Bloemfontein road and found great quantities of ducks, coots and waders and about 500 flamingoes (Greaters). They looked incongruous with the background of mines and their buildings and tips, but Phil took some photographs of them.

So we set off homewards and reached Johannesburg after dinner at a roadhouse.

A special feature of our trip had been finding in quantities the caterpillars of the Thorn-tree Emperor Moth, which Phil remembered from her youth and which, because of their enormous size, great profusion, and propensity for falling to the ground and being trodden on by her bare feet, had been one of the causes of her dislike of big caterpillars.

There were two ornithological adventures worthy of record. Just before arriving at Westminster we stopped to look at some Egyptian Geese and Yellowbills on a dam near the road. After a few minutes a female Spurwing [Spur-winged Goose] with 5 small downies swam out from the near shore. This was my first sight of downy Spurwings. They were extremely yellow and their bills pointed downwards. They looked not unlike downy Canvasbacks.

The second ornithological observation was as follows:

On January 23 1962 at Kroonstadt in the Orange Free State I was watching a thermal up-current which had drawn in some smoke from the town, when I noticed a flock of birds in tight formation circling in the core of the thermal and gaining altitude very rapidly. The wind drifted them overhead and I was astonished to find that they were Greenshanks. There were between 80 and 100 in the flock and having climbed some 3,000 ft they headed off in a north west direction at very high speed, still in a tight flock. They lost height rapidly, but soon found another thermal and the process was repeated. Although they spent most of the climbing time circling round, they frequently changed direction and sometimes weaved around, obviously looking for the strongest lift. At the top of the second climb they were lost to view. During the 8–10 minutes they were under observation they had not flapped their wings at all.

I have not been able to find any previous record of flocks of waders using this technique – which is exactly similar to that of the cross-country glider pilot.

Thorn-tree Emperor Moth
larva, *Gynanisa maia*,
26 January 1962.

Greater Kudu bull,
Tragelaphus strepciceros.

During the month in South Africa that followed, we saw so many exciting things and met so many people working in the wildlife conservation field, that my diary becomes a series of species lists and a kind of address book, with only a brief note of our itinerary.

We went to the Kruger Park and stayed for a couple of nights at Skukuza driving out from there each day. We saw our first Greater Kudu, our first Sable, our first Tsessebie and our first leopard. Altogether we listed 27 mammal species and 88 birds. From there we went to the island of Inhaca, off Lorenzo Marques, to swim on Santa Maria Reef and there we recorded 112 species of fish. Lists of animals seen are evocative only to the list-maker. As I run my finger down the column of names in the diary twenty years later I can see again the sunshine and the light playing on the kudus' horns, the brilliance of the blue that flashed from the back of the Angola Kingfisher, the expression on the face, once I had found it, of the Sargassum Fish, *Histrio histrio*, in a patch of weed on the edge of Santa Maria Reef. So long afterwards I cannot conjure up an image of Smith's Woodshrike, *Eurocephalus anguitimeus* nor of the Sabota Lark, *Mirafra sabota*. I could not for certain identify Jardine's Babbler, *Turdoides jardineii jardineii*, nor yet the Cuckoo Finch, *Anomalospiza imberbis*, but we saw all those birds during our three days in the Kruger Park.

After Inhaca we went to the Natal Parks with our old friend Jack Vincent, who played so great a part in creating them. We saw our first wild White Rhinos with Ian Player, then Chief Warden at Umfolozi and Hluhluwe and our first Nyala in Hluhluwe and Mkuzi Parks. In the False Bay Reserve, in the northwest corner of Lake St Lucia, Pink Pelicans, herons, darters and cormorants were breeding and later, on the east side of the lake, we watched large concentrations of Hottentot Teal, and even larger flocks of White-faced and Fulvous Whistling Ducks, with lots of Yellowbills and Egyptian Geese and a few shovelers and Cape Teal. There were vast flocks of Ruffs (like winter knots in Britain) which settled among stilts and Hottentot Teal. That day we saw two crocodiles. Two days later we saw Blue Cranes (Stanleys) with young and a Wattled Crane at the Giant's Castle Reserve, which had a beautiful 'camp' with a garden of indigenous flowers that brought in Malachite and Lesser Double-collared Sunbirds.

From Natal Phil and I went back to Arusha and the Ngorongoro Crater [in Tanzania], which she had not seen before, and on, for the first time for both of us, to the Serengeti Plains.

White Rhinoceroses,
Ceratotherium simum simum.

Hluhluwe+

Mkuzi. 16ᵗʰ + 17ᵗʰ Feb.

Nyala
Tragelaphus angasi.

SUNDAY 25 FEBRUARY

Set off for the Serengeti Plains with John and Jane Hunter from their home at Oldeani, in their modified diesel Land Rover. He is currently Chairman of the National Parks.

Just past the entrance to the Ngorongoro Conservation Authority Area we found a very interesting (and as yet unidentified) chamaeleon. It was crossing the road, was relatively fast moving and aggressive, trying to bite me when I picked it up. At the gape it had reddish marks, tending to increase the apparent size of the mouth. It had an incipient single horn on the tip of the snout – a horizontal line, a rather elongated shape and very long tail. The basic colour was brownish with small red

'The Oldeani Monster' – still not positively identified in spite of reference to the principal experts in the field. It has been suggested that he was perhaps a female and related to *Chamaeleo jacksoni merumomontanus*. But we believe he was a male and we think he may have been new to science, and as yet undescribed. He lived for a year and a half at Slimbridge and the bottle containing his remains has been mislaid and possibly destroyed in error. Perhaps he should now be described as *Chamaeleo oldeanii* – the Oldeani Chamaeleon.

dots. It became known as the Oldeani Monster – and is probably a male. We have brought it with us. It is just possible that it is a juvenile of the giant Meller's Chamaeleon. (This proved not to be the case.)

Then on to Leakey's camp. He was away but his wife Mary showed us fossil bones of all shapes and sizes (down to a chamaeleon's jaw and rodent teeth 2 million years old). She took us down to the digging sites and showed us where the *Zinjanthropus* [primitive man] skull was found.

Stone circles (evidence of some kind of dwelling) were the most recent discoveries – also 2,000,000 years old – whereas most of the rest of the human evidence was 30,000 years old.

Then on across the Serengeti Plain. Sandgrouse, Tommies and a few Grant's Gazelles, giraffes, a Kori Bustard on its nest of two red-brown eggs.

Near a kopje called Naabi, having motored for nearly an hour through continuous scattered herds of Tommies, we came to the wildebeest – we reckoned 40,000 – and many zebras too. We turned down towards them to see some lions under a lone tree (full of vultures and one Abdim's Stork). The lions were rather wild. The noise when we stopped among the wildebeest was delightful. There were great numbers of calves.

Later the grass got longer – a few Topi, but not many animals at all; quail jumped up all round.

MONDAY 26 FEBRUARY

Opening ceremony at the Michael Grzimek Memorial Laboratory at Banagi. It was performed by Dr Gerstenmaier – Speaker of the West German parliament.

Jacques Verschuren (ex Congo Parks) now established at Banagi was also present. He described how 80–90% of wildebeest and zebra breeding areas are outside the park in Masai grazing area south and east of the boundary, and there is a rumour that Fosbrooke is planning to fence the boundary with the conservation area. (Later Starker Leopold told me in Nairobi that he did not think this was imminent).

After lunch at Seronera we went to the Turners' to photograph the Rock and Tree Hyraxes. Myles Turner (wife Kay) has been Assistant Warden for many years since getting bored with being a white hunter. He is second in command to Gordon Harvey (Chief Warden of the Serengeti).

Before lunch he had taken us over to Joy Adamson's* camp. She told us all the special pleadings about why she should be allowed to see Elsa's cub Jespah again. Not all of what she told was true. One of the conditions under which the Trustees had agreed to have the cubs released in the Serengeti was that they would revert to being wild lions and would not be kept aware of the link with human beings by any further intervention on Joy's part. For one concession allowing her to take food to the cubs (the third or fourth concession), Joy had agreed that if it were granted she would leave the cubs alone and never make any further attempt to see them. On this understanding the concession was granted.

Since then however, more concessions have been sought because of the arrowhead which was in Jespah's flank before he was moved and which on all veterinary advice should be allowed to remain there – but which has been playing on Joy's imagination until it has become an obsession. Joy is quite unbalanced about it. At first I wondered whether her blackmail, that she would 'expose the Trustees' in the third Elsa book, should not be met with a final concession against a document of legal force binding her to let the cubs alone thereafter. But having discovered that such a document (though without legal force) exists from a previous concession which was 'positively the last', I am bound to agree that the Trustees have no choice but to be firm and let her do her worst.

After tea John Hunter took me for a flight over the breeding concentrations of wildebeest and zebra. In $1\frac{1}{2}$ hours we reckoned we saw 105,000 gnus and about 40,000 zebras. The herds stretched for mile after mile across the open plain.

TUESDAY 27 FEBRUARY

We began our return to Oldeani in the Hunters' Land Rover before dawn. After crossing the black cottonsoil area and three rivers (now dry, but impassable in the rains a few weeks ago) we struck out to the eastwards across country to find the great herds we had seen north east of Naabi Hill the night before.

Just after sunrise we came upon a herd of more than 30,000 zebras which we had missed on the flight. They barked their high pitched call incessantly 'qua-ha, qua-ha', (which is how 'quagga' is pronounced in Afrikaans).

After photographing them in the early light, we went over a terrific bump, which broke the beer bottles in the back. Having stopped to assess damage we decided to have breakfast, with zebras in all directions. We were perished with cold, and unfortunately the sun was obscured

'Ngorongoro',
Chamaeleo bitaeniatus,
25 February 1962.

*Joy Adamson (1910–1980), painter and author. She is best known for her accounts of lions in Africa, for example *Born Free*, *Elsa*, and *Living Free*.

203

by thick cirrus cloud and gave us little heat. Nevertheless we felt warmer after breakfast, as we motored through the incredible herds of wildebeest – not less than 60,000 in the next hour. From the wildebeest – and more zebras round a rather delightful rocky outcrop, we came into the Tommy country, still with many herds of wildebeest at first. The Tommies ran to cross in front of us – they seemed to run for the enjoyment of running fast.

Just before rejoining the 'road' from Ngorongoro to Seronera, (this euphemistic term refers to a rough track grown high with grass in the centre and deviating whenever there are serious obstacles or roughness to avoid) we saw a couple of black dots in the distance ahead. Jane Hunter bet John two shillings they were rhinos. As we approached it became evident she had won her bet. There were in fact 3 rhinos (six shillings) – a mother and two young, one 2 year old and one 4 year old.

We pulled up about 60 yards away downwind. After a few moments the old lady woke up, got up, started towards us, and then began a fast trot directly at us. She was charging. John had been saying that the ground just ahead was so rough we could not expect to make a fast getaway, and so he decided the best thing was to keep absolutely still. At 10 yards she paused and stood looking at us, then turned and trotted away to about 50 yards again, rounded and faced us again. We waited. She made as if to charge again once or twice but seemed to think better of it, and when we started up and moved off, she trotted away in the opposite direction.

We had lunch half way down the Ngorongoro crater, under trees with a splashing waterfall and some interesting butterflies including a tiny blue *Syntarucus* with two eyes on the underwing next to a small 'false antenna'.

Down on the crater floor were baboons, a pair of Crowned Cranes with 4 babies and Greater and Lesser Flamingoes in the swamp. We circled the Lerai forest looking for elephants, but without success. It was a strange contrast with my last visit when the salt lake had been dry and the borders of the forest teeming with gazelles, zebras, hyaenas and birds. Everything seemed to have gone to the far side of the crater at this season.

And so back to Oldeani and next morning – 28 February – to Nairobi in John Hunter's plane, with Phil and Jane sitting in the back seat.

On 1 March we left Tanzania for Khartoum to be followed by a week's snorkelling in the Red Sea off Port Sudan.

THURSDAY 1 MARCH

We arrived at Khartoum and were met by a young man, Gasim M Soliman, from the Forestry Department whose car had failed to turn up – so we took the bus to the Grand Hotel, overlooking the Nile. We had about 3 hours' sleep and then the young man arrived to take us back to the airport, just after dawn.

A brand new high winged Turbo-prop Fokker Friendship took us to Port Sudan at 25,000 ft in an hour less than the scheduled flight which was normally flown by Dakotas. This was the Fokker's first run on this route.

We were about to board the bus to the hotel when a Sudanese arrived to say he was the Assistant Commissioner and that the Commissioner

Blue butterfly (*Syntarucus* sp) found on the inner slope of the Ngorongoro Crater, 27 February 1962.

himself would shortly be there to greet us and bring us into Port Sudan. We must only wait because the plane had arrived an hour early. But we did not have to wait an hour for Salih Mohed Tahir, Commissioner for the Red Sea Hills, a big man with a gusty laugh whom we came to know quite well, and to like very much, during the next few days.

The Commissioner (whom we addressed as your Excellency) brought a typed copy of a full programme carefully worked out, which occupied the mornings and left the afternoons free. With minor modifications, it was a very enjoyable programme. With sympathetic understanding, the first morning was dropped, and in the afternoon we went to the Marine Gardens in a glass bottomed boat. The coral was rather poor but the fishes were interesting. The Gardens are inside the harbour mouth on the north side, with a cable on pylons, along which the boat is pulled with boathooks. This cable was lined with Sooty Gulls as we approached. At the far end was a Brown Booby and, on a post by itself, an Osprey which allowed us to come within 20 feet. There was a new and interesting *Chaetodon* with a whitish head, and the most characteristic fish was a greyish surgeon fish with streamers and orange spots which was everywhere – perhaps *Acanthurus lineatus*.

Zebrasoma veliferum.

We spent some of the afternoon catching grasshoppers for our 8 chamaeleons.

FRIDAY 2 MARCH

The Commissioner and the young Fisheries Officer, Dr Mohamed, took us to the dead city of Suakin (pronounced Suwakin). Following behind was a Willys 'Land Rover'. Suakin was the principal port of Sudan until the beginning of the century. In 1905 when ships were growing bigger and the harbour of Suakin was incapable of expansion, work was begun on a new harbour 40 miles to the north. It was completed and officially opened in 1909 as Port Sudan, and from then onwards the town of Suakin was dead. The number of inhabitants fell from 30,000 to 3,000 and the great buildings began to fall into disrepair. Now 50 odd years later it looks as if it had been bombed. Everywhere the houses are falling down into great heaps of stones and rubble.

Acanthurus lineatus.

We went for a tour of the harbour with the Commissioner in an outboard motor boat, then back to the Rest House to change and out again to a part of the reef we had selected.

The water was murky, but the fishes were very good. I wrote down 34 species, but we must have seen more than 50.

Back to Port Sudan for a late lunch, hoping that the remaining spring leaves of the car would last the journey!

Acanthurus triostegus.

SATURDAY 3 MARCH

Out in the Fisheries boat – a sturdy tub with an antediluvian engine – to the famous Wingate Reef – about an hour's trip, starting at 8 am.

At the western corner of the reef lies a ship on her side and there are various beacons. Lieutenant Commander Frank Paddison, senior Pilot of the port, had lent us a chart which helped us considerably.

The boat was anchored near some coral heads easily visible and it was evident that for the first time since our arrival in Sudan, we were going to see the real thing. As soon as my mask was under water I could see small fishes 40 or 50 feet below me. Three others came in with me, Dr Mohamed, the Fisheries officer, and two of the crew.

Naso lituratus.

I swam in to the main wall of the reef. This was it. Here at last the water was clear, much clearer than it had ever been at Inhaca. Here the corals were more brilliant than we had seen since Fiji, and the fishes were absolutely fabulous. The star turn was an angel fish (or conceivably a *Chaetodon*) with a basic colour of yellow vertically striped with pale blue outlined in black, with blue and magenta stripes on the anal fin. (Later found to be *Pygoplites diacanthus*.) I also had a fleeting glimpse of *Pomacanthus imperator* – the diagonally striped angel fish. Great clouds of orange and pink *Anthias* surrounded the coral heads. I had my best views of the yellow *Chaetodon* with the blue opercular blotch. In the deep water, where my companion warned 'big fish' there were some fine rock cod and some medium sized fish with huge eyes which hovered about in the gloom at extreme visibility. Later I saw many of these, and discovered that they were *Monotaxis grandoculis*, and that they could change colour rather easily. I saw a small barracuda.

After about three quarters of an hour I returned to the boat, and saw down below, near the anchor chain, a small shark. It was no more than $3\frac{1}{2}$ ft long and was brownish. It was interested only in moving on without attracting attention.

Pygoplites diacanthus.

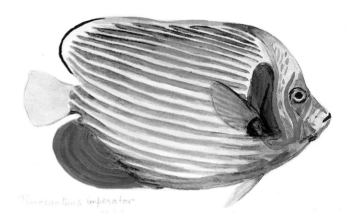

Pomacanthus imperator.

The most beautiful sight against the deep blue of the deep water were the shimmering shoals of golden red *Anthias squamipinnis*, with their puzzling mixture of larger pink-purple individuals [which were simply the males, as I afterwards discovered], and in other shoals of apple green *Chromis caerulea* mixed with a duller, greyer species. Everywhere, too, were the little yellow *Pomacentrus sulfureus*; and there were seven species of *Chaetodon*.

The most ubiquitous fish was a colourful surgeon fish, maybe *Acanthurus lineatus*, which was most numerous on the plateau at the top of the reef.

There was perhaps a height of 18 inches of water over the top of all the reefs. In summer, we were told the water of the Red Sea is about this amount lower, so that the tops of the reefs are then barely submerged. The rise and fall of tide is negligible – at springs no more than an inch or two, but there was a current where we anchored on that first day, though not at all strong.

On my third swim on that first day I went over to the inside of the reef, where a sandy sea bed was about 25 feet down. I saw a White-tipped Shark about 6 feet long which came towards me along the coral

Juvenile *Monotaxis grandoculis*.

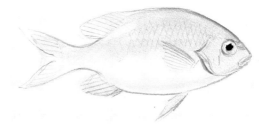

Chromis caerulea.

Adult *Monotaxis grandoculis*.

Juvenile *Pomacentrus sulfureus*.

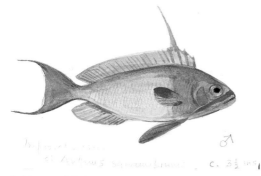

Anthias squamipinnis.

Adult *Pomacentrus sulfureus*.

edge. I backed away facing it and it turned slightly away, and went on about its business. Swimming free just below it was a remora (sucker fish) about two feet long.

SUNDAY 4 MARCH

We returned to the Wingate Reef and anchored in almost the same spot. For the most part the day was overcast and much of the under-water brilliance was missing. I swam for an hour, accompanied by the oldest member of the crew who had no flippers and was dreadfully thin. The poor man, I suddenly realised, was almost dying of cold, so I quickly returned to the boat. Thereafter it was agreed, to the crew's great relief, that we need no longer be accompanied.

We left the reef early enough for me to have a short swim at the harbour entrance. I was anxious to see the large shoal fishes which show sickle shaped fins above the water. Unfortunately the water was very murky, but I found a shoal and the fish themselves were very curious and swam up in a semicircle. They were Milkfish, *Chanos chanos* (I think, as they were a little too deep for *Elops saurus*). The largest must have been about 4 feet long.

After two more visits to the Wingate Reef we decided to try a new spot on:

Painting on board the boat at Port Sudan.

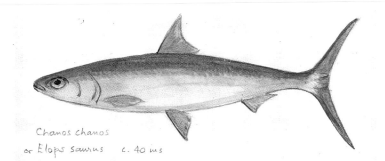

Chanos chanos or Elops saurus   c. 40 ins

TUESDAY 6 MARCH

On the previous day the captain of our boat said 'Tomorrow, Christmas perhaps', which at first puzzled us. It meant that the festivities which conclude the fast of Ramadan are a holiday, but that the next day was only, as it were, Christmas Eve.

In spite of this the boat duly arrived for us at 8 o'clock, and this time we proposed a change. We began by diving from the felucca over the wreck of the *Umbria*, an Italian ammunition ship scuttled there after being taken in prize 22 years ago. The ship is a large one, with nothing showing above the water but a davit and some other stanchions just awash. On the wings of the bridge and among the boat deck rails there were most of the local coral fishes, and much coral which had grown extensively during the 22 years.

Looking over the end of the upper bridge deck we came upon as decorative a crowd of scarlet *Anthias* as we have seen anywhere. This little fish is one of the great glories of the Red Sea coral. Against deep water a shoal of 100 or more is an unforgettable sight.

Phil joined me and we swam above the angle of the starboard boat deck and the ship's side, sloping endlessly down into the blue deep. Parrot fish, blue tang – much bluer than we had seen before, with brilliant yellow tails, grunts and chaetodons, pecked away at the corals growing in clumps on the edges of the plates and the guard rails.

I swam down to the stern, accompanied by a shoal of black surgeon fish with white bands round the caudal peduncle. Dimly in the depth I could just make out the gigantic starboard propeller. The ship had a counter stern.

But by comparison with the natural coral this was poor stuff. It was quaint and I found myself thinking of the people who built the ship, and the fate of her, and the collapse of dreams – but for the naturalist there was nothing special. A barracuda watched me as I swam back, lurking, head slightly down. He was only about $2\frac{1}{2}$ feet long.

Zebrasoma xanthurum.

I re-embarked in the felucca and we rowed over to the reef immediately to the west. This was excitingly different. The coral forests were feathery. There was stagshorn coral in profusion – purple tipped. The colour here was predominantly fawn – whereas the coral colours on South Wingate were predominantly magenta pink, blue and purple.

Phil decided to come swimming when I was far away, and we met face to face as I returned. It is a great joy to me that Phil enjoys the fishes so much.

We rejoined the boat which had been away trying unsuccessfully to catch fish, and we moved to the reef immediately to the north of *Umbria*. Here Phil and I swam again. I went in first and saw two of the huge hump-headed parrot fishes, and a Black-tipped Shark which I followed for a while. It had curious stripes on its sides which may help in identification. It also had a remora stuck to the top side of one pectoral fin, presumably upside down.

WEDNESDAY 7 MARCH

A trip to Sanganeb Lighthouse about 13 miles from Port Sudan, in the fortnightly tug. We swam, first in the lagoon, and out to the edge – the water much warmer. Phil was in for over an hour without getting cold. Lots of *Rhinecanthus* trigger fish and a new *Chaetodon* – large specimens of *C. lineolatus.*

I had a second swim on the southern coral face. It was fabulous, clear water, great depth and wonderful fishes. It was a fitting farewell to the Red Sea.

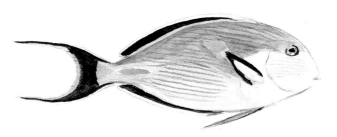

Acanthurus sohal.

CHAPTER 12

Zambia

DIARY 11   1969

We first visited Zambia in 1969 on a holiday with our children, Dafila then aged 17 and Falcon aged 15. We arrived in Lusaka at the beginning of August and went a few days later to Lochinvar, a farm on the south side of the Kafue River flood plain. I had played a minor part in getting it formally accepted as a reserve.

WEDNESDAY 5 – THURSDAY 6 AUGUST
Two lovely days at Lochinvar, to which we flew from Lusaka in a Piper Aztec, in bumpy air, passing over Blue Lagoon where we met the first of the Kafue Lechwe herds. We came down to 50 feet over masses of waterbirds – White-faced and Fulvous Tree Ducks, Reed Cormorants, egrets, Spur-winged Geese, Comb Ducks, Open-bill Storks, Glossy Ibis. It was exciting trying to identify all we saw. Some large-birds may have been Woolly-necked Storks or perhaps Wattled Cranes – possibly both. To the west of Blue Lagoon there were great concentrations of lechwe – many thousands altogether.

Kafue Flats from the air.

Then we turned north heading for Lochinvar. On the banks of the Kafue – out in the middle of the floods were two groups of native huts – was a fishing village. The grass emerging from the flood water was very green. There were occasional pelicans in small groups and even singly. We had to avoid soaring birds – mainly Open-bill Storks.

Beyond the edge of the flood the country was still flat but the grass was dry and brown. We headed south for a little hill, Sebanzi, and passed over a small herd of wildebeest. Eventually we spotted the Lochinvar strip with a Land Rover going out along it. We landed without difficulty although the strip was short, and were met by Bill Greasly (Warden) and his wife and Bob Dowsett (ornithologist).

Kafue Lechwe.

We embarked in 2 Land Rovers to drive 8 miles back towards 'the Flats' – the flood plain. We were heading for a tented camp beside the Nampongwe stream. On the way we saw a Black Chat, a Lilac-Breasted Roller, lots of Capped Wheatears, a pair of Crested Cranes and many soaring vultures. At the camp there were Red-billed Teal, Blacksmith Plovers and Greenshanks which have been there all through the northern summer (why?) and Common Sandpipers (apparently already arrived from the north). The camp consisted of three green tents and one square mess tent, plus a tin cupboard as a latrine, which stood 50 yards back from the Nampongwe, and had been used for some weeks!

We then set off in the open Land Rover, and headed north towards Chunga (= Big tree) which is a fishing camp, 2 miles away at the normal edge of the highest flood.

We travelled along the road, then turned back along the edge of the flood where there were lechwe and Crested Cranes and a Fish Eagle's nest in a tall tree – and on the right a continuous ribbon of ducks, cormorants, Lily-trotters, Pied Kingfishers, Blacksmith Plovers and egrets in 3 sizes. Where the Nampongwe runs out into the swamp there was a huge concentration of many hundreds of White-faced Tree Ducks with a few Fulvous. From the corner we followed the stream back to camp past 3 delightfully confiding Oribi, which stood for pix by Phil.

An excellent lunch of 'Kate and Sidney' pie – a short siesta – and then out again to Chunga – seeing a Grey-rumped Swallow building a nest in a hole in the middle of the road (well spotted by Falcon). From Chunga we turned right this time. The fish offal had attracted many vultures, crows and Marabous.

Along the shore was an endless fringe of ducks, cormorants and darters, punctuated by closely packed bunches of pelicans, and beyond them a mass of lechwe. Falcon, looking for bones for his collection (comparative osteology) spotted first a Nile Monitor which provided good pix before finally making its way into the water, and second a curled up lechwe lamb pretending not to be there.

Eventually we came to a point from where we could go no further out towards the river as the black earth became too soft for the vehicle. At this point we saw a tree full of pelicans with nests. These were the small species – Pink-backed – and it was apparently the first record of breeding in Zambia. We watched a pair of Fish Eagles catch a cat-fish.

White-faced Whistling or Tree Duck.

And so back along the edge of the flood. The sun went down behind the haze as an orange ball, and the sunspots were clearly visible with binoculars and even detectable to the naked eye. Some Spurwings stood for their photograph in the red track of the sun's reflection.

Sunset over the
Kafue Flats, Lochinvar.

Back at camp in the cool dusk, the wood fire looked inviting. I sat and wrote up my notes, while Dafila played her guitar. It was all very beautiful and satisfying. Bill Greasly and his wife came down by Land Rover for supper and we talked of Lochinvar and lodge sites and dams which would make the flood permanent, possibly a rather bad idea.

Next morning, 6 AUGUST, we went out along the same route as we had taken in the afternoon. The light was from the opposite side which lit the birds at the water's edge. The pelicans were a magnificent sight and we got fairly close to one bunch of nearly 600, some of which were flying from the roost on land into the water to fish – with hundreds of attendant Reed Cormorants and a few darters.

By 10.30 we were already late for 'breakfast' though we had had a snack before departure, but we decided to go out from Chunga in a boat with an outboard motor – a large fibreglass dinghy, susceptible to the breeze that was blowing from the south east. But it was possible to get much closer to the egrets and Reed Cormorants than it had been with the Land Rover. We had good views of pygmy geese among the waterlilies, and African Pochard, and passed some distance from some hippos, approaching the pelican flock from the water and against the light.

In the afternoon we went up into the dry plain, seeing 22 new species of birds, zebras and wildebeest. Then to the hot springs in which you can scarcely bear to hold your hand and to the top of a delightful little hill called Sebanzi where they plan to build a lodge. This seems very sad as it is interesting habitat which would be ruined. Also it must be the wrong place for a lodge – with so little to see in the way of mammals.

FRIDAY 7 AUGUST

To Livingstone. Driven out to the Mosi o Tunya ('smoke that thunders') Hotel by the Manager – Peter Costello. The hotel is within 300 yards of the falls. We were no sooner installed than the monthly fumigation of the rooms began. A man with an extremely noisy motorised pack on his back and a mask on, was pumping Dieldrin* (sold to them by Shell) which filled our rooms and the corridor with blue fog. It was, at least, not very good PR within half an hour of our arrival. It was almost impossible to breathe in there as we tried to get our binoculars, cameras, etc before going out to the Victoria Falls.

What can one say of the Victoria Falls? Like the Taj Mahal they are said never to disappoint. To us all they were so far above expectation as to be wholly memorable. Falcon was perhaps most excited but so were we all.

We had seen them first from the air, our next view was of the Eastern Cataract through the spray – the smoke that thunders. There were millipedes which Phil photographed along the damp path. A friendly guide – a young Zambian with a pleasant smile – took me to the bridge where, after formalities, we were allowed to walk half way across. Here was a yellow line and a white line. One represented the Zambian border, the other, 3 feet further on, was the Rhodesian border. No one seemed to mind if we crossed into Rhodesia, which we did for fun.

The view of the falls from the bridge – which carries road and railway – is only moderately good. There was an Augur Buzzard soaring in the gorge, doing very tight turns so as to keep in the upcurrent caused by escaping air counteracting the air carried down by the water. The gorge is in a zigzag pattern. The remarkable thing is its narrowness, so that you can look across at the lip of the falls from about 50 yards exactly opposite. We climbed down towards the Devil's Cauldron, but landslides during the very heavy rains this year had damaged the path at various points. It was a series of rocksteps and wooden steps, many carried away by falling rocks. It was labelled 'Dangerous'. About half way down where it was already impressive and drippingly humid, we turned back up again. The best views of all, as the sun got lower in the west, were along the falls from the east end. It was very beautiful indeed and we stayed there until the sun was a deep red ball just above the edge of the cascade.

SATURDAY 8 AUGUST

David Hoys took us to the small fenced game park where we met Stewart Campbell – now seconded to the Tourist Bureau. I was required to inspect the Rangers and watch a display of marching. Then in a Land Rover round the park – 2 square miles of it. A bull Sable was rather tame and allowed Phil to approach on foot. There was a tame hippo which had taken up with some buffaloes, and quite a nice lot of water birds including the Rufous-bellied Heron and several Greenshanks. The best thing in the park was a close view of a mother White Rhino with a small calf. They were very tame and Phil was able to walk up quite close to them for photographs.

Later we went to a kind of embryo orphanage zoo. It had duikers and

Sunset at the Victoria Falls.

*Dieldrin and other pesticides had, at this time, been banned in Europe and the USA but were still being exported to Third World countries.

White Rhino with her calf,
Ceratotherium simum,
Livingstone Game Reserve,
8 August 1969.

Cheetah.

8ᵗʰ August. KAFUE NATIONAL PARK.
Ngoma & Toly's Loop (Toly's Loop) with Cecil Evans.

Dabchick
Reed Cormorant
Grey Heron
Purple Heron
Little Egret
Yellow-billed Egret
Squacco Heron
Rufous-bellied Heron
Hammerkop
10 Saddlebill
Glossy Ibis
Sacred Ibis
Whitebacked Duck
Redbilled Teal
African Pygmy Goose
Knob-nosed Duck
Spur-winged Goose
Lizard Buzzard
? Wahlberg's Eagle
   or Verreaux's Eagle
20 African Fish Eagle.
Swainson's Francolin
Moorhen
African Jacana
Wattled Crane
Blacksmith Plover
Wattled Plover
Greenshank
Ringnecked Dove
Lilac-breasted Roller
30 Pied Kingfisher
Malachite Kingfisher
Little Bee eater
African Hoopoe
Richard's Pipit
Yellow vented Bulbul
Capped Wheatear
? sp/ Cisticola
Grey rumped Swallow
African Sand Martin
40 Magpie Shrike
? Fiscal Shrike
Lesser Blue-eared Glossy Starling
Oxpecker Redbilled
   " Yellowbilled
? White browed Sparrow Weaver
Red billed Fire Finch
Blue Waxbill
Yellowfronted Canary.
White winged Black Chat?
50 Grey headed Bush Shrike?

Rufous-bellied Heron

Defassa Waterbuck
Wildebeeste
Zebra
Reedbuck
Oribi
Roan

Buffalo
Warthog.
Serval
10 Vervet Monkey
Baboon
  (Papio ursinus)

Star Turns

Pygmy Geese among
  pink, blue & white
    waterlilies
Herd of 400 Buffalo.
Roan Antelopes (3)
Saddle billed Storks with
  a full sized young one.
Pair of Wattled Cranes.

? Arnott's Chat.

Species list for 8 August 1969.

Wattled Cranes and ducks walking loose, and cheetahs (4) and a Spotted Hyaena in cages. There were also snake and crocodile pits and the crocs had bred. Rather a rush to catch our plane after lunch.

A DC3 took us to Ngoma in the Kafue National Park where we were met by Cecil Evans, who runs the hotel. We had 2 rooms in a corrugated green roofed bungalow in an agreeable but inward looking compound, and after settling in Cecil took us in an open Land Rover round Toly's Loop. To me the best bit of this was a series of pools covered with waterlilies and pygmy geese, with a few White-backed Ducks. We also saw a herd of 400 buffalo and 3 Roan Antelopes.

SUNDAY 9 AUGUST
Cecil Evans took us round the Nkala Loop, which showed us our first Lichtenstein's Hartebeest – very red with a diagonal across the hind quarters dark above and pale below. We also saw some very tiny baby Warthogs and got close to a Serval in long grass which flushed and ran at about 20 yards.

MONDAY 10 AUGUST
In the afternoon Doug took us to the safari camp just north of Kalala Island. We went out to look at Puku – our first sight of them – a beautiful russet, almost chestnut brown, but heavily built by comparison with such antelopes as Impala.

There were hippos in the river where we went down to the bank to fish for our supper. Dafila caught a Silver Barbel – a catfish *Shilbe mystus* – of about 1 lb, which was put back as they are inedible. I caught four of the small golden olive 'pike' which have an adipose fin. I had one strike from a large silver fish – probably large-mouthed bream – *Tilapia*, but I missed hooking it. We were fishing with short casting rods and a very small spoon, and trying to cast against a fresh wind.

The camp was lovely – I only missed Dafila's guitar. We had an excellent barbecue supper (including our fish) and then went for a night drive seeing hippos, gennet etc. A lion was moaning nearby when we were back in camp and another answered from the other side.

Puku (Senga Kob),
Kobus vardoni senganus.

On 11 August we flew to Blue Lagoon.

TUESDAY 11 AUGUST
Up early for a cold drive. We did not see very much but it was pleasant and we saw a few birds. Then after breakfast back to Ngoma, to be ready for the Charter Aztec out to Blue Lagoon, the home of Ronnie and Erica Critchley. At Ngoma Lodge I had a brief meeting with Alex Paul – the Shell representative. He said it was a fair question to ask Shell Chemicals what they were selling to the Zambians (Dieldrin).

We flew low down the Kafue Flats – seeing large numbers of cattle and later some birds and Kafue Lechwe, also several flocks of up to 40 Wattled Cranes. It was hot and bumpy and Phil with a tummy upset was not enjoying it. The wind was stronger than expected and we didn't find Blue Lagoon where we expected it. However a few minutes later it came up almost ahead. We landed and taxied up to the front lawn to be met by Ronnie and Erica.

Following the formation of the World Wildlife Fund in 1961, conservation attention in Africa had been directed mostly towards

Kenya, Tanganyika and Uganda. The Critchleys felt that Zambia was missing out on the substantial grant support that the other countries were getting. I had corresponded with them on the subject, and had met them in England, where I had been enormously impressed with Erica's vitality and energetic devotion to the conservation cause. She was a small woman, in contrast to her very tall husband, but she lacked nothing in determination and had a splendid sense of humour. They were to become our dearest friends, but this was the first time we had been to Blue Lagoon which they had set up as a wildlife reserve.

The house stands on a barely perceptible rise above the flood plain among fine tall trees. From the doorstep hundreds of lechwe and a Bushbuck were in sight – also a great many kinds of birds (three species of plovers on the lawn). Champagne restored Phil's spirits and Dafila played the guitar before lunch. After a marvellous curry in a house full of Jack Harrison's watercolours, we went for a drive in the Land Rover.

Lots of quite tame Oribi, and lechwe, a pair of Saddle-billed Storks, a Secretary Bird (the first we have seen on this trip) and five Denham's Bustards – large with white spots and sandy rufous sides to their necks. Later we drove down a bumpy road to the edge of the flood water – to the blue lagoon. Here a Goliath Heron, many Black-headed herons and Cattle Egrets all new for this trip. Lots of lechwe and ducks.

On the way back towards the house we found a pack of wild dogs. Two came towards the Land Rover. On the side of an anthill we saw 5 puppies which were outside the burrow that was their den. By the time we had thrown biscuits to and photographed the two inquisitive ones – one of them very beautifully marked – and moved on towards the anthill, the puppies had retired down their hole. Two other adults were quite tame. The party seemed to be 4 adults and 5 babies.

At about 4 o'clock we took off for Lusaka.

Saddlebill.

Lechwe at Blue Lagoon.

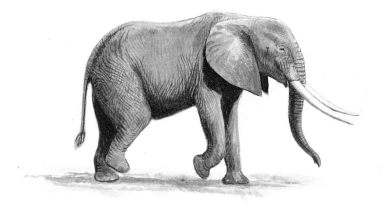

One elephant stood for some minutes on two legs with the other two raised. Why?

On the following day we had lunch with the President [Kenneth Kaunda] and his family at State House which was totally and delightfully informal. Our travels thereafter took us to the Ruaha Park in Tanzania where we saw our first Roan Antelope, to the Kenya coast at Watamu, Jadini and Shimoni for fish-watching (and to see the reintroduced Sable Antelope in the Shimba Hills) and thence up into the Masai Mara.

THURSDAY 3–SATURDAY 5 SEPTEMBER

Masai/Mara. Keekorok Lodge. Driving out with the senior driver (African) and an armed warden.

The game viewing was exceptionally good. The main herds of the plains game had moved up into the north, and a great number were in the Mara.

Close to the lodge were big herds of wildebeest, zebra, Topi, buffaloes, and smaller numbers of Impala, Kongoni, Tommies and a very few Grant's and waterbuck. There were many giraffes, a few elephants and we saw two rhino. In the two days (and a final morning) we saw 22 different lions and one pride which had treed a leopard in a *Euphorbia* and were keeping guard below. Apparently lions *hate* leopards.

Grant's Gazelle.

Bare-faced Go-away Birds eating desert dates, *Balanites aegyptata*.

Sable Antelope
Hippotragus niger
Shimba Hills
27th August 1969.

Females + calf.

Adult ♂

Topi

Topi, *Damaliscus korrigum*,
Mara, September 1969.

The leopard in this tree was extremely difficult to see, and looked very uncomfortable. He was totally unphotographable, only minute areas of his spotted skin being visible from any one point. Manoeuvring the Land Rover among the lionesses I managed to see the tip of the leopard's nose from one point and his balls from another. It was *not* a good view of a leopard, even if he was only 20 feet above us. But the incident was of some interest.

In the afternoons of both days big storms developed. On the first it broke and the tropical rain fell on a young male lion which tried to shelter at the side of an anthill (termite hill) very unsuccessfully and looked very sorry for himself, and very funny.

But the unforgettable part of our Mara days, to be savoured and enjoyed at the time (and in retrospect for the rest of all our lives) was the

Lion.

thrilling profusion of gnus and zebras and Topi. Nature was being rarely prodigal. Here were numbers and diversity in a magnificent display under a dappled sky on the rolling plains of the Mara. It was a sight to take the breath away. It is not always that one recognises the golden moments of life when they are actually happening, but this time I believe we all did.

By the time we left on the morning of 5 September – Falcon and I by air, Phil and Dafila with the Tatham-Waters – we had seen in $2\frac{1}{4}$ days 25 species of mammals and 71 of birds.

Other special delights were a litter of Silver-backed Jackals quite close to the camp, and some young hyaenas looking up at us from a culvert under the road directly below and 6 feet away. As we flew out we took a turn over the Mara River to see a concentration of wildebeest estimated at over 100,000. We saw not less than half of them. Incredible.

CHAPTER 13

Zambia and Malawi

DIARY 22   1974 AND 1977

We returned to Zambia in 1974. We hoped to help Cindy Buxton's endeavours to persuade the Zambian government to allow her to make wildlife films for Anglia television. We left in early October.

MONDAY 4 OCTOBER
A desperate day of trying to finish things off – a picture of Red-breasted Geese; a design of a Blue Tit for a series of bird medallions I am designing for Pinches and another of an Osprey, papers on the future of IUCN Commissions, letters on the WWF approach to King Faisal, and on the Wildfowl Trust's financial needs – £95,000 this year and £100,000 next.

A rushed departure with one infuriating packing omission – the Zambia diary of five years ago, which got forgotten in the rush.

Aubrey Buxton [of Anglia Television and Cindy's father] met us in the Airport lounge.

TUESDAY 5 OCTOBER
We were met at Nairobi airport by Cindy Buxton and John and Sandy Hopcraft who were still trying to rescue their Lake Nakuru research and education project. At 10.45 we took off from Nairobi in a Cessna 310 6-seater to fly to Lusaka – 1,200 miles at 180 knots. We had a head wind for the last part and the flight lasted 6 hours 10 minutes.

We were met by Peter Miller, Chairman of the Wildlife Conservation Society of Zambia ('Willy Consocz' – my irreverent abbreviation) and its Executive Officer, Ian Tanner, John Clarke plus wife and son Ian.

In the VIP lounge we met first Mrs Kalulu with 3 children, and afterwards in the corridor as we were leaving Solomon Kalulu. He used to be Minister for Wildlife and Tourism but now has a more important post in the Inner Cabinet and is one of HE's (=Kenneth Kaunda) special friends and protégés.

Juvenile Gymnogene.

John Clarke, head of the Game Department, drove us in to the Intercontinental Hotel where we are staying. The immediate object is to set up two or more film projects. Cindy wants to do bee-eaters and Whale-headed Storks (latter in Bangweulu Swamps). John Clarke and Cindy call it 'Bang-wella'. I remember it from 5 years ago as 'Bang-way-ulu'. I am playing a game to get as many people as possible to pronounce it, and see which wins! ('Bang-way-loo' wins.)

MONDAY 7 OCTOBER
Shopping in Lusaka – food for our trip and a copy of the *Field Guide to the Birds of Zambia* (not in the 2 top bookshops, but finally found in the gift shop of our hotel).

11 am – a visit in blue suit to the Department of Lands, Natural

Resources and Tourism with John Clarke, Aubrey and Cindy (Buxton). The Minister (Dr Mulenga) is recovering from an operation. We saw the Permanent Secretary Basil Monze – a quiet man who doesn't miss a trick. He took us in to see the Minister of State, deputising for Dr Mulenga.

We referred to the Order of the Golden Ark which KK (Kenneth Kaunda) has agreed to accept from Prince Bernhard and to the letter Aubrey has brought from Prince Philip, and to WWF, and then Aubrey did his spiel on Anglia's filming plans which Cindy will start off in January. Aubrey's claim is that Anglia is so much more respectable and conservation minded than any other TV outfit that it should perhaps be exempted from the £2,000 fee which is normally charged.

Away in the chopper driven by Jack Uys on a 45 minute trip to Lochinvar. Big expanses of the flood were virtually empty of life, but there were concentrations of Open-bill Storks and I saw some Glossy Ibises, Reed Cormorants, Great White and Little Egrets, and white-winged plovers which turned out to be Long-toed Plovers as we later discovered. A Ground Hornbill flew up from close to the Lochinvar Lodge. Waiting for us were the Warden, Gerry Griffin, and the biologist Tim Osborne, from California, with his wife and baby daughter.

Further studies of the immature Gymnogene or Harrier Hawk, *Polyboroides radiatus typus*, which I drew to confirm identification on a different day. I did not have time to draw the beautiful grey adult we saw on 8 October.

TUESDAY 8 OCTOBER

A bird walk with Tim Osborne round the lodge at 7.00. From the slight elevation of the lodge site there is a good view across the savannah area of the flats – some wildebeest with calves were about three quarters of a mile away. A Gymnogene flew across – the 'eagle' that looks like a huge grey hawk with yellow cere and legs. There was a continuous flight of doves apparently coming from the hot springs at the foot of the hill which had been shown to us last time as the proposed new lodge site. That plan has been abandoned, thank goodness. There is an Iron Age site on top of the hill, and a Stone Age site at the hot springs at its foot. A new plan is being talked about for a lodge on stilts at the lower end of the park by the river. It would have sewage disposal problems. Another idea is houseboats. Pollution might be the principal stumbling block.

After breakfast we went off to the flats. At one point along that bird-lined shore we turned inland a little to investigate a point to which vultures were plummeting down. It turned out later to be a long dead Oribi. About 20 vultures were there – mostly White-backed with 3 Lappet-faced and one large pale bird – several inches taller than the Whitebacks. It had bluish skin below the eye. Tim Osborne became greatly excited about it because it was clearly a Cape Vulture, hitherto unrecorded in Zambia. He was familiar with the bird as he had ringed a large number. This however was not one of them as we checked its legs carefully.

We drew up alongside the green Fiat to tell of our discovery, and I was astonished to hear Tim ask John Clarke when he would get his licence through to take specimens. Evidently the Cape Vulture would be taken as soon as it came through. The timing of the request appeared to make the issue of the licence less imminent!

The light on the birds along the water's edge was better than on the previous evening. Eventually we reached and set out in the boat. Although we often got rather closer to birds than in the cars, the concentrations were less spectacular. We found far more Long-toed Plovers –

with their very white wings – further out in the flood plain.

Lesser Jaçanas – a nesting Goliath Heron with 2 well grown young which the girls walked back to photograph, a Purple Gallinule, but most particularly a pair of Spotted-necked Otters, which kept abreast of the boat, swimming under the crust of vegetation and surfacing in the open pools to crane their white necks – with small brown spots – the better to see us.

Having returned to the vehicles, various vicissitudes followed the bogging of John's car in a creek which had not dried out sufficiently.

We spent the next few days visiting Chibembe, Norman Carr's camp on the banks of the Luangwa, and Chikune in the Bangweulu Swamps where we saw the Shoebills which Cindy was later to film so successfully. On the following Tuesday (15 October) Aubrey and I had an audience with the President, Kenneth Kaunda, at State House in Lusaka, which I recorded thus in my diary:

KK was as good-looking and charming as ever, only a trifle greyer than 5 years ago – and looking taller than I had remembered. He talked well and reminisced on his school days when wildlife could be seen in places where it no longer is.

He was easy, talked well, missed nothing. A man of immense authority and stature. Utterly impressive, and yet engagingly human. Every bit as spell-binding as we had found him last time.

Before we flew home from Africa at the end of the week, we flew up to Lake Rudolf with the Buxtons (Cindy at the controls most of the way) to Koobifora, headquarters of the anthropologist Richard Leakey (son of Dr Louis Leakey) who flew over from his camp by the lake shore to the formal airstrip where we had landed a mile away and quickly ferried us over to the beach. He is a strikingly competent low altitude pilot. His fossiliferous areas are fascinating to walk over. Fossil bones are littered over acres of ground at a density of at least one every square yard – mostly fish bones, but after rains there are always major finds including ancestral hominids. Richard has strong views about conservation in Africa. He believes there should be greater emphasis on African 'grass roots'.

The purpose of our third visit to Zambia in 1977 was two-fold: I was to be the international representative to the Wildlife Conservation Society of Zambia's anti-poaching week, and later to sign agreements on behalf of WWF with both the Zambian and Malawi Governments for the Conservation Coin Collection (CCC). We flew to Lusaka, which was to be our base, at the end of July. We were to be based at the home of the Society's Chairman, Peter Miller – a beautiful farm just outside Lusaka where he lives with his family. My first engagement was to address an outdoor evening function in the Copper Belt and Philippa decided to stay at Lilayi – the Millers' farm – while I went off to Kitwe.

FRIDAY 22 JULY

To Kitwe with Ian Tanner. Met by a reception committee.

Taken off to watch birds at Chembe Dambo by Brian Coates – excellent ornithologist and Free Church minister (which I didn't guess till

I was told at the end of the day).

The Dambo covers some 300 acres but, although it belongs to 'Willy Consocz', it is much disturbed by Africans fishing and at weekends by whites in small boats. The waterbirds were therefore surprisingly scarce. However the extensive water-lily cover of large parts of the lake carried a number of rather widely scattered pygmy geese with a few tree ducks and Yellowbills. We thought we had seen Whitebacks, but on further consideration I think they were Fulvous Whistlers.

We found a few parties of passerines while walking through the Miombo woods (*Brachystegia*).

Bright coloured birds were: Orange-winged and Green-winged Pytilia and Black-headed Oriole (more). Golden-breasted Buntings and Yellow-eyed Canaries were fairly numerous. Pied Kingfishers were prospecting nest holes in the banks of the small boat 'harbour' at the clubhouse where we had an excellent chicken and salad lunch.

The evening started at 8.30 and we got to bed at 1.20. It was a Winter Extravaganza at the Show Ground – ie out of doors and mighty cold and windy. There was a sort of a cabaret. The tables were interspersed with charcoal braziers. The food came an hour late. A blond local wife called Wendy sang contralto with a band for most of the evening. The opening performance was a group of 3 pipers who played pipe marches and *Amazing Grace*. There was also a band called the Mantis with a coloured girl singer doing songs from the musical *Zulu* now playing in London.

Somewhere in the middle of this, and some energetic dancing to keep warm, I had to make a speech on wildlife conservation and the Anti-

Temminck's Courser

Lilayi
31.7.77.

Palm Swift.

poaching campaign. The showground public address system did not help the timing of my jokes! *The Ivory Poachers*, which we had brought with us, was shown after my speech.

Two days later we made a trip to Blue Lagoon. The indomitable Erica Critchley had died and Ronnie, her husband, had left Zambia, but the house had been kept going by special instruction of Kenneth Kaunda, though no one seemed to be sure what ultimate plans he had in mind for it.

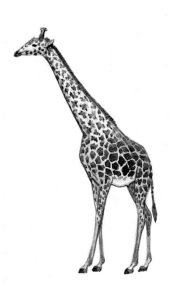

Thornycroft's Giraffe.

SUNDAY 24 JULY

We took about $1\frac{1}{2}$ hours to get to Kweeze – the village of Blue Lagoon. We arrived at precisely 10.00 – our expected time of arrival. The headman – Peter Chibango was there but few others. Peter Miller suggested we go to Blue Lagoon (the house) and come back at 11.00.

There was a small herd of 5 Roan just before we came to the homestead. They were fairly tame and we had a splendid view of their long droopy ears as they looked at us. They were all females. The trees round the house were teeming with birds. The figs were ripe and there were quantities of Green Pigeons, Greater and Lesser Blue-eared Starlings, Amethyst Starlings, White-rumped Babblers . . .

To the village of Kweeze, where the headman had assembled everyone. There were exchanges when we arrived between him and the 150 villagers – 'One Zambia' reply 'one nation' – 'one leader', 'Kaunda'. Then the national anthem sung mainly by the children of the village Chongololo Club. (Chongololo = millipede. These conservation clubs for young people have been set up all over the country and are playing a vital part in conservation education in Zambia.)

Then speeches punctuated by dances and songs. It was all rather informal and quite delightful. Peter Miller made quite a long speech to which I had to reply. This was all done through a villager who acted as interpreter. Then we had a break and went to see the site of a proposed clinic which the Beit Trust have financed, although there are currency exchange problems. Then back and more songs, speeches and dancing. At last it was over.

The last hours of daylight we spent on the causeway, which was covered with lechwe and large birds. We had exceptionally good views of Painted Snipe and a distant view of Denham's Bustards. Grey-headed Gulls and Long-toed Plover flew past with Sacred Ibis – and at one point a huge flock of Common (Red-winged) Pratincoles. A small flock of White-winged Black Terns passed – and lots more. At the end were 4 or 5 hippos. One mum with a very small baby was curious and swam up fairly close. We watched the sunset and on the way back saw a Marsh Mongoose (which at first we thought was an otter), a Marsh Owl and lots of Fiery-necked Nightjars.

We bathed and dressed rather smartly for dinner (me in my blue Marks and Sparks summer suit). It was a convivial evening with an excellent dinner. We had a toast to the memory of Erica, and talked about the future of mankind, space travel and the search for extra-terrestrial intelligence. It had been an extremely enjoyable day.

We left Blue Lagoon late the next morning and returned to Lusaka for a late lunch.

TUESDAY 26 JULY

11 am – to Zambian National Tourist Board with Peter Miller.

12.30 – State House for lunch with HE Kenneth Kaunda. About 30 people at lunch. Press and TV. When Kenneth Kaunda came in I was facing directly away which was *almost* embarrassing. He was most cordial in greeting both Phil and me. There was a jocular atmosphere. At the long table I was on the President's right with Phil at the other end on the right of the new Minister of Water and Natural Resources, Kebby Musokatwane.

There was some jest about having a Catholic grace, which was said by one of the ministers present. Our old friend Solomon Kalulu was there, and his wife. Opposite me was Aaron Milner, Minister of Home Affairs whom I had sat next to at dinner a few days before. I set out to make conversation and it went reasonably well. Then the radio was brought in so that KK could listen to the news, which was largely about him. This occupied about 20 minutes or more. When it came to the closing headlines he switched it off.

We had quite an interesting discussion about world affairs, the UN, world government (which KK believed would come). I asked if for a few minutes after lunch I could see him to discuss business – he agreed.

Then he made quite a long speech about me – very flattering – I was a citizen of the world 'we love you for what you are doing . . .' and many other nice things.

I had not realised this would happen and I would have to reply. At first I was rather overwhelmed – and said so. But thereafter I managed better – virtually without funnies(!) But it seemed to go down reasonably well. After that coffee which KK himself poured for all the guests.

Then I was led away to his room for the *tête-à-tête*. I deemed it politic to complete my business in under 10 minutes – and this I managed to do.

What was to be the future of Blue Lagoon? Could he go there himself from time to time? That would be the best of all solutions. 'But I suppose you wouldn't have time.' 'Well there are times when I have to

Black Lechwe, *Kobus leche smithemani.*

225

read a lot of papers, and I will go there to do that – rest assured I will go there.'

It would be good if the park could stay open at least to day visitors, I suggested, though I recognised this posed some problems of a confidential nature. No answers came on that point. (It was a critical time in the birth of Zimbabwe.)

I told him that we had heard that some soldiers had been trying to shoot on Blue Lagoon – as we had heard the day before from the game guard we had met on the road. He said he would personally look into it.

He seemed annoyed that nothing had been done about Zambia joining the Conservation Coin Collection and said he would try to expedite it. He was keen for Zambia to take part in it. He would try to arrange for the contract to be signed after my return from Malawi. We then returned to the main party (after KK had crossed the room to switch off the air conditioning – 'you see we're trying to save energy here').

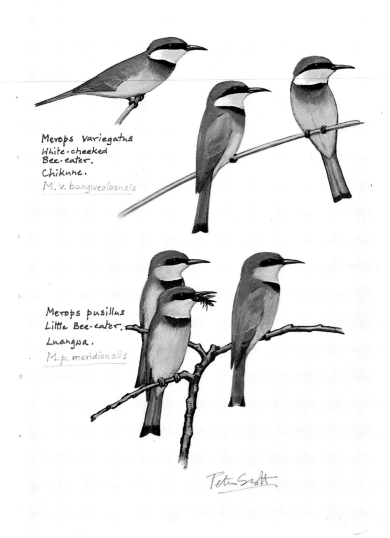

Merops variegatus
White-cheeked
Bee-eater.
Chikune.
M. v. bangweoloensis

Merops pusillus
Little Bee-eater.
Luangwa.
M. p. meridionalis

Peter Scott

And so we took our leave – and Solomon Kalulu showed us one of KK's paintings of a girl running away from a hyaena, in the passageway to the main reception room.

It will be interesting to see if I get to sign the CCC Agreement before leaving. (I didn't.)

Since the success of her Shoebill film, Cindy Buxton had been filming extensively in Zambia, and was now down in The Valley – Luangwa We flew down to join her at Chibembe New Camp and also spent one night with Prince Bernhard at his camp at Mwamba. Cindy took us to Luambe Park to the north of Chibembe and to Nsefu Reserve to the south. We had a special excitement.

SATURDAY 30 JULY

Chibembe New Camp.

Two elephants under the full moon outside our chalet (wooden grasshut) pulling branches from the trees. When the first one woke us it was pushing branches against the roof and wall. 'Did you hear that?' said Phil. 'Yes I thought it was you.' We looked out of the window and the elephant was within 3 feet of the head of Phil's bed, reaching over the roof.

Later he walked out in front of our hut and pulled branches off the small trees. Another elephant came along the river bank and crossed 10 yards from our door while the first one continued to feed about 20 yards away. The second animal passed between our hut and the next, came to a grass screen and pulled it down towards him – then walked over into the swimming pool area. There was no water in the pool so he walked over to one side and broke the screen down reaching up for more branches. Then finally he walked across the area and broke yet another screen down to get out. It was 4.30 am and they'd been round our hut for an hour.

That evening we returned to Lusaka whence Phil flew home to England and I went off the following evening to Malawi to sign the CCC agreement.

MONDAY 1 AUGUST

00.15 – Arrived at Blantyre – Chileka Airport, Malawi.

Met by L P Anthony, F L Mambiya, J Chipaka and David G Anstey [creator of the Malawi National Parks]. Conducted to VIP lounge, thence to car and 10 mile drive to the Mount Soche Hotel in Blantyre. In the car with me was James Chipaka, General Manager of the Reserve Bank of Malawi who has been handling the Conservation Coin Collection arrangements.

I am to sign the agreement on Tuesday at Club Makokola at Mangochi at the south end of Lake Malawi. Hope there may be a chance to go fishwatching in the lake but the programme is very tight. I have brought a mask and fins from Lusaka.

A delightful time in Lengwe National Park with David Anstey, 'G D' Hayes and Elias J Kambalame (Assistant Manager of Administration of the Reserve Bank of Malawi). The park is 50 miles from Blantyre over a mountainous and very rough road.

The main feature of the park is a good population of Nyala – *Tragelaphus angasi*. At one time they were said to be down to 15 individuals

Southern Carmine Bee-eater,
Merops nubicus nubicoides,
Luangwa.

Chestnut

Böhms
Bee-eater
Merops boehmi

but with park protection there are now at least 2,000. There are hides on stilts, overlooking water holes which are well designed and built, holding about a dozen people sitting down.

When we entered one hide there was nothing in view save a sleeping Hammerkop. Out of the side window 'G D' Hayes drew my attention to some birds. He is 75 and deafish, so our whispered conversation was difficult. He reported Böhm's Bee-eater – all I could see was a sunbird with a yellow breast. Eventually I found one of half-a-dozen Böhm's Bee-eaters – very elegant birds indeed.

Then a herd of about 15 Nyalas came to drink. I could see the old male's nose wrinkling as he drank. It began to rain quite heavily as we had our lunch from generous cardboard boxes. I drew the bee-eater and the Nyala bull in this book.

TUESDAY 2 AUGUST

08.20–11.05. From Hotel Mount Soche (pronounced So-chay) in Blantyre to Club Makokola 14 miles north of Mangochi on the shore of Lake Malawi, in a large and comfortable chauffeur driven Renault.

We stopped briefly at the Government Rest House at Zomba – until recently capital of Malawi and still the seat of the parliament. Then down from the highlands across the Shire River and past a part of the shore of Lake Malombe to Mangochi, once Fort Johnston. And so to Club Makokola – a typical beach resort hotel with round chalet rooms, thatched and quite attractive.

The object of the exercise: to sign the CCC agreement with the Governor of the Reserve Bank of Malawi (equivalent to the Bank of England), J Z U Tembo, who was attending a Board Meeting for 3 days at Club Makokola.

228

The signing on behalf of WWF and IUCN was duly performed – with Press photographers and was followed by a lunch at which I sat between the Governor and the MP for the region. After lunch the Governor made a short but graceful speech which must have been inaudible at the far end of the long table because of the electric fans. The hotel's normal guests were sitting at small tables along the lake side of the room. My speech followed with some talk about land use policies and a few funnies – 'the pig', the 'elephants found', 'the fossil footprints', 'the moron' – less than 10 minutes.

We received a message just before lunch that there would be no signing of the CCC agreement with Zambia in Lusaka on Wednesday or Thursday as I had hoped, so there was time to alter the Malawi programme to get in some fish-watching in the lake.

After lunch I changed into shorts, and in a few minutes David Anstey and I were off in his Land Rover about 25 miles up the road to Monkey Bay and the Fisheries Research Station, with the mask, snorkel and flippers lent to me by the Zambian Sub Aqua Club.

Lilac-breasted Rollers were very numerous on the drive north. It was already 3.30 by the time we reached the Fisheries Station and were met by Dr David Eccles, and at once went aboard a small motor fishing boat. Dr Digby Lewis joined us in a sleeveless wet suit top. We chugged out to a small bay among the rounded rocks of an island just offshore. Fish Eagles were all around, 5 or 6 in sight in the tree tops.

The boat was tied up to a rock and the 4 of us went over the side – Eccles, Lewis, Anstey and me. Visibility was about 20–25 feet. The scene was quite beautiful. The bay was teeming with fish, many of them very brightly coloured – pale blue, deep blue, yellow, green and brown. The spots and stripes were striking and there was apparently some mimicry. Males were different in colour and in some cases in fin lengths. Nearly all the fish were *Cichlidae*. The adaptive radiation was amazing. What are the isolative factors which produced from the original cichlid stock such an amazing diversity? Apparently this is a result of extreme territoriality, total commitment to habitat, and perhaps also to mouth brooding of the young. In the rock dwelling species a patch of sand is an uncrossable ocean and the same applies to a weed dwelling species. A further factor is that there are many underwater craters isolated from each other by deep water. For shallow benthic species these provide 'island' habitats as promising for speciation as the Galápagos Islands. So Lake Malawi is full of ecological islands.

The water temperature was 23°C. After 40 minutes we were getting cold and came out. We had been watching perhaps 25–30 species of fish and the scene was comparable with a good coral reef without the colourful corals and other invertebrates. The fish were quite tame so that one could see them well. It was amazing how many of them were comparable in shape and habit to marine reef fishes.

And so to the Eccles home to meet his Australian wife and their 3 year old son William who had been down on the jetty. David Eccles is Rhodesian – tall with a small moustache and a high degree of enthusiasm.

Digby Lewis and his wife and almost born baby arrived for drinks. He showed me his pen and ink drawings of fish which were outstanding. I liked him *very* much. He and David Eccles and I had a fascinating Darwinian and Hennigian discussion. Hennig says that generic nomen-

Doves

Red-eyed,
Streptopelia semitorquata.
'Coo coo cook –
Koo-kuk coo', the
fourth syllable slightly
stressed, the last 2
lower in pitch.

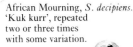

African Mourning, *S. decipiens.*
'Kuk kurr', repeated
two or three times
with some variation.

Cape Turtle or Ring-necked,
S. capicola.
'How's father,
how's father.'

Laughing, *S. senegalensis.*
A quiet gentle
descending
'Cooroocoo coo
coo coo'.

clature should be based on the estimated point of divergence from the evolutionary tree rather than the amount of morphological change – which is all very fine and large but depends on the correct assessment of the lines of the past family tree (no easy task). Anyway the 'flocks' of species in Lake Malawi are one of the great evolutionary wonders of the world.

WEDNESDAY 3 AUGUST
I left Club Makokola at 8.40 with David Anstey and Maguire (David's 'bearer'). We went first to Norman Carr's newly built house close to the beach at Madzidzi Bay. Norman [who invented Walking Safaris] was in Zambia but the caretaker let us in. It is a most attractive house on a very beautiful site.

By watching the doves that were singing in the trees above I discovered that the African Turtle Dove has a far greater repertoire than I had thought. The 'Poor Father' call [of the African Turtle Dove] is made by the same bird as the 'Who-C-r-r-r-eouw' and the 'Who ah who'. (What do Laughing and Red-eyed Doves say?) Then on to Lilongwe, by a side road through a very pretty forest reserve, which took us up the escarpment to the high plateau – 3,700 feet.

David Anstey is an interesting man. On the journey we discussed the ethics of hunting, of culling, of strict protection and eventually of doubtful means being justified for good ends. I was surprised that he was prepared to accept that culling should be done by inexperienced hunters provided they were paid enough. He is much preoccupied with the total land use scene. We talked about the necessity to plant eucalypts for firewood all over the country. He's a very direct man and not always very tactful. But I get the impression that he's an achiever. He seems to get things done.

On arrival at Lilongwe, I was installed at the Capital Hotel – brand new and everything working (unlike the Mount Soche Hotel in Blantyre where the 'royal suite' telephone was not). I had lunch off the fruit sent by the Permanent Secretary to the Ministry of Agriculture and Natural Reserves – whose guest I was in Lilongwe. The Ministry's acronym is normally rendered as MANURE.

After lunch we went to the new Nature Sanctuary which is really remarkable. In the middle of this new Capital City with its reasonably good architecture, beautiful landscaping and gardening, they have set aside 300 acres of wild land – half of which has already been fenced (only 4 ft high so far). A fine education centre has been built and is already in use.

I was whipped in at once to talk to a party of ex-patriate children who were watching a feature film, which was interrupted in mid-stream for me to talk. Some were very young. It was quite difficult. I encouraged them to become naturalists, and not much more.

Then we went round the first half of the nature trail. The 300 acres incorporate both banks of a river and the forest on either side. The nature trails are on one side only and there are some roofless hides with the shutters hinged at the top. From the first one I had an excellent view of a Henglin's Robin on a sand bar in the river.

The planning of this excellent facility – which must be unique for a capital city – has been done by an American Peace Corps worker,

Warren Starns and his wife Barbara. It is really a fantastic achievement. The area holds a number of crocodiles, a leopard, several hyaenas, lots of bush pig, a few Bushbuck and lots of duikers. 172 species of birds have been recorded so far and there are 130 species of trees (with a numbering system for their home-made field guide). They are planning an animal orphanage as an educational tool. I suggested planting flowering and fruiting trees near the headquarters and near hides to attract birds.

They have a nice aquarium tank full of local cichlids. I suggested some vivaria for chamaeleons and lizards. They have two largish pythons, but have released their puff adder and cobra.

And so, just in time for our appointment with Michael Scott, the British High Commissioner, in his office. He has only been in Malawi for a few weeks. He stressed the point of getting a form of words from the Overseas Development Agency to cover projects in Malawi (and elsewhere).

Michael Scott was previously in Nepal and had been to Tiger Tops. He is a tall man with a well trimmed beard and an agreeable sense of humour. He told a nice story about a diplomat in a car who had run into a cow and killed it – in Nepal. It seems that the order of capital offences in Hindu law is that it is always applicable to those who kill a Brahmin priest or a cow. Thereafter the punishment may be progressively reduced for killing a man, killing a male child and killing a woman (the lowest for which the death penalty may be called). The diplomat's situation was serious. An incident was imminent. There was only one solution. The court decided that the cow had committed suicide.

After the High Commissioner, we went to see the Permanent Secretary to MANURE – Mr Mtwale – as a courtesy visit. There had been a plan for me to show two films – the *Ivory Poachers* and *Refuge* – which were in my suitcase. However there is film censorship in Malawi and although it would be legitimate to show the films in private 'behind locked doors' part of the object would have been to get some black Malawians to see them. The PS thought it wouldn't be wise and so the plan was cancelled. Instead a group came for drinks to the Capital Hotel and I 'held court' in my Marks and Sparks blue summer suit.

After the party broke up I went to dinner alone in the hotel and wrote this diary. Some of the fisheries' boys were still around when I came out of the dining room so I stayed to talk a little. When I finally went off to my room at 10.30 it was to paint a Nyala for David Anstey till after midnight – with a call, for 5.30 to fly to Blantyre, to Lusaka, to London. Anyway I finished it – even if its head *was* on the large side.

Namaqua, *Oena capensis*. Rather silent, 'Twooh hooo', the first syllable explosive.

Tambourine, *Turtur tympanistria*. A mournful series of 'Du du du's', ending in a rattle, does not descend the scale.

Emerald-spotted Wood, *T. chalcospilos*. One of the most characteristic sounds of the bush, 'Du du . . . du ; du . . . du du du dudu dudu', the final run descending quickly.

Bathydraconidae
Gymnodraco acuticeps(?)

$\frac{1}{3}$

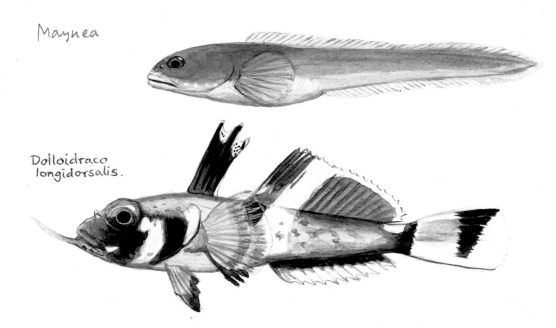

Notothenidae
Trematomus
bernacchii

? White may be caused by damage, but Carleton thinks not.

$\frac{2}{5}$

Maynea

Dolloidraco
longidorsalis.

All drawn from live specimens in the aquaria in the
USARP Biology Lab at McMurdo Base.

CHAPTER 14

Antarctica: Ross Island
and the South Pole

DIARY 9   1966

From an early age I had been determined to make my way in life without trading on my father's reputation as a famous explorer*. As I saw it, his achievements in the Antarctic precluded me from going there, and indeed from becoming knowledgeable about the continent and its history.

At the age of 57, however, having made a reasonably successful career as a painter, writer and broadcaster, and having travelled quite widely around the globe, it became evident that regarding Antarctica as a 'no-go' area was a rather pointless vanity. So when an invitation to go there to make a film for the BBC arrived from the Admiral commanding Operation Deep Freeze, based on Ross Island in McMurdo Sound, from where my father had based his two expeditions (in 1902 and 1911), I gladly accepted.

Included in the invitation were a BBC producer, Christopher Ralling, and a cameraman, Charles Lagus, with whom my wife and I had travelled ten years earlier in Australia, New Guinea, New Zealand and Fiji. But at that time the Antarctic was a stronghold of male chauvinism, and my wife was not invited. The diary I wrote (No 9 in the series of 48 such books) was mainly for her and the children to read.

My Qantas Boeing 707 took off just after noon on New Year's Day, 1966. I was bound first for Fiji for some snorkelling and then New Zealand where the expedition was to begin. I spent a week in New Zealand gliding, filming and preparing for the ardours of the Antarctic. I don't think that I quite realised then that the journey was going to be not only physically demanding but also emotionally stirring. Of course I was aware of the 'sentimental' aspect of the journey which the press were keen to emphasise but the impact it was to have on me came later as a surprise.

THURSDAY 13 JANUARY
The adventure is on. We assembled in the overseas lounge of the airport, had breakfast, wheeled our hand baggage (chiefly cameras) out to the waiting Hercules transport plane and climbed in. Inside it is like a great storage hangar. We sit in seats along the side with cargo in the centre. The seats are canvas with net backs and quite comfortable.

It's 2,280 miles to Williams Field and it will take us 8 hrs 20 mins. In my father's time the voyage took a month.

*Captain Robert Falcon Scott RN commanded the National Antarctic Expedition of 1901–1904 in the *Discovery*. He sailed again for the Antarctic in the *Terra Nova* in 1910. He and his four companions hauled a sledge 800 miles to reach the South Pole on 17 January 1912, 34 days after the Norwegian party led by Roald Amundsen. All of Scott's party died on their way back from the Pole, 100 miles short of their base camp, the hut at Hut Point, Cape Evans.

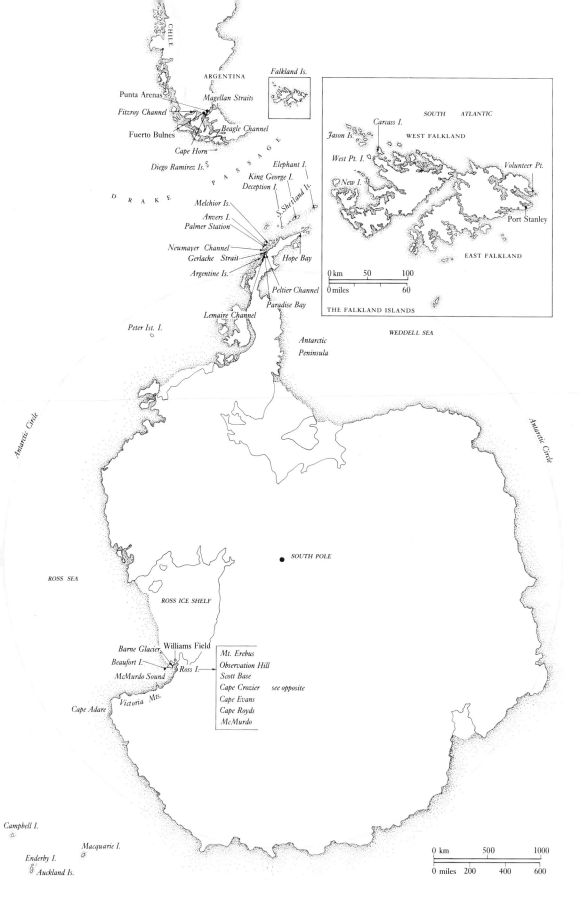

CHILE

ARGENTINA

Falkland Is.

Punta Arenas
Magellan Straits
Fitzroy Channel
Fuerto Bulnes
Beagle Channel

Cape Horn →

Diego Ramirez Is.

D R A K E

P A S S A G E

Elephant I.
King George I.
Deception I.
S.Shetland Is.

Melchior Is.
Anvers I.
Palmer Station
Neumayer Channel
Gerlache Strait
Argentine Is.

Hope Bay

Peltier Channel
Paradise Bay

Lemaire Channel

Peter Ist. I.

Antarctic
Peninsula

WEDDELL SEA

SOUTH POLE

ROSS SEA

ROSS ICE SHELF

Barne Glacier Williams Field
Beaufort I.
McMurdo Sound *Ross I.*

Cape Adare

Victoria Mts.

Mt. Erebus
Observation Hill
Scott Base
Cape Crozier   see opposite
Cape Evans
Cape Royds
McMurdo

Antarctic Circle

Antarctic Circle

Campbell I.

Macquarie I.

Enderby I.
Auckland Is.

Falkland Islands inset:

SOUTH   ATLANTIC

Carcass I.
Jason Is.
WEST FALKLAND

West Pt. I.

Volunteer Pt.

New I.

Port Stanley

EAST FALKLAND

0 km   50   100
0 miles   60

THE FALKLAND ISLANDS

Main scale:

0 km   500   1000
0 miles   200   400   600

I made these notes about Antarctica in my diary from a series of articles by Mike Daley in an Australian newspaper:

'Chi-chi' for Christchurch
Mt Erebus 13,000 ft.
Icecap 16,000 ft of ice, in places.
McMurdo 'City' holds 1,000 people.
International Geophysical Year was 1957–58.
Annual precipitation – 4″.
90% of the world's fresh water is down there.
Cross* on Observation Hill is of jarrah wood.
Amundsen–Scott station – 30 men in summer, 18 in
    winter. Club 90 and Post Office. Ham Radio.
White-blooded fish without red corpuscles and
    therefore without haemoglobin, (*Notothenidae*).
Adelie Penguins in homing experiments have an
    'escape direction' – north northeast. There's a cut off
    point after which homing takes over.
Antarctic cooperation could be the pattern for
    space exploration.
Ultimate colonisation (?21st Century).
Support from farming the ocean.
Living under transparent domes, nuclear power.

3.15. Crossed the Antarctic Coast. Mountains looking superb in clear sunshine. At 5.0 pm precisely we landed at McMurdo – on the ice shelf at Williams Field.

*This cross, 9 ft in height, was erected in January 1913. It bears the inscription

In Memoriam
Capt R F Scott RN
Dr E A Wilson,
Capt L E G Oates Ins Drags,
Lt H R Bowers RIM
Petty Officer E Evans, RN

Who died on their
return home from
the Pole. March
1912.
To strive, to seek,
To find,
And not to
yield.

From the overheated interior of the LC 130F Hercules, *City of Christchurch*, we emerged into a strong wind blowing snow like mist, though it wasn't very cold. We hustled across to a couple of waiting helicopters with their rotors spinning. In a few seconds we were airborn again and flying down from the ice, over two large Weddell Seal colonies and round the corner to the Helopad.

I was abandoned on arrival (Chris and Charles came in a later helicopter) but a Lieutenant Fermo guided me on a 400 yard walk through the 'city' past the church to the Ross-Hilton (the VIP bunkhouse). It was later decided I should share the Press Hut with Chris and Charles. This is a 'Jamesway' hut (corrugated iron half cylinder-type). We went over to the mess hut, just opposite, for a typical American service meal – very good, but not for my figure. A cafeteria with compartmented trays and an ice cream machine on a press button which was almost enough to put one off one's meal. After dinner and a tour of the city Carlton Ray (an old friend with whom I had done some snorkelling and SCUBA diving in the Exuma Cays, Bahamas) turned up in Ken Moulton's office – the Swiss Chalet, and took us first to the Ward Room and then to the biology lab where we heard his hydrophone recordings of whales and seals, and saw some live fish.

FRIDAY 14 JANUARY

Over by Nodwell – tracked vehicle – to Scott Base, the New Zealand headquarters. Leader of the New Zealand party is Mike Prebble, we also met red-bearded John Murphy in charge of public information. The scientific leader is Dr Andrew Porter – we'll meet him when we go there next Monday.

The buildings are connected by a covered tunnel – and the whole thing is *much* more attractive and agreeable than the sprawling 'frontier' town of McMurdo – although of course enormously smaller. From McMurdo to Scott Base is about 2 miles over the neck of land connecting Observation Hill to Ross Island. There's a main road leading out onto the ice and thence across to Williams Field which is a patch of ice cleared of snow surrounded by aircraft and small huts – a cluster of dots far out on the Ross Ice Shelf.

While we were there – an hour perhaps – the wind freshened and it turned a lot colder. Early this morning it was balmy warm. The sun was quite hot. Breath showed, but it was like a nice fresh wintery morning in England. When we emerged from Scott Base it was blowing a cold wind from the south east and low clouds were hiding the lower slopes of magnificent Mt Erebus (nearly 13,000 ft) – which we saw for the first time from Scott Base, as you can't see it from McMurdo.

Back at our Press hut, after a very rough journey in the Nodwell, Charles had found a new young American camera-man and sound technician named Charlie Brown who is to be attached to us from now on.

This afternoon we are to go out and film an interview with Carlton Ray, preferably with seals in the background. Questions to ask Carlton Ray in the interview – your third year down here?

1. Seals and their incredible underwater sounds – do you know which noise belongs to which species and what they mean?

2. Underwater swimming: Can you describe SCUBA diving under the ice?

3. General: Is intensive zoological study good sense at the end of such an extended supply line? What is the biggest thing, in your view, to be found out down here?
4. What is the future of the Antarctic?
5. Do you feel as if you were on the frontier? A part of the heroic age?

Precisely at 2.0 Carlton Ray arrived in his Nodwell – a more comfortable type than this morning's, and we went over the saddle road towards the airfield. We carried the equipment about 300 yards over the snow which lay on the sea ice, and eventually reached a group of 8 Weddell Seals scattered about.

Having set up the cameras, Carlton and I walked into a silent shot and talked to two of the seals, which made virtually no attempt to bite, and were moderately upset, but unable to do much about it except roll over on their backs, open their mouths and hiss. The party nearest us consisted of two males and a pup. The pup had a conspicuous wound on its back.

Having filmed the last of our three as it slithered into the water of a small pool near the hillside – and full of brash ice like a daiquiri – we set up a sound shot and Carlton talked well about the hydrophone recordings he had made, and about the 'skin diving' (actually wet-suit diving) which he did last year, but hasn't done this year. Having completed the piece we found that the tape recorder wasn't working properly and the sound was *not* on the tape – or rather it was impossibly distorted. The fault was not immediately to be found and as we were all very cold by this time, operations were abandoned. Nomiyama, the Japanese Embassy 1st Secretary at Wellington, has been with us all day – a cheerful little man. The tape recorder has nominally been repaired, but the cause is undisclosed and may have simply been the cold. Chris and Charles have been out filming around the base.

Mount Terror,
Ross Island and
the Ross Ice Shelf.

I have been 24 hours in the Antarctic. I suppose it has not been *very* different from what I had expected. The nearest I have previously seen to McMurdo City is Yellowknife on the Great Slave Lake (in Canada). Interesting, but not really very attractive. In the distance the scenery is superb – the mountains unbelievably beautiful, Terror and Erebus, White Island and Black, and the broken jumbled ice at the edge of the barrier. But the bases, and especially McMurdo, have made no concessions whatever to the aesthetic. There has been no attempt – or virtually none – to make any of it look nice. The USARP (United States Antarctic Research Program) Office is called the chalet because the end of it was dressed up to look like a Swiss chalet. The Chapel outside looks reasonably agreeable as a building, and inside is quite well designed and pleasant. No doubt it is expensive here to do more than the bare minimum, but even then one would expect some architectural standards to be set up.

The enthusiasm of the workers – like Carlton Ray – is one of the most heartening things about the place, and I find Ken Moulton – the Senior USARP representative a very friendly sympathetic character.

Yet somehow it is exciting to be here. There are indefinable things which make it very special, and the little square wooden hut on Hut Point, down beyond the icebreakers, built by my father in 1902 may have something to do with it.

SUNDAY 15 JANUARY

We should have taken off from McMurdo at 8.0 bound for Cape Crozier and Bill Sladen's 150,000 pairs of Adelie Penguins colony at the other end of Ross Island – a 45 minutes helo-flight – but after standing about on the helopad for 20 minutes, Carlton Ray, who was to have gone with us, went to find the pilot who said it had been cancelled because of weather (though no one had thought of telling us). So it looks like another day in the big city, although the weather doesn't look so bad.

But by 11.30 we took off in the helo with the 2 New Zealanders who are to mark the 5,000 young Adelies of this year's program – George Lowry and Doug Crawford. A 35 minute flight, a smoke canister to determine wind and a landing on a small shelf high on the hill overlooking the penguin rookery. The camp consisted of a single Jamesway hut – semicircular, snug and wholly appropriate. The camp was tidy and altogether attractive. The helicopter had gone again, the skuas had returned to their nests (McCormick's Skuas). It was rather reminiscent of the Perry River camp at Radio Hill [in the Canadian Arctic]. Below was the teeming rookery full of big chocolate coloured chicks, and the delightful chatter of the quarrelling, calling, displaying adults.

We went in for coffee, then out for filming among the penguins. Then down the long hill to the beach through the oblivious hordes. The most unexpected things to me were the vast number of long dead dried and frozen chicks which littered the ground – about one per square yard in some areas – and the pink stains on the white breasts of many penguins derived from the krill they eat – the stains being excretory or regurgitatory 'accidents'. At the shore – with its black sand I took pix with my Instamatic. Bill talked all the time about his penguins which was wholly fascinating. It is a wonderful study he has made and is making. Current work is concentrated on 'teenagers' (they don't breed till 4 years old). All marking now is confined to young birds so as to

The Adelie is somehow the most appealing of the world's 17 species of penguins.

Opposite: studies of Adelie Penguins, one is carrying a flipper-band. The red stains are spilt krill juice. The bird with the extended flippers is performing the 'ecstatic display'.

have known-age birds. The oldest of these are now 4 year-olds and some are breeding. The only exception to the young-birds-only banding rule is for adults in which small radio transmitters have been planted (by operation) in the abdominal cavity. These measure temperature, and I listened to the radio pulse emitted by one, while sitting in the little green tent down by the shore, with John Pedersen.

Also down there was a red-bearded American, Robert Wood, who is studying skuas. We looked out for one of the four Leopard Seals patrolling that shore, but we didn't see any of them. We climbed back up to the Wilson Hut as the main camp is called. Bob Wood took me to see his skuas which had nests with eggs and new-hatched young within a few yards of the camp. His study area contained 120 pairs. 95% of his marked pairs had remained faithful over the 4 years of his work there.

Bob had just caught a skua with a hand net in mid air as it dive-bombed him when the helo could be heard approaching. There was a new plan for Bob Wood and George Lowry to go back with us, which involved stopping the helo motor – which is tricky to restart. However, it restarted and soon after we said our farewells and were on our way back. Bill Sladen will be flying back to Chi-chi on the 25th with me.

For the first time since our arrival in Antarctica, we got the real feel of exploration and frontier. This was what the whole operation was for – whether the study is penguins or ionosphere, lead fall-out or seals, glaciology or geology, cosmic rays or fish with antifreeze blood.

So safely and cheerfully we returned to our Press Hut at McMurdo, which has two stoves, a small armchair space round one and a larger working room with tables along each side of the other. In between are the two berthed cabins separated by half height partitions with a space underneath, presumably for heat distribution, which also successfully distributes noise.

We continued our filming during the next few days, even pitching a camp solely for this purpose. This wasn't my kind of work and by the middle of the week it was getting me down.

WEDNESDAY 19 JANUARY

This job is difficult because so much of it is phoney. We go out with dogs and motor toboggans and make camp 4 miles from base, all for show – all so as to be filmed doing it as if we had been doing it for months on some long and rugged journey. It is bogus and rather hard not to feel a charlatan. A dude way of doing it. And yet we *are* doing a job, getting a film record, telling other people what it's all like. That's our job and I suppose we must do it, and mustn't feel *too* shy about it.

These gloomy thoughts came to me only the day after I had tele-phoned Phil at Slimbridge, from Scott Base – the New Zealand head-quarters. The call came through at 1.40 am in England and she reported that, for the first time, there were over 100 Bewick's Swans on Swan Lake in front of our house at Slimbridge. She told me after-wards that when the operator woke her the following conversation took place:
'Will you accept a transfer charge call from Scott Base, Antarctica?'
'How much will it cost?'
'Oh, come off it, Mrs Scott . . . it's your husband calling.'

239

Her Scottish ancestry momentarily took charge.

There's a saying at Scott Base 'Choose your friends well – you may have to eat them'.

THURSDAY 20 JANUARY

A morning of catching up on notes and checking equipment for the Pole . . . In two journeys we were helicoptered out to Williams Field where the Hercules was waiting with engines running and turbo-props spinning. I was ushered onto the flight deck, and, soon after take-off, into the co-pilot's chair. The pilot, Dave Hilton, was charming and welcoming: 'The instrument panel is less complicated than *Sovereign*'s' (a reference to the 12 metre yacht which I had helmed unsuccessfully in the 1964 challenge for the America's Cup) . . . We flew for nearly 5 hours to Plateau Station at 11,500 ft, then on for 2 hours with cabin pressure at 9,000 ft to Pole Station.

We shall arive at 10 pm. The radio operator is calling 'South Pole Radio, South Pole Radio, South Pole Radio' at this moment. We are to circle a couple of times for Charles to take movies. What a way to arrive – sweaty hot in an overheated 'Herc' – a giant aircraft that can carry more stores in a single load than all the Dakotas could do in a season a few years back. Yet somehow the change is stimulating.

I am quite certain that my father would be delighted with these developments, delighted with the thought that there is a reason for so many people to be here, delighted that his own effort 'without the reward of priority', and with its tragic ending, should be remembered and acclaimed by the frontiersmen of today.

But with all these modern developments there are new dangers, new technical problems, new things to go wrong. Research in Antarctica is still mainstream science on the frontiers of knowledge, some of it pure science, some applied. Techniques for use on the moon, for studying the upper atmosphere, for studying fall-out and pollution – especially of lead, as well as glaciology, geology, zoology, climatology and oceanography. And all of it is international – a blueprint for other cooperative research, in the deep oceans, maybe, or on the moon. What I see of man's Antarctic activity so far looks quite good to me.

Soon after landing at 10 pm we were met by Lt Griffin, doctor and commander of the base. Pole Station is reached by a tunnel into the compressed snow, leading to 'rooms' cut out with huts set up inside. We went to the mess for a late meal and in due course back to the sick bay where the six of us sleep in a minute overheated room. And some slept less well than others.

FRIDAY 21 JANUARY

We overslept because no one called us. Then rigged ourselves up in outdoor layers and went forth into $-33°$ Fahrenheit. In due course we were all assembled in the Nodwell – a smaller version than the New Zealand one – and after pointing out the above-snow features Lt Griffin said 'And now if you are all ready we'll go out to the Pole and I can show you that area'. So in the little Nodwell we trundled out to the Pole, and began to take photographs. We were at or around the Pole for the next 2 hours. We took stills and we shot film, I shook hands with Griffin, I looked up at the American flag which now flies from the Pole, I walked towards the Pole, I stood in front of it, alone and in

various groups – a photographic bonanza.

I remembered that 54 years ago my father was also involved in taking photographs at the Pole. It made the whole distasteful business a fraction more bearable. 54 years and 3 days. We could quite easily have come here on the 17th January – the day my father got to the Pole. In a way I am glad that we didn't. It demonstrates that our objectives here are not a sentimental journey.

The sun shone brightly and was warm on our faces, although minus 33°F is 65° of frost. We were dressed in our heavy clothes which consisted of a string vest and brief pants, wool vest and long wool pants (long johns), thick woollen shirts, thick woollen trousers, jersey, windproof trousers with a thick liner buttoned-in, windproof parka with a thick liner buttoned-in (the liners have towelling), muffler, nylon-fur hat, fur trimmed hood, 'thermal boots' with an air space between two layers of white rubber, and wool gloves, inside plastic gloves, inside big bulky mitts on ribbon round the neck. And dark glasses against snow blindness.

In all these clothes it was quite hard to move – indeed in the rarefied atmosphere (the Pole is 9,200 feet above sea level), putting them on had been a major effort leading to much breathlessness. However walking around at the South Pole I was perfectly warm. Charles was working, often in bare hands. The official Pole which has not really been confirmed as the precise position, is 400 yards out from the station. There's a large box beside it, buried deep in the snow. No one knows what the box is. Griffin thought it was a latrine. It may once have contained instruments. It is anchored 6 feet down in the snow.

Standing at the Pole one is far enough away from the station to feel the emptiness of the snowfield all round.

Away to the horizon in every direction the snow is flat and unbroken but for the masts and the few buildings around the station – 'Great God, this is an awful place' my father had said. And awful it must have been with a prospect of 800 miles to walk back – and Amundsen's tent already there. For us with 400 yards to walk back to a snug overheated camp under the snow it was not awful. Yet it had a certain wonder born of the realisation of its immense isolation. It was incredible that people could have come here looking for the near-abstraction of the earth's rotational axis; it was no less incredible that they should have made a scientific station here, supplied exclusively by air, that men should choose to spend a whole year in the middle of this featureless white expanse. Yet this is what has happened and we are privileged to see it happening at first hand on a sort of unreal tourist trip. As we filmed out at the Pole one of the three Hercules aircraft that would come today landed on its skis and taxied up to the station. For some of the time we were outside there were tiny ice crystals floating in the air which shone like fireflies in the direction of the sun.

Completing our film as we walked back, we went down one of the tunnels into the bowels of the snow, along the frozen passages and into the mess hall. From now on we spent the day underground. The filming team went up again after lunch to film the arrival and departure of another Hercules.

Leader of the scientists was a young Polish American studying aurora phenomena. Also there was Mike Gadsden, a world authority on auroras who was visiting briefly to plan the programme for the winter – with its 11 days of continuous twilight.

We managed to get a quorum for a sound sequence round the bar in Club 90 – playing dice, talking about the prospect of women in the Antarctic and about what brought each of them down here. Like our previous sequences only a small proportion will be worth using. It was 10.30 when I turned in, in the sick bay, where we all sleep. It is next door to the radio cabin where Barry Woodberry, the Australian ionosphere man, was talking to Melbourne by ham radio.

As our stay came to an end my thoughts about the Pole crystallised and I summarised them in my diary:

The South Pole – A conclusion –
'Great God, this is an awful place.' (My father's diary).
Awful because of its monotonous flat immensity . . .
Awful perhaps because of Amundsen's tent, and being forestalled . . .
Awful for the cold and the wind . . .
Awful for the prospect of walking 800 miles back . . .

Since then the place has altered little on the surface, but underneath is the snug warm camp with all its machinery. I wonder if even in his most optimistic mood my father could have imagined flush toilets and computers, generators, and Club 90 under the snow at the Pole. Surely not. The circumstances have changed *too* much. A plane will take us in less than 3 hours to Hut Point. No gnawing doubts about the lateness of the season, no appalling disappointment at Amundsen's secretly changed plans, at his priority at the Pole, at the lost race, at the vanished daydreams. No dietetic problems with scurvy beginning to take its effect. No fears for personal survival.

Yet because of the intangible significance of the earth's rotational axis – the Pole still has a magic and majesty which can be felt. It is the South Pole. It is still there, just like Everest, even though both were conquered long since.

The South Pole may be overlaid with the trappings and jokes of civilisation, there may be a bar in Club 90, an airhostess's recorded voice to announce the arrival of planes, a post office to frank the mail, but it is still the best place to study cosmic rays, the phenomena of the aurora, the ionosphere, and the effects of isolating men in low temperatures.

The Pole itself hasn't altered much since my father's day and I find it stirring that people have come here, and still come, to this one particular spot on the unbroken expanse of flat snow because of its wholly intangible significance as the southern end of the earth's rotational axis.

Who can guess what further developments there may be at this spot, in man's never-ending pursuit of knowledge. But I doubt if anyone here will ever know the desolation of spirit which that small band of men must have felt when they got here in 1912, and during the two months of their unsuccessful return journey.

We left the Pole the next day returning by Hercules to McMurdo, circling Mt Erebus to give us a marvellous view of the smoking crater close beneath us (see photograph on page 245).

SUNDAY 23 JANUARY

A quiet morning at McMurdo with some interesting data from a glaciologist called Tony Gow, who explained how the fish work themselves to the top of the ice if they get frozen into the bottom. Apparently it only happens near islands.

He told me that my father's last camp was now probably 14 miles to seaward of its original position and about 50 feet down.

At 1.00 pm the helicopter picked us up and took us the 15 minute flight to Cape Evans, where we landed beside the old *Terra Nova* Hut. We had to dig the snow away so as to get into it.

My father's hut at
Cape Evans with Mount
Erebus in the background.

Inside it was fascinating – so much is left just as it was in 1911. We filmed outside first, and I went along the edge of the sea, where the ice was undercut. Off shore were many bergs. There were penguin tracks and seal tracks in the snow, and many skuas on the hills behind. I walked up and found 2 well grown young skuas. I was sharply clipped on the head 6 or 7 times by the parents.

After that we came into the hut to film the interior shots – which the others are still doing while I sit at the table in my father's corner where Ponting's famous photograph was taken, and write this diary from the top of the last page. It's very cold, of course, but the sun pours in through the window. The background to the Ponting photo now looks more austere without the books and portrait photos. But it's an evocative place, and does not have the rather gloomy blubber-smoke-blackened air of total dereliction that we found in the hut at Hut Point. This is, surprisingly, a cheerful hut even though it bears little relationship to its condition when it was being lived in.

One striking thing we have found on this trip is how much better the people who have been here some time can stand the cold. This was especially noticeable at Scott Base.

Hanging above the table here is a big tow-net for plankton. Opposite is Wilson's bunk and next to it Ponting's dark room. Over in the far corner is the Physics lab, still full of bottles and Bunsen burners. And as I write Charles and the American Charlie Brown are flashing away with their still cameras.

I do find it strange and rather moving to be sitting here in this alcove, having lived for so much of my life with the photo of my father sitting here.

I find I have not described the scene adequately. Mount Erebus is a supreme backcloth. On the other side 15 yards away is the shore with great lumps of ice heaving in the swell and beyond them stranded icebergs. The compacted snow is undercut by the sea. There are penguin tracks along the shore and a seal hauled out recently beside the hut. To the north the Barne Glacier ends with a wall of ice where the last icebergs were calved. Just behind the hut is a small fresh water lake with open water around which the skuas congregate. On the little hill is a cross in memory of Mackintosh and Hayward who were lost crossing the sea ice from that point in 1917.

Altogether my father's hut at Cape Evans is in an extremely beautiful place, and the old hut itself is of great interest. Somehow however the preservation of these huts is a new thought and the result is a new kind of museum piece. But it bears about as much relation to the hut when it was in use as a stuffed bird does to a living bird – and is to the same extent depressing.

MONDAY 24 JANUARY

The helicopter for Cape Royds was to leave at 10.0 and before that we had to climb Observation Hill for some filming. We got a Nodwell, which Charlie Brown, our entertaining Apache assistant drove, and it took us to Nukipoo, (the nuclear power station) which is about $\frac{1}{3}$ of the way up. After that it was quite a steep walk. Chris, with his long legs went up fastest, then Charles, then Nomiyama, and I brought up the rear – taking it slowly as befits my years!

At the top is the cross of jarrah wood with the Tennyson lines 'To

PS on Observation Hill.

strive, to seek, to find and not to yield', (from *Ulysses*) and the names of the polar party. This was where the fruitless watch was kept for them in February and March 1912.

Back at the hut came a telephone call from Art Kranz, Commander presently in charge of the Base: would I come down to his hut, where Chris and Charles already were, playing the US equivalent of Vingt-et-un? This I did and lost about $1 in an hour. I was then asked by Commander Kranz to make a drawing for him. 'A penguin?' 'Why not a lovely girl?' So I started to draw a nude standing girl, which ended up very realistic. Whilst I was at work Charles addressed the Cdr as 'Lootenant' which took a good deal of living down. The Cdr also disclosed that he was married with 5 children of whom he showed pictures. It seemed doubtful whether he really wanted my little drawing, but he said he had a feeling for 'that sort of thing' – by which he intended to mean art and culture, but Chris who was fairly well away, got the giggles. The whole episode was fairly hilarious, and Art Kranz was left with a drawing labelled 'Girl' and signed – which Chris hoped the *Daily Express* would not get hold of!

TUESDAY 25 JANUARY

Our last day at McMurdo. Much colder with a strongish south east wind blowing over the saddle from Ross Island.

When we had first got out to Williams Field the visibility had been down to 200 yards, but true to its regular habits in these parts the weather changed suddenly, and as we took off Mounts Erebus and Terror were clear as a bell.

Mount Erebus with Mount Terror beyond, taken with my Instamatic as we returned from the Pole.

We turned back to the north passing over McMurdo City, then out over the sound with the Ross Island coast on our right. It was up-sun and it looked stupendous, lit exactly opposite to the day we returned from the Pole. I hope my photos come out – I took several of this scene, culminating in 2 shots with Cape Evans in the foreground and Erebus behind with its plume of smoke blowing far to leeward towards us and the shadow of the smoke coming down the mountain – almost like a lava flow.

Further on was Cape Royds and the little bay of ice where we had seen the Crabeater Seals.

Later I arranged for Bill Sladen to come up to the flight deck at Coulman Island, where he had been to see the 33,000 Emperor Penguin rookery on the sea ice at the northern end of the island.

It was 30 miles to the east of us – and so was Hallett Station, and farther north Cape Adare with a colony of 750,000 Adelies – studied by Murray Levick, with the Northern Party. This was also the site of the first overwintering in the Antarctic by Borchgrevink in 1899 (who had been the first man to set foot on the Antarctic continent in 1895). We could just see the low beach where the penguin colony is (though some climb 1,200 ft to their nests). There was a mirage which made the beach difficult to see.

Soon afterwards we crossed the north coast of Victoria Land and headed out for New Zealand – 2,300 miles from McMurdo.

Goodbye to the Antarctic. I wonder if I shall see it again. I wonder if I could have kept away from it if I had allowed myself to go there as a young man. There is no denying its tremendous appeal. Cold and inhospitable it may be, but oh the exquisite beauty of it – and the challenge that is still there, however much man's travelling and living techniques may have changed.

Imagine a continent as big as North America with one small town and a few scattered villages, most of them empty in winter.

And so at 5.40 we landed smoothly and safely at Chi-chi. Dave Hilton was sitting next to me as the pilot, who had flown us around Erebus, made the landing – his first on wheels for 6 weeks. It was a beauty.

I had occupied some part of the journey writing up this journal for Phil, part of it in writing a message to the youth of Japan for Nomiyama and part of it reading the abbreviated *Eye of the Wind* (my autobiography). I have read and corrected 180 pages.

Cdr Mike Goodwin met me on disembarkation. I returned to the White Heron Lodge Hotel and a very much needed bath. There were some lovely letters from my darling Phil and my darling Dafila – with drawings of the new swans.

After my bath I had a very pleasant and stimulating dinner with Bill Sladen, Carlton Ray and Alan Cox. Then I painted some chaetodons, as an aide-memoire from the *Barrier Reef Fish Book*, which is borrowed through Bernard Stonehouse, and will have to be given in today before I go.

I left Auckland the following day for Fiji where I snatched a few more days' swimming amongst the colourful fishes. I returned to a dank and misty England at the end of the month.

CHAPTER 15

The Falklands, South Shetlands and the Antarctic Peninsular

DIARY 10 1968

Philippa and I have made 24 voyages with the Lindblad Travel organization, most of them in the MV *Lindblad Explorer*. In January 1968, however, the Explorer was still being built, and we were to join the *Navarino* – a Chilean ship – for a cruise from the tip of South America via the Falklands to the Antarctic Peninsula. We would be going to the opposite side of the Antarctic Continent from the part I had visited two years before.

MONDAY 29 JANUARY
After drawing the bill pattern of the last Bewick's Swan at Slimbridge at 2 pm – Hawkster, a Boosey/Hawkes cob cygnet, ringed G027R – we drove to London for the inaugural cocktail party and dinner for the Animals Magazine/Houlder Bros/Lindblad tour in the *Navarino*.

In the Abraham Lincoln room in the Savoy Hotel we met a proportion of our fellow travellers. Peter Warner of Houlder's was in the Chair (he has done all the organising at the British end). I had to make a short informal speech; it was followed by an excellent talk about the Antarctic from Sloman of the British Antarctic Survey.

Very comfortable night in a luxurious suite at the Savoy. An auspicious start to the venture.

TUESDAY 30 JANUARY
Met up with the party and, after a BBC TV interview, embarked in a Pan Am Boeing 707 which left at 11.15 for New York. Some clear air turbulence (CAT) on the way and a late arrival at 7.30 GMT.

An hour or so at John F Kennedy Airfield – with transfer to Pan Am Departure Building. Mrs Lindblad and Rosalie Howard met us and told us that the *Navarino* had failed to get to the Antarctic with the tour being led by Roger Peterson. This was because of a failure of the steering gear near Cape Horn, which had occurred on 19th January.

After some lack of organisation by Pan Am, we finally embarked on another 707 – the Pan Am Clipper *Glad Tidings*. In this we flew for five hours to Caracas [Venezuela], and afterwards heard that No 4 engine was dry of oil on arrival. It was topped up, but found still to be leaking. The 'nuts were tightened' and after half-an-hour of delay we moved out for take off. When the pilot opened the throttles, as he put it 'No 3 engine let go on us'. The throttles were very quickly closed and we taxied back. The plane's name was beginning to seem rather inappropriate.

Rumours that a new plane would be sent began to percolate. Later when dawn had broken we transferred to the new plane which came in as we were sitting in the bus waiting for it. As I write this, just as the

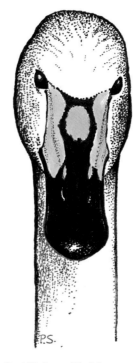

Bewick's Swan, 'Florin' showing the black and yellow pattern known as a 'Pennyface' – one of the three basic patterns within which there is sufficient variation for every swan to be identified and individually named. (Since 1964 4,500 of these swans, which breed in Arctic USSR and winter in England, have been recorded and named. The coded details are now stored in the Wildfowl Trust's computer.)

jets are running up in the new plane, the smell of impending breakfast makes us very hungry. It is 12.15 GMT on

Caracas airport, humid, overcast and devoid of animal life, was rather a depressing place. As we taxied out, a cloud of 2–300 birds rose from some rubbish dump half way up the hillside and started to circle in a thermal. These were presumably Turkey Vultures (or Black Vultures – or both). And so to a landing at Asunción (Paraguay) after flying over the Gran Chaco.

A small sparrow with chestnut spots at either side of the chin – and some House Sparrows were in a garden outside the airport – the only birds Paraguay had to offer us. But as the Boeing 707 pulled round to the tarmac in Buenos Aires (BA) there was a flock of 70 Glossy Ibises in the grass, paying no attention whatever to the jet passing within 30 yards of them. There were oven birds with rufous rumps on the way into the city – where we stayed at the Plaza Hotel.

At the dinner I made a presentation to Francisco Erize – a young photographer with a beard who had won the Animals Magazine photographic competition with a picture of Elephant Seals at the Valdez Peninsula. [He has led some of the later Lindblad cruises.] The prizes were a gold medal with my little fawn on it, and a pair of binoculars. All this had been thrust into our hands at Heathrow by Nigel Sitwell. However, the presentation served in lieu of a speech, which was one good thing about it.

THURSDAY 1 FEBRUARY

A bus to a different airport and in the bus to the foot of the ladder leading up into a BAC one-eleven jet – a privilege only previously afforded to the Duke of Edinburgh, we were told.

With us came Alexander Nesviginsky (of Astra – agent for Lindblad) – leaving his wife and a somewhat frightening American lady to deal with our baggage problems. Also with us was Francisco Erize leading a group of six of the previous tour which had failed to get to the Antarctic. They were going to the Valdez Peninsula – over which we flew before landing at the oil town of Commodoro Rivadavia. A hot wind blew across the pampa. It was 29°C. Phil and I went into the airport building to buy postcards for the children and some chocolate for 'iron rations'.

Then on to Rio Gallegos – an hour at 450 mph – where the temperature was 9°C. Here we were met by Jaime MacMahon who was to take charge of us for Lindblad.

From here on it was to be buses – two of them. But we began with a drama. Charles Tuckwell, a 60 year old company director from Braintree, Essex, came breathless and clapping hands to pockets – 'My passport . . . I must have dropped it in the plane – or in the taxi which brought me from the plane'. The BAC one-eleven had never stopped its jets, but now its ladder was up and it was ready to go back. Alexander Nesviginsky and Tuckwell jumped into a taxi and raced out to the plane. I watched through binoculars as it pulled up just behind the plane. They rushed forward to where the pilot could see them. The jets were revving up but it had not begun to roll. I saw them shouting up to the pilot. Then the tail ladder was lowered. They climbed up and searched . . . and found the passport.

Meanwhile, Guy Bowles – a farmer from Fordingbridge – had put *his* passport in his baggage about to be put, as we thought, into a lorry to travel separately across the Chilean frontier to Punta Arenas. This problem was also solved happily – and the luggage was eventually all loaded onto the roofs of the buses. And so away on the 6-hours drive in bright sunshine.

Quite soon we began to put up little flocks of waders from the roadside which flew along beside us, often for some distance. There seemed to be two sizes of them. They were seed snipe – *Thinocorus*. The smaller species *T. rumicivorus* was certainly there – the larger, *T. orbignyanus* possibly.

The grey gravel road rolled across the brown pampa, and the horizons were broken by volcanic hillocks and craters. Two hundred yards to our right we saw three guanacos, and a little later a fox. It was 75 km to the Argentine/Chilean border, where there was a long delay – perhaps longer because of strained relations between the two countries.

There were 3 beautiful Buff-necked Ibis (Bandurria) near the Argentine post, and later we walked out and almost trod on a seed snipe which ran a few feet around us. We watched a small grey bird with a russet tail, and saw a larger grey passerine with a buff stripe along the wing – the Dark-bellied Cinclodes.

We finally set off again and were a much shorter time at the Chilean post. Then a long drive, passing large numbers of Upland Geese. The great majority of males were white with only perhaps one in 8 or 10 bar-breasted. Darkness fell only half-an-hour or so before our arrival at Punta Arenas – where we had a late dinner in the fairly comfortable Hotel Cabo de Horno.

Guanaco,
the lowland camelid
of South America.

FRIDAY 2 FEBRUARY

A morning tour of the city and visit to the museum was a part of the programme we decided to miss. At eleven we embussed for the $1\frac{1}{2}$ hrs drive to Fort Bulnes, south along a coast road. We finished with quite an impressive bird list of which the most memorable features were a fleeting glimpse of two Chilean Eagles in the high forest country near the fort, a view from a wooded promontory of penguins, albatrosses, skuas, diving petrels and cormorants, and a close look at a little flock of Winter Plovers – *Zonibyx modestus* – on the way home.

There were two species – at least – of Antarctic Beech on the Fort Bulnes promontory. These I took to be *Nothophagus antarcticus*, and *N. betuloides* though *N. pumilo* may have been there too. I am not sure which is the evergreen one. The commonest tree had a somewhat dentate leaf. The leaf of the other had a smoother edge and was a little more shiny. Many of these leaves were turning yellow and the branches had a flattened appearance.

There had been some complaint that we had not stopped on the way out to look at birds – and so on the way back we did so fairly frequently, getting a really wonderful view of the little dotterel or Winter Plover –

Winter Plovers,
Charadrius (*Zonibyx*)
modestus.

Albatrosses

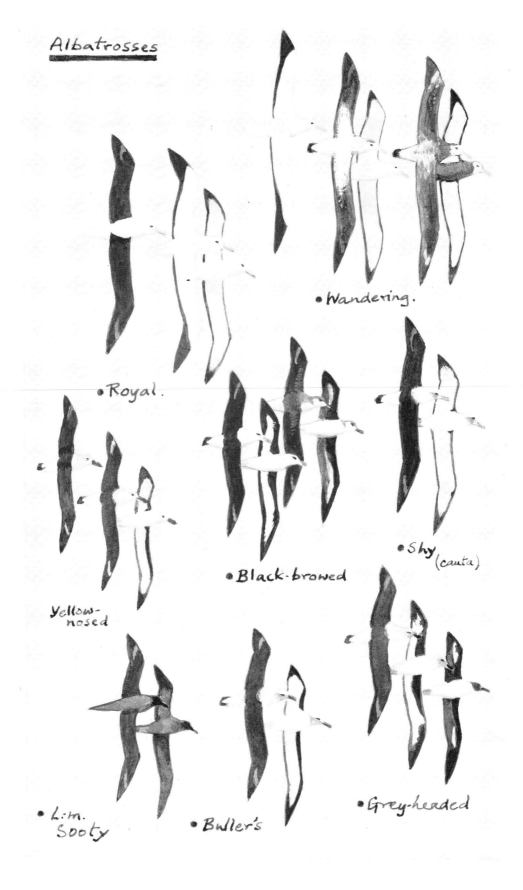

• Wandering.

• Royal.

Yellow-nosed

• Black-browed

• Shy (cauta)

• L.m. Sooty

• Buller's

• Grey-headed

in a flock of a dozen or so, with (probably) White-rumped Sandpipers, on a little gravelly point. Later we saw the Spur-winged Plover (alternatively called the Chilean Lapwing and known locally as Queltegue or Tero-tero) very well, with a Chile Teal and some passerines. The bus had a microphone and I was able to communicate some enthusiasm about all these birds. It is agreeable to find that I can still impart some interest to marginally committed bird watchers!

The best moment of the day was certainly when the bus decanted us among tall Antarctic beeches on the promontory beyond Fort Bulnes just before lunch, looking out across a grey sea, smooth in the lee of the land. We were perhaps 60 feet up a steep slope and below on the water were a number of Magellan Cormorants and 5 Magellan Penguins. Further out were Black-browed Albatrosses in flight over the rougher water and a hundred or more were sitting on the surface looking like huge black-backed gulls.

Magellan Cormorant
or Rock Shag.
Phalacrocorax magellanicus

Head + neck all black in summer
Chin throat + foreneck white in winter.
Underparts white.
Red face + throat
Feet flesh.

Guanay

A Magellan Penguin looks at you with both eyes to make sure – first one, then the other.

There were a number of skuas – the Southern Great Skua – *Catharacta skua* – wheeling about, among Dominican and Brown-headed Gulls. And low over the water were small auk-like diving petrels – probably *Pelecanoides magellani*. It was on the way up to lunch that I saw a group of three black tyrants – at least one of them with a quite conspicuous chestnut mantle. This is illustrated by Crawshaw (1904) as *Centrides niger*, but is presumably *Lessonia r. rufa*. Altogether quite a good day.

SATURDAY 3 FEBRUARY

There was a division of the party into four groups. Phil and I took the largest group, in a fleet of seven taxis, to look for birds around the pampa lakes to the north of Punta Arenas. The second group was to have lunch at a ski club on the hill overlooking the city, and to walk in the woods to see birds. Unfortunately a trip to the mutton factory was added to this excursion, and some at least of the party did not care for watching the animals being slaughtered – although others are said to have remained for some time fascinated by the spectacle. It takes all sorts to make a world – and with no more public executions to watch . . . !

Our youngest expedition member – tall rather shy artist Lavinia Blair didn't go to the Frigorifico but walked in the woods and saw *Scytalopus magellanicus*, the Magellanic Babbler, and the Thorn-tail, *Aphrastura s. spinicauda*. We were envious.

Magellanic Babbler,
Scytalopus magellanicus.

The first stop for our motorcade was on the outskirts of Punta Arenas to look at a most remarkable mammatus cloud formation. To the west over the Cordillera was an ill-defined lenticular arch, with some small lenticulars below it. Then in the sky above and to the east of us, the cloud was cascading down in extraordinary streaks and blobs to about 1,000 ft out over the Magellan Strait. There was also a wind shear which gave the streaks a herringbone kink. It was altogether memorable and the party had something to talk about till we got to the next stop, by a lake with Great Grebes on it.

At a small river where 15 years ago I had filmed Crested Ducks, we stopped and the crowd of us walked down a small tributary stream, which was a dry hollow. This enabled us to get close to some ducks I had seen from the road. The scheme worked well and we had good views of Crested Ducks and Brown Pintails, a White-tufted Grebe, White-rumped Sandpipers, etc. Three Bandurria flew over quite close and made their gorgeous metallic call. Later many Magellan Geese came down to the water. On the way back some of the party saw a Cassin's Peregrine being mobbed by terns, and we all saw many Darwin's Rheas.

We botanised a little on the way back, and ate the berries of *Empetrum rubrum* and *Berberis buxifolia.* The *Chiliotrichum* was in flower.

A little further was a lake with a lot of geese. We stopped to see them and Capt John Cadwalader (joint leader of the tour) said this was where he had seen flamingoes two weeks earlier. As we pulled away from the lake I looked back into a part of the shore which had been in dead

On the day when these five penguins were drawn as a personal key we saw an unidentified duck.

ground and there were 4 flamingoes. One was *very* bright pink for a Chilean, but Chileans they were. The weather was sunny and hot.

We were heading now for Estancia Maria and took a side road up through Antarctic Beech woods. At one point we looked down on green paddocks with many Upland Geese and about a dozen Ashyheads, quite close and easy to see. Here we heard (and some saw) Austral Parakeets (Magellan Conures). Another memorable spot was a little opening in the trees with a marsh covered with Bandurria and Tero-tero, which rose a couple of times and settled again while many of the party took pictures. One group found a baby seed snipe – grey and unspotted.

At Estancia Maria we turned left to return along the Fitzroy Channel and almost at once, as the road came to the shore, we saw a group of large white birds bobbing up and down in the short steep sea just off shore. To my astonishment they were Black-necked Swans – not that I did not expect to see them in the Fitzroy, but that I had never imagined them in such a seaway. They were feeding avidly, swimming hither and thither to pick up the food from the surface, and even racing each other to each titbit. But what could the food have been? Floating weed or plankton? We shall never know. There were 35 swans in the group, but no young.

That day produced not less than 35 species of birds for our party.

SUNDAY 4 FEBRUARY

We embarked in the *Navarino* although we did not sail till 4.30 pm. It was a calm sunny afternoon as we cast off, leaving behind a strange Canadian composer, Cecil Meade, who was a member of the first (unsuccessful) cruise and who had longed for a place on this one. He was apparently working on an Antarctic composition.

As we steamed northward up the Magellan Straits we saw all the usual sea birds as well as an Arctic Skua all the way from the far north. Near Isla Magdalena the sea was full of penguins and sea lions. Many of the sea lions were lying in little groups with their fins out of the water. Each has 3 fins out and keeps the fourth in the water for manoeuvring. What can the function of this be? Is it perhaps a heat regulation mechanism? Presumably a flipper that is drying cools more quickly than if kept in the water. We saw the same thing with the Galápagos Sea Lion.

Some of the sea lions were porpoising. It was suggested that these might have been fur seals but I rather doubt this.

Andean Condors soaring.

Southern Sea Lion bull, cow and calf.

Magellan Straits
4 February 1968

Commerson's & White-bellied Dolphins

The star turn of the whole day for me were the dolphins. They were first seen coming in to our bow wave and surfing on it. 'What', someone asked me 'are the dolphins with white over their backs?' They were unknown to me, and I began by suggesting they were really showing white bellies. But then I saw them myself. They had black heads, but the middle part of the body was all white – top and bottom – and the tail black again. We must have seen a hundred or more. At one stage two of a different kind came in – rather brownish with white belly only.

These black and white Commerson's Dolphins are apparently usually found in narrow straits, and almost always are seen in the narrows of the Magellan Straits.

It was a wonderful calm first day for the whole party to get settled into the ship and everyone was glad to be on our way. Spirits were high and there is a satisfactory feeling of unity in this strikingly heterogeneous group. Some of the American contingent have not yet been assimilated by the British party, but on the whole the omens are good.

We sighted the West Falkland coast the next day.

TUESDAY 6 FEBRUARY

A beautiful bright almost calm morning, as we steamed into Port Stanley, past pairs and family parties of Falkland Flightless Steamer Ducks, *Tachyeres brachypterus*. We were taken ashore in the boat of the Customs Officer, past two males and a female Kelp Goose under the wall in front of the town – where there was also a pair of steamers.

The town is rather like a Scottish fishing village, quite attractive in the sunshine. The principal shop is the store of the Falkland Islands Company – whose General Manager came out to talk and help us. We bought postcards, a map, stamps etc.

We were due to lunch with the Acting Governor (the Governor being in England) and were lucky to be able to thumb a lift to Sullivan House, where the Colonial Secretary – now Acting Governor – lives. He is Tommy Thompson, who paints with considerable talent, and grows begonias and schizanthus.

We ate Upland Goose and quantities of memorable, large and rather dark strawberries. It was all very good.

While at Stanley we heard the bad news that the Royal Marines had laid on a night exercise with a hovercraft and illuminations on Volunteer Beach. This is the breeding beach of the King Penguins. According to Ian Strange [Falklander and conservationist] the first pair returned to this beach twenty years ago after an absence of 60 years (? were they birds that had been reared there, or is Volunteer Beach especially suitable to King Penguins). During the last 20 years the colony has built up to 22 pairs, which has been kept secret – thus the Marines would have had no means of knowing. The exercise had taken place only a couple of nights ago. The Acting Governor knew nothing about it till I told him but said at once he would look into it and let me know whether the penguins had been disturbed. He also said that there was one other small colony of Kings.

We talked about the bounty on goose beaks [a fee paid for every goose shot], no longer paid by the Government, but still paid by some farmers to their employees.

Male Falkland Island
Steamer Duck,
Tachyeres brachypterus.

Opposite:
Commerson's Dolphins,
Cephalorhynchus commersoni,
with two unidentified dolphins,
possibly the White-bellied,
C. albiventris, riding
the *Navarino*'s stern wave.

King Penguin,
Aptenodytes patagonica.

Rockhoppers *Eudyptes crestatus*
Westpoint Island
7 February 1968

Above:
Macaroni Penguin –
these three penguin
species were all seen
on West Point Island.

Westpoint
Island
7 Feb.

Magellan Penguin *Spheniscus magellanicus*

There are still a great many geese, and indeed they have increased greatly as a result of sheep farming (like the kangaroos in Australia). Short grass is no doubt much better for them than tussock grass, as food.

After lunch Thompson drove me to the broadcasting station to interview me for a regular radio programme which he runs. The questions were good and I was able to get in quite a good plug for conservation.

Johnny Rook
(Forster's Caracara),
Phalcoboenus australis.

We left Stanley later that afternoon and spent the next day at Carcass and West Point Islands with their wonderful profusion and variety of very tame birds – penguins, albatrosses, geese, ducks, shags, night herons, terns and four species of birds of prey including Forster's Caracara, locally known as the Johnny Rook. A special feature of Carcass Island, which at that time belonged to Cecil and Kitty Bertrand (Philippa and I have been there twice since) was the Elephant Seal 'rookery' at the north end of the island, from which we could look across to the Jason Islands. Len Hill of Birdland at Bourton-on-the-Water in Gloucestershire was with us in the *Navarino* and soon afterwards completed the purchase of the Jasons to become a 'penguin millionaire'.

At West Point Island which belongs to Roddy Napier we went to the Devil's Nose, a rocky headland among steep cliffs with a rookery of Rockhopper Penguins interspersed with breeding Black-browed Albatrosses or 'Mollymauks'. My diary for that day ends:

in the gathering dusk we waved goodbye to the Napiers and chugged out to the *Navarino*, passing four or five Night Herons sitting on the kelp and bouncing up and down over the waves – quite a remarkable sight. And so we returned on board after a splendid day. The Napiers came out and sailed round the ship with Ian Strange in his boat *The Gleam*. We weighed anchor and sailed for the Antarctic.

Next day the sea was slight but we were crossing the stormy Drake Passage and by nightfall the wind was freshening and the sea rising. The Antarctic Convergence* was crossed at 2.30 am on 9 February and by dawn it was blowing Force 8 – wind speeds 40 knots and the sea very rough indeed. Antarctic Petrels were around most of the day. At 11 am we crossed latitude 60° south and were, by the terms of the Treaty, in the Antarctic.

Early on 10 February we sighted Bridgeman Island with two icebergs, their tops were brown with what was probably volcanic ash from the recent Deception Island eruption. The next 2 days were spent at King George Island and Half Moon Island seeing more Elephant Seals, our first Weddell Seals, a breeding colony of Giant Petrels (Giant Fulmars) and another of Chinstrap Penguins.

At lunchtime we set off for Deception Island and at 5 pm, with a full gale blowing snow showers horizontally, we came through the spectacularly narrow gap in the island's wall known as Neptune's Bellows into the huge crater bay, where we anchored close to the huts

*This is the line (which varies from 50–60° south) at which the cold and less salty water flowing from the Antarctic sinks beneath the warmer and more salty water flowing south.

of one of the two recently abandoned British bases, and to two large oil storage tanks among the ruined buildings and machinery of the long-abandoned whaling station. We were the first to visit the island since the personnel of the stations had been rescued from the eruption two months earlier.

Elephant Seal, which is a more accurate name than Sea Elephant.

Sea Elephant.

MONDAY 12 FEBRUARY

By morning the wind had died down and blue sky was showing. We had our usual 'council of war' up in the Captain's cabin with John Cadwalader and Jaime MacMahon, and decided to send one boat on into the crater to explore the results of the eruption two months ago while another boat went ashore at the nearby, but abandoned station.

We were rather crowded in the boat and cluttered with our life jackets, but it was quite warm as we went with the wind along the north shore of the crater, past the abandoned Chilean station, with a tattered emergency flag on the headland. Beyond the station, somewhat embedded in ash, we could see steam rising from a little bay. This was a fumarole. The bay steamed and there were steaming points all up the shore. Some of the water was sulphurous yellow and here I trailed a hand over the side. The water was warm and as we moved forward it became too hot to keep my hand in the water.

We tried to land in this bay, but in the end all we succeeded in doing was to clog the water cooling system with ashes in the shallows. However we chugged on round the shore to a new island – about 70 or 80 ft high with two small craters on it – and some steam rising. This island of perhaps 100 acres was immensely impressive. It was just 2 months old, with a crater lake on the side nearest to the Argentine station half buried in ash. We had engine problems with the boat and had to stop a couple of times on the way back to clean the water cooling system.

The only wildlife we had seen on the trip, apart from the 50 or 60 Cape Pigeons, with a few Kelp Gulls and Wilson's Storm-petrels round the ship, had been a Weddell Seal on the first point (where on the return journey there was what I took to be a Crabeater Seal, and 30–50 Kelp Gulls downstream of the hot water along a lee shore picking up what was presumably 'cooked' plankton.

After lunch the second party went off to look at the vulcanicity, while the morning party went ashore. The base is depressing. The derelict

buildings of the whaling station, the tumbled machinery, the scatter of old and wrecked boats, of collapsing huts, of piles of barrels and tubs (presumably for the whale oil) – all these things lent a sad air of desolation to the scene. The new British huts were neatly green, but even around them was the chaos of untidiness which seems to be inseparable from Antarctic bases. There was evidence of a lot of ash having fallen, but otherwise no startling effects of the recent eruption on the base could be seen.

Deception Island:
The old whaling station and more recent British hut silted up with volcanic ash.

The *Navarino* at Deception Island with Neptune's Window in the background,
11–12 February 1968.

In the morning the sailors had painted the ship's name and the date in white twice, once on each of two large round storage tanks on the island. Other ships' names were on the tanks, but none so prominent as the *Navarino*. Another message on the tank in huge letters read 'Going home, Jim?' We wondered who Jim was and what the joke had been.

There are very tame Sheathbills along the shore. We came to some steam rising from a trickle of yellow sulphur water emerging just above the tide edge. This was almost too hot to the hand.

Further along the extensive strand were quantities of whales' bones, many of them skulls. One or two Chinstrap Penguins sat around, and were being filmed by Franz Lazi and his team. Ahead of us was a low saddle in the island's rim and we decided to walk up there to look for Cape Pigeons breeding. Eugenio Callegari and Terry Bassett were already climbing at a steeper and higher point where I could see many Cape Pigeons on ledges. Our saddle was only a half saddle. At its crest was a 100 foot vertical cliff to a small beach on which lay a Leopard Seal which we photographed from almost directly above.

I moved along the steep slope out on the ledges among the large grey downy chicks of the Cape Pigeons with a few adults in attendance. There were also Wilson's Storm-petrels flying in and out of holes on the cliff above.

Phil and I walked slowly back along the shore in the balmy sunshine, stopping for me to take an Instamatic photo of a conversation piece between Phil and a Chinstrap.

We cogitated upon the derelict whaling station and the mess it had left behind. What should one think of the whalers who had set it up, with their grasping greed and lack of foresight? They were none the less adventurous and courageous men. Yet the plundering of the whale stocks for economic gain was surely an inferior activity of man. Was our method of exploiting the Antarctic for tourism better? We felt it did not do so much harm and that we should not be put to shame by future visitors to this remarkable island.

Back at the little tumble down jetty there was no boat from the ship, and the boat which had gone to see the fumaroles had not returned. Phil decided to wait there while I walked on round the bay to a seal which had hauled out of the water. A few minutes later the volcano boat came round the corner and the boat from the ship set out to the shore. If I hurried however, I thought I could get to the seal and back before the rest of the party, straggled along the beach, could get back to the boat. So on I went. The seal was very obliging and I took a

Chinstrap Penguin,
Pygoscelis antarctica.

Leopard Seal.

number of photos of it. I had taken it to be a Crabeater but when I got close I thought it was a Leopard Seal, and later sightings confirmed this. Then I had a lively half mile walk back arriving in a muck sweat. That night we sailed for the Melchior Islands – or rather early on the morning of

TUESDAY 13 FEBRUARY

We arrived at a small base at about 7.0 am and Jaime went ashore to find it deserted. We quickly decided to weigh anchor again and move on to Paradise Bay. It was a morning of almost dead calm and the islands and passages we passed through were of great beauty.

The Chilean base at Paradise Bay which is on the mainland of Antarctica is set up in the middle of a Gentoo Rookery. We anchored very close to the shore; Gentoos and some Chinstraps were porpoising all about the bay. There were also a number of shags, and some Crabeater Seals from time to time.

Gentoo Penguin brooding two young on its nest of stones.

Chinstrap
Pygoscelis antarctica

Gentoo
Pygoscelis papua

Chinstrap Penguins (above) and Gentoo Penguins. The Chinstraps are more southerly in range and when the two meet they are dominant and rather aggressive. The gentler Gentoos are divided into a northern and a southern subspecies. These are only distinguishable by the size of the bill which is slightly larger in the northern race.

Within a few yards of the landing place Gentoos were lined up to welcome us. They were extremely tame and phlegmatic, indicating that they are well treated by the Chileans.

Some had about half grown chicks, and surprisingly quite a number had eggs. The explanation of this was evidently that the base had been empty until the Deception eruption on 4 December after which the 30 men were moved to Paradise Bay. No doubt this disrupted the birds with eggs in some parts of the rookery around the base and quite a large number had renested.

There were Chinstraps nesting in two places among the Gentoos – one up on the cemetery and the other across the tidal beach which makes this base an island at high water. The new Gentoo nests had what appeared to be twigs built into them, but these were old moulted tail feathers.

By easy stages, and in rather a crowd, we made our way to the further penguin rookery where we watched both species coming ashore and swimming under water.

I noticed a very curious movement in which the swimming penguins roll from side to side while using their feet and flippers evidently to scrape themselves. Two explanations occurred to me. The first is the obvious one – that they are washing. A second possibility is that they are brushing off any crustacean (or other) ectoparasites which may attach themselves. The water round the shore was alive with a species of amphipod growing to about an inch. I cannot help thinking that the penguins were taking these as they cruised underwater, clearly visible to us on the rock above, frequently altering course. When on the surface we observed once more how they constantly dip their heads, presumably mainly to look out for Leopard Seals or Killer Whales.

We climbed up towards the Chinstraps, and came upon a very solicitous pair of Sheathbills. They obviously had young and were running almost round our feet. The larger of the two, which I took to be the female, was the more agitated. Whenever the small male came within reach she pecked him viciously. Eventually I found the nest hole, and could just see a baby in the deep shadow. Eugenio Callegari whom I directed to the nest with Terry Bassett said they had found two young.

At the top of the rookery the Chinstraps were established, with Gentoos on the outskirts – indicating Chinstrap supremacy. We watched the feeding routine in both species. The Chinstrap chicks were further advanced than the Gentoos. The soft grey of the Gentoos with their white breasts makes them by far the prettiest penguin chicks we have seen.

We ambled pleasantly back past a spectacular snow wall covered with icicles and with a cascade of freshwater pouring out from near its top – as a regular waterfall.

And so back on board with our appetite for penguins more or less sated.

The base itself was pretty disastrously untidy and unattractive, but even that couldn't spoil this beautiful anchorage among the steep snow-clad mountains.

That evening the Chilean tug-sized supply ship berthed alongside us for a party. Language was a principal stumbling block, but the party apparently went on until the Chilean ship sailed at 1.00 am and even

Sleeping Gentoo.

later for the *Navarino*'s Officers – till 4.00 they say. But we had been in bed since 11.00.

We sailed from Paradise Bay early the following morning cruising down the Neumayer Channel in rare Antarctic sunshine, through the Peltier Channel, anchoring near Palmer Station on Anvers Land where we went ashore. We left the following day.

THURSDAY 15 FEBRUARY

An early start from Palmer Station to go through the Lemaire Passage to Argentine Island – the British Base F. I made a cardinal error in waking Phil at the advertised time of 5.00 am when we were due to enter the narrows. But we were an hour behind time and it was a grey cloudy morning with a strong westerly wind.

Up on the upper bridge it was cold and cheerless for the first half hour. Then we turned downwind into the Lemaire. From a distance the astonishingly narrow cleft appeared to be completely blocked by icebergs. This was a part of the trip which we had been told would be touch and go. We advanced slowly and cautiously. The mountains rose vertically on either side of the rift. On the left was Cape Renard with twin peaks like a fox's ears. The tops of the higher mountains, which included Mount Scott, were alas hidden in cloud.

The Lemaire Channel is perhaps the most famous beauty spot in the Antarctic Peninsula. Like the Taj Mahal it did not disappoint, even though the mountain tops were hidden. The forbidding walls rose almost vertically on either hand as we threaded our way among the icebergs – in some places so thick that the channel ahead appeared to be completely blocked.

The lack of sunlight produced one dramatic effect. In a world of black and white with a slate coloured sea, the blues and green of the icebergs shone out with incredible brilliance. The blue was almost luminous and many of the bergs were in fantastic shapes, with caves and holes like Henry Moore sculpture.

Among the bergs were a few Adelie Penguins porpoising – a few seals – Crabeaters mostly with one or two Leopards. Also in one place there were porpoising Gentoos. The cloud hid the peaks, but the main walls of the channel rose almost 1,000 feet before they met the cloud base. The ship moved slowly among the icebergs, the bergibits and the growlers (small icebergs). She is not strengthened for ice and the Captain was taking no chances.

South of the Lemaire we emerged among islands and presently ran past some low islands to the east which carried an enormous rookery, presumably of Adelie Penguins. All of the islands were pink with the krill-tinted droppings. The colony covered at least 3 islands and must have run into scores of thousands at the least.

It was still only 8 in the morning when we slowed and stopped opposite a tiny channel leading among low rolling islands. Through the crack we could see the buildings of the British Base F, Argentine Island.

The Captain announced that he could not anchor here, and that he could remain only half an hour. He had hoped to steam up and down but there was so much ice that this was not apparently practicable. Furthermore backing down presented the hazard that growlers and

Adélie
Pygoscelis adeliae

bergibits could be sucked into the space between the hull and the propeller and might even break a blade.

It was arranged that only Phil and I and the BBC man (Jefferey Boswall) should go in in the boat with Jaime to bring the mail and the sheep and wine which were our presents to the base.

We chugged in, passing very close to a group of Crabeater Seals which provided excellent photographic opportunities. We were directed by some of the base chaps round to a little dock on the far side. We were all dressed up in our Antarctic clothing – red parkas and trousers, gloves, woollen helmets, the lot. The boys who met us were in shirt-sleeves.

Nothing that I have seen in the Antarctic compares with the clean and orderly state of this station. They are working on the ionosphere, seismology, geomagnetism and meteorology. They have a very good ham radio installation. There was a line of huskies close by, which had had 4 puppies. Up till recently it had been a place of retirement for elderly huskies, as they are less used at that base than on other British stations.

We tried to get the latest weather information, and while this was being obtained by radio I signed copies of my two editions of *Eye of the Wind* (or maybe one was *Happy the Man*). They had baked a lot of tarts and things for all of our party, expecting 60, but the dozen of us (with the Chilean boat's crew) ate a few.

When I commented on the tidiness of the station, the leader said 'Well, we put in quite a lot of work yesterday!' But it was marvellously well done and we wished like anything that all the *Navarino* passengers could have seen it.

Crabeater Seals
on an ice-floe.

A blast on the *Navarino*'s siren hustled us back into the boat for the 15 minute chug out to where the ship lay. Back on board, we moved on at once and for the next three hours the surroundings were of superlative beauty and interest. To me this was the peak of the expedition.

The cloud lifted and a watery sun emerged. The ship moved slowly forward among pack ice which looked as though it would bar our passage. There were many bergs and bergibits and seals and penguins on the ice all round us. The ship proceeded in fits and starts with frequent stops to coast forward almost to a halt. Some Adelie Penguins stayed on an ice-floe till we were very close, and a Leopard Seal provided some good photos when he stayed sleeping until his floe was hit by the ship. Another floe carried a single young Adelie of the year who was determined not to get wet and stayed firmly on his ice as it was bumped and drifted down the port side.

So we passed through this wonderland of ice and out at last into the open water. Once clear of the ice we steamed out to the westward and then turned south for our dash to the Antarctic Circle*, which we reached at dusk, about 9.0 pm.

Phil broke a bottle of champagne over the stem, and we all drank to the occasion when the Captain sounded the siren for the crossing of the magic line. We were the first tourist ship to penetrate the Circle on this side of the Antarctic. On the other side the *Magga Dan* – with Lars Lindblad on board – was on its second trip of the season into the Ross Sea (and of course well south of the Circle).

There is no doubt we have been exceptionally lucky with the weather. But now the wind began to rise and by next morning . . .

FRIDAY 16 FEBRUARY

It was blowing hard as we headed due north for Diego Ramirez and Cape Horn. Light-mantled Sooty Albatrosses were the most numerous bird species as they had been on the evening before (with the possible exception of the ever-present Giant Fulmars). The Silver Grey (Southern) Fulmar was also there in numbers – extraordinarily gull-like in flight – indeed at Melchior I had seen two in calm conditions and been convinced that they were an unknown gull! I had drawn them without correctly identifying them. Then there were Cape Pigeons and Antarctic Petrels together.

Wilson's Hour-glass Dolphins, *Lagenorhynchus wilsoni* (probably a synonym for *L. cruciger*, see page 267).

On the previous day I had twice seen small flocks of 30–50 Antarctic Petrels sitting on icebergs. After the first sighting I happened to be looking at the book made from Wilson's sketch books, which has a drawing of a flock on an iceberg. The later sighting confirmed the identification. But for me the zoological climax was a group of 3 – perhaps 5 Wilson's Dolphins – *Lagenorhynchus wilsoni*.

Steaming north we left the Antarctic and rounded Cape Horn. We sailed up the Chilean coast to Puerto Montt where we left the *Navarino* after twenty-one wonderful days and 4,026 miles of travel! We came home by way of Buenos Aires, and Rio de Janeiro where we were on:

*The Antarctic Circle is that line of south latitude at which the sun does not set on midsummer's day.

Wilson's Hour-glass Dolphin ?
Lagenorhynchus wilsoni
Fri 16 Feb. 1968

FRIDAY 1 MARCH

I telephoned my friend and colleague on the IUCN Board – Dr José Candido de Melo Carvalho who came to fetch us at 10.30 and looked after us all day. He took us up into the National Park of Tijuca which is surrounded on three sides by the city. It is marvellous that so much primary rain forest can exist so close to one of the world's principal cities. The first great thrill as we went further up the park road to the Corcovado itself was our first morpho butterfly. It flapped slowly with frequent glides above the road, the sun catching its wings in blue flashes of incredible brilliance. It was huge, almost bird-like and immensely impressive. José told us that it was a male of *Morpho anabixia* and that at the beginning of the season, when newly emerged, they flew much faster than now.

There were many cars in the car park below the Christ statue, with souvenir shops clustered round the steps leading to the foot of the statue itself. Butterflies mounted in various ways – from rather tasteful groups and single specimens to 'pop art' paintings decorated with them and trays of solid morpho wings. José told us of some new work by a student who had discovered how to breed them in captivity which might lead to a controlled exploitation and remove the pressure on the wild stocks. The wings are without doubt exquisite things. Can one deprecate the use of the mortal remains, which last for ever (virtually), of an insect which naturally lives only a few months, except on grounds of endangering the survival of the species? What of aesthetic values? Why do we not find a stuffed peacock aesthetically satisfying? Or a stuffed hummingbird? Is it aesthetically unbeautiful? Or has fashion created a resistance since the plumage trade threatened species and legislation was brought in? Or is it merely anti-Victorianism?

Without the overlay of civilisation and culture any child or adult who is not colourblind could not fail to think the feathers of a bird of paradise or the wing of a morpho butterfly superlatively beautiful. Perhaps the bird skin can evoke the thought 'Oh, poor bird' but scarcely as strongly in the case of the butterfly.

We deprecate the magpie in humanity – the collector's mania, partly for its effects on rare creatures, partly also for the wish to *possess*. Perhaps we should not wish to capture and *possess* a morpho butterfly. Rather should we delight only in seeing it fly high in the glade of a tropical rain forest. But of course it is also (and differently) marvellous to see one at a range of 1 foot – even dead and preserved.

Down the years different people with different cultures will resolve these conflicts differently. The only thing which must be aesthetically and morally wrong would be to exterminate morpho butterflies so that future generations can no longer enjoy them – either alive in the forest glade or as decoration for an ashtray.

Leaves of forest trees, *Cunoniaceae*, growing to 60 ft high at Puerto Lagunas, 24 February 1968.

Philesia buxifolia, Puerto Lagunas, 24 February 1968.

Desfontanea spinosa.

Opposite: Wilson's Hour-glass Dolphin, *Lagenorhynchus wilsoni*, was described by Dr Edward Wilson who saw them from the *Terra Nova* on my father's expedition to the Antarctic in 1910. It now seems probable that this is a synonym for the Hour-glass Dolphin, *L. cruciger*, which was described in 1824; the distribution of the black and white patterns on dolphins is subject to considerable individual variation. The birds are: Light-mantled Sooty (left) and Black-browed Albatrosses.

CHAPTER 16

The Sub Antarctic Islands and the Ross Sea

DIARY 14 1971

Phil and I were joined by our daughter Dafila on our second Lindblad trip to the Antarctic. We were to visit the Ross Sea side of Antarctica this time (South of New Zealand) so I would have the opportunity of showing them some of the places I had visited in 1966. We left Slimbridge at the end of January and flew to Auckland boarding the *Lindblad Explorer* (LE) in the early evening of Friday 5 February. The Auckland Islands were reached a day later but we did not go ashore until the next day.

SUNDAY 7 FEBRUARY

Alas a morning of low cloud and drizzle which persisted for the first 2 hours of our visit to stupendous Enderby Island.

Two qualities made it as good as any wildlife island we have seen since the Galápagos. The first was a rich diversity of bird species and the second the extreme tameness of almost all of them. The wildest seemed to be the introduced blue-grey and black rabbits, and the Giant Fulmars. The skuas were absurdly tame, the penguins agreeably tamer than the Yellow-eyed are supposed to be. The endemic shag, and the Red-billed Gulls were also very tame and the Red-crowned Parakeets were quite easily approachable. The New Zealand Pipit was the tamest of all, followed by the New Zealand Bellbird, with the endemic Auckland Island Tomtit (flycatcher) only slightly less so.

Enderby Island.
7.2.71

Yellow-eyed Penguin,
Megadyptes antipodes,
Enderby Island,
7 February 1971.

Red-crowned Parakeet,
Cyanorhamphus novaezelandiae,
Enderby Island,
7 February 1971.

The 'pièce de résistance', as far as I was concerned was a close range view of the flightless Auckland Island Teal, brilliantly spotted by Keith (Shackleton) from the Zodiac when we were looking at shags. He was on a ledge in a cave about 10–15 yards away, and finally walked down into the water and swam into the cave, through which daylight was showing from the far end. The bill was quite blue.

For the last hour on Enderby the rain had held off and we went up onto the closely rabbit-cropped turf with Hooker's Sea Lions all around – and deep into the woods as well. There were freshwater pools full of crèches of tiny baby sea lions.

During lunch the LE steamed south to a fjord of Auckland Island called Hanfield Inlet which had an impressive waterfall. We steamed up the fjord with good speed, seeing large numbers of Sooty Shearwaters, which landed on the water and dived all in one movement – practically flying into the water. When they came up they burst out of the water and were at once flying again. This to me was new behaviour. Was this for feeding? We saw a skua trying to keep a shearwater underwater, but it got away and soon outdistanced the skua in the air.

MONDAY 8 FEBRUARY

A pleasant and amusing trip in 3 Zodiacs to the head of the fjord to trace an abandoned settlement. On the way along the shore we saw a pair of Tuis – glossy black birds with an elegant tuft of feathers in the middle of the breast. They were chasing moths in a crazy vertical pursuit over the water and high into the air.

At the head of the bay was a small flat island at the mouth of the river. There was a strange periodical tidal surge which at one moment left the boats high and dry and then flooded in five minutes later.

Meanwhile those still on the island were in retreat from a young bull sea lion. On the way back to the ship we passed close to the mouth of a small river. Far up under the trees in the dark was a duck with apparently an enormous bill. I had only a fleeting glimpse and believe it may have been a New Zealand Shoveler. Anyway, it was certainly not an Auckland Island Merganser, now generally believed to be extinct.

From a point high up on the open greensward, where much larger numbers of rabbits were in evidence than yesterday, I looked across the rata forest to the heathland on top of the island and saw a Royal Albatross at the nest. I set off to try to get to it, but it was clearly not going to be possible to do so in the available time, and after going about a quarter of a mile I turned back.

Deeply cut watercourses were virtually uncrossable and hidden in the scrub. Being 7 or 8 feet deep they could have been very difficult to get out of if one had fallen in. Back on the beautiful green turf among the sea lion cows and pups and the birds I found Phil getting pix of parakeets, tomtit and the really beautiful windswept rata forest.

The last half hour on this exquisite island was idyllic and absolutely memorable. It seemed to me that neither the island nor its incomparable wildlife had suffered in the least from two invasions of 60 plus tourists on the two consecutive days.

Dafila looked inside the tiny hut near the landing and found it full of baby sea lions sleeping in rows. And so we said farewell to lovely Enderby Island, and sailed away towards Campbell.

During the night it blew up and the little ship rolled a lot. Apparently

Fjordland Crested Penguin,
Eudyptes pachyrhynchus,
Enderby Island,
8 February 1971.
This lone bird was possibly sick or injured. It was far from its normal range, but was positively identified by the white flecks on its cheeks.

the stabilising device could not be used because the tanks were needed for fuel and the stabilizers only work when they are half empty.

TUESDAY 9 FEBRUARY

A misty moist day for our arrival in Perseverance Harbour (Campbell Island) – to be met in a boat by the leader and deputy leader of the New Zealand base who came on board, Derek Laws and Bryan George (in thin shorts!).

We were to go ashore on a trek to the col behind and to the north of Beeman Hill, to the breeding colony of Royal Albatrosses. It was a hill walk of approximately 5 miles and most of the *Lindblad Explorer* passengers set bravely off on it in their red Antarctic anoraks. There were two routes – one each side of Beeman Hill and half the 'redcoats' went by each. We walked round by a bay to the old camp which was occupied by a temporary group studying the effects of sheep on the island. A fence has been put up right across the island and the sheep virtually eliminated from the northern half. The effect on the vegetation will be studied, after which it is likely that the sheep will be eliminated from the other half of the island also.

It was a very gloomy day – low visibility – almost a fog and at times quite heavy rain. There are virtually no trees on the island, only heath (*Dracophyllum*) which grows in places to 10 or 12 feet but is mostly much shorter. Some of the party decided to turn back. Others had already gone far ahead so that when I reached the col where we had to turn sharp left the path was more or less deserted, with visibility about 200 yards. Somewhere ahead, I knew, were Phil and Dafila and I became concerned about whether Dafila should be doing anything so tough so soon after her appendicitis operation.

A party of Japanese came back past me, including the little old lady with the golden smile. Then another party including Julia – the young Argentinian girl – who said that Dafila was in some pain, but determined to go on. This worried me more. Then out of the mist came Dafila with one of the Campbell Island boys. Very wisely she had decided to turn back. Next I came up with a group including Phil who had the New Zealand boy's rucksack complete with one of Roger Peterson's cameras. The whole back-pack was nearly as big as Phil herself. As usual she wouldn't let me take it, as we were almost there.

The path was quite a quagmire, and I had on my Alaskan overboots which are enormously bulky and heavy, and wished I had simply had straight rubber boots.

At last we came over a rise to find two long suffering Royal Albatrosses – vast, and friendly-looking, sitting on flamingo-like nests and surrounded by redcoated tourists clicking cameras at them.

There was no question in my mind that the long climb had been infinitely worth while to see the great birds in their wild breeding grounds in standard weather conditions. Of course it would have been nice if the rain had stopped and the sun had come out and the visibility had allowed us to look out across the whole island. But it was not to be. I reckoned that one of the incubating birds was a male, the other a female. There were a few dark spots on the heads of the albatrosses which appeared and disappeared as I remembered seeing also on the nesting bird at Tairoa Head near Dunedin [back in 1956]. These were clearly *Mallophaga* (feather lice). Apparently they also have ticks.

Royal Albatross,
Campbell Island,
9 February 1971.

Pleurophyllum speciosum,
Campbell Island,
9 February 1971.

Beaufort Island and
Mount Erebus.

Occasionally the female bird on the nest clappered her bill, and occasionally both turned away from a too close camera. But their immense dignity was never seriously ruffled. One felt they came out of the whole affair far better than any of the human beings!

After perhaps 20 minutes with the birds Phil and I started back, looking critically at some of the plants as we went.

Dafila got back apparently none the worse a little after we did. For her and for Julia one of the boys from the camp had climbed up, caught a non-breeding Royal Albatross and brought it down to show them – thereafter releasing it in Perseverance Harbour, where in the afternoon I went with Lars in the Zodiac to look at Elephant Seals, Campbell Island Shags, Grey Ducks and sea lions. It was still rainy and dull. The Elephant Seals in the grass were reminiscent of those on Carcass Island in the Falklands.

As evening drew in on Saturday the Victoria Mountains of Antarctica appeared over the horizon and the next morning we went ashore briefly at Cape Hallet and then headed south once more.

MONDAY 15 FEBRUARY

At breakfast time we were approaching Beaufort Island and beyond in a clear blue sky was Ross Island, with Mount Erebus dominating the scene. The volcano remained visible for most of the morning as we steamed up to Cape Bird and along the Ross Island shore. We had quite a good view of a family party of Killer Whales which were quite close to the ship. Many more were further away near the shore at Macdonald Beach, named after 'Captain Mac' who is with us and has had a great career in Antarctic exploration, this being his 36th journey down to the ice.

Peter, Phillipa and Dafila Scott in the hut at Cape Evans.

The south wind was now blowing at gale force, and the possibilities of landing at Cape Royds and Cape Evans seemed slender. We sailed past Royds and on past the Barne Glacier finding enough shelter at Cape Evans and the Zodiacs put us all ashore. There was much less snow round the hut than when I had last been there and much more debris and rubbish was visible, including the remains of a lot of Emperor Penguins and some seals.

Although our visit had been cleared with the New Zealanders at Scott Base we had no key. It had been arranged that we would cut through the padlock of the lock of the *Terra Nova* Hut with a hacksaw and put a fresh padlock on when leaving. Keith (Shackleton) had the equipment, but the hacksaw was, in his phrase, 'merely polishing the padlock'. The only thing seemed to be to cut through the hasp which could quite easily be renewed – and in any event we were likely to be the last visitors this season. So Keith sawed through the hasp – the work of a few seconds and we were in.

I passed a message back for Dafila and Phil to come as I felt they should see the inside of the hut before it was filled with red coated tourists. So they stood just in front of me on the threshold for a few moments while our eyes became dark-adapted. I took a great deal of pleasure in seeing my two darlings standing there looking at the interior scene which had moved me so much when I had first seen it 5 years ago.

Then we moved in and the flashes started to flicker and the shutters to click. My father's den was the corner we spent some time in. There is an Emperor Penguin skin on the table there, as well as a bound volume of the *Illustrated London News* – with a piece on the Kaiser as a farmer.

Even the milling LE passengers could not spoil this enchanted place which had seen so many moods, in which men had been happy and bored, hopeful and heartbroken. Only a few men had ever lived there – but they were men whose adventures and attitudes had caught the imagination of the world. The aura of the Cape Evans hut has a quality which does not (at least for me) pervade the other huts to anything like the same degree.

With Phil and Dafila I climbed the hill behind where the cross commemorates Mackintosh and Hayward.

The view was superb. The bitter wind on the top of the hill was blowing in some snow. The possibility of a blizzard and 'white-out' had to be considered. Back on the beach Lars was starting to load the Zodiacs in a hurry for the return journeys to the LE.

On return to the ship I heard that Roger Peterson had a strangulated hernia of the oesophagus which was causing some alarm and Dr Roy Sexton had been up all night with him. He had been injected with every known remedy to no avail, and there was talk of intravenous feeding and of having him flown out from McMurdo. This clouded my day more than a little.

During the lunch period the Captain took the LE close under the foot of the Barne Glacier. We cruised along within 30 feet of the 60 ft ice wall which was incredibly beautiful. There was a brown line waving along the glacier stratification, which must have been dust from the latest Erebus eruption. This daringly close approach to the glacier face was characteristic of Captain Ars, who is really a rather splendid man.

The snow still came in showers and the wind was blowing 25 knots, but in spite of that it was decided to make a Zodiac landing at the Shackleton Hut* at Cape Royds, which we had passed in the morning. The ship lay beam on to the wind drifting rapidly down but creating enough lee for getting into the Zodiacs. We went away in the first.

There were several hundred Adelie Penguins but almost all of them were moulting adults. There was no sign of either the albino chick which had been there on the last LE trip, or of the single Chinstrap which had come ashore for the first time during the LE party's landing. It began to snow as we walked round the little lake towards the old hut and the chill factor must have been very high, as the wind was very strong. Dafila was first into the hut followed by Phil and Keith. It is much smaller than the Cape Evans hut but has a very agreeable feeling about it. The portraits of King Edward VII and Queen Alexandria looked as fresh, pinned up on the wall, as they had been on my last visit 5 years ago. The *Illustrated London News* had a full page portrait of Herbert Asquith – 'the new Prime Minister'. I showed it to Dafila as 'one of your grandmother's boyfriends and Kip's great grandfather'.

Looking at the fast ice off Cape Royds.

We took a careful look at the acetylene-making plant over the door. Keith commented on its Emmet-like qualities. John Smith was making notes on the contents of the shelves.

On the way back to the shore I took a look into the much smaller new hut where I had tea last time I was there. There was really very little difference between it and the old Shackleton hut except that the dates on the newspapers were more recent and the food on the shelves had different labels! Sixty years is, after all, not such a very long time. I called Phil and Dafila over to look at it – then on down to the landing place with a little time to look at the penguins. I could only find six young of the year. All the rest (some scores that I looked over critically) were adults moulting – probably Bill Sladen's 'teenagers'.

The re-embarkation operation was not going to be easy. Getting off the beach was not too difficult though one had to be careful on the ice-covered stones. The plan was that the ship would drift past beam on to the now very strong wind, and we would go out in the Zodiacs as she came past.

Ice on the fo'c's'le and on the ship's bell.

Unfortunately we pushed out too early and had to steer upwind through a short steep little sea. The Zodiac ahead got through without too much trouble, but a big wave reared up ahead of us and swept green into our boat. Fortunately it was the only one, and we were soon in the lee of the ship. She was drifting to leeward so fast that we had to turn outwards in order to get alongside. The green water had soaked a good many of us leaving icicles hanging from our parka hoods.

The LE steamed south to reach McMurdo Base at 7.00 in the evening and berthed alongside in berth No 3 with the ship's stern opposite the *Discovery* Hut. There was no old ice in the Sound nor in Winter Quarters Bay, but for the latter part of the approach we had been cutting

*Major Sir Ernest Henry Shackleton (1874–1922) was Commander of the 1907–1909 British Antarctic Expedition. Their ship, *Nimrod*, reached the Ross Barrier in January 1908 where they had hoped to land. When that failed, they made an attempt to land on King Edward VII Land but were eventually forced to Cape Royds, McMurdo Sound. Members of the expedition reached the top of Mt Erebus in March 1908 and the South Magnetic Pole in January 1909. Shackleton was also Commander of the 1914–1916 Antarctic Expedition.

My view from the Hercules over the top of Mount Erebus (taken 5 years before) looking across McMurdo Sound to Victoria Land.

through new soft pancake ice, and there was enough of this between the ship and the shore to make berthing quite difficult.

That evening we managed to get a lift with one of the Scott Base vehicles up to Nookipoo so as to start our climb up Observation Hill at half way up. We started at 11.00 pm and were at the top 35 minutes later. We met an earlier party from the ship coming down, and Keith turned and came back up with us. It is a steepish path-walk, and was made a little more difficult by a recent snow-fall.

The view under an intermittent midnight sun was glorious, and even McMurdo City looked colourful and attractive at our feet. That evening a Hercules transport plane – its maintenance apparently overdue – had been taxi-ing out on Williams Field at about 6.00 pm for take off and return to Chi-chi, when one of the engines had caught fire. Eventually the engine fell out. There was only a small crew on board and as soon as the machine came to a halt they managed to get out. The plane then caught fire completely and was almost totally burnt out. In any event it was a write-off. We could see it, quite close to the control tower out at the field. This is the third write-off aircraft accident this year with, miraculously, no loss of life.

The sun was on the cross, illuminating the Tennyson quotation 'To strive, to seek, to find and not to yield' – and selected by Cherry Garrard. Facing the sun the wind was fierce. As we moved over onto the lee-side just below the summit I remarked to Keith, referring to the bitter wind, 'that was remarkably unpleasant'. I think Keith thought that was the sum total of my impressions of the summit of Observation Hill, and he was quite shocked. This started a discussion on how much we are all affected by being in these places with their rich historical overtones.

Of course it is impossible to ignore the influence of the explorers of the heroic age. For me the personal connection is almost cloying. I cannot read the diary messages and last entry without tears. Observation Hill and the Cape Evans Hut (and last time the South Pole) are the nearest topographical links with the diary. But even then these places seem remote from the reality of 60 years ago.

I suppose I am not cut out to be a historian. Or is it that I am leaning over backwards not to be inundated by the fulsome sentiment of the tourists? It is no good to pretend that I am not moved – and perhaps most of all by being able to show these lovely places to my beloved Phil and our darling Dafila. The places themselves are *so* real, *so* unmushy, so fantastically beautiful. Nothing can spoil them, but I am perhaps too busy trying to make sure nothing does. If that gives the impression that I am unmoved by these places then that is quite a false impression. But what is of most interest to me is what man is doing here now.

The LE was a welcome splash of red in the harbour below as we made our slithering way down the hill.

We passed the church and in the main street among the unbelievable wirescape we passed the hut labelled the Ross Hilton and the Press Hut, in which I had stayed last time – the last on the left overlooking the harbour.

McMurdo wirescape.

As we returned to the ship a somewhat roisterous group from Scott Base was leaving. Dafila wisely hung back so as not to coincide with them at the gangway. Too much alcoholic hospitality seems to be one of the quite serious problems of the advent of a tourist ship in these parts. It is a great pity.

Too many impressions for one day. They couldn't all be adequately savoured, but there were strong ingredients. The best news was that Roger Peterson was better and the oesophagus was clear. Plans to fly him and Barbara (his wife) out could happily be abandoned.

We steamed south out of McMurdo harbour two days later to see Emperor Penguins and then turned north towards Macquarie Island and on to Hobart, Tasmania, where the cruise ended on 25 February 1971.

Emperor Penguins,
Aptenodytes forsteri,
in McMurdo Sound,
17 February 1971.

CHAPTER 17

Antarctica and the Falkland Islands

DIARY 30 1978
DIARY 33 1979

It was not until seven years later that we were again in the Antarctic; then we spent four weeks in the *Lindblad Explorer* going to the Antarctic Peninsula via the Falkland Islands. The passengers were for the most part members of the World Wildlife Fund's club called 1001 – A Nature Trust. Founder of the 1001, and then President of WWF International was The Prince of the Netherlands (Prince Bernhard) who came on the trip. Also with us that time (with his wife Daku) was Sherpa Tenzing who, with Sir Edmund Hillary, made the first ascent of Mount Everest.

A special feature of that cruise was the incredibly good weather – a calm Drake Passage both going and coming back, and fantastic weather in the famous Lemaire Channel.

FRIDAY 20 JANUARY

Sailed early (0600) from Paradise Bay in brilliant sunshine and glass calm sea, out through the southern entrance, with the mountains perfectly mirrored. In the Gerlache Strait there was a light breeze to make the sea blue. There was not a single cloud in the sky, though a tiny horizontal wisp hung half way up one of the mountains to the south.

On the bridge there was talk about Cape Renard, known in BAS circles as Una's Tits, at the northern entrance to the Lemaire Channel.

The Lemaire Channel.

A Snow Petrel flying
with Antarctic Petrels.

Once in the narrows the sea was once more mirror calm. Ten years ago the cloud had been down over all the peaks, but this time the visibility was unbelievable – 100 miles plus.

The impact of this passage through the Lemaire amounted to something like a mystical experience. Everyone was aware of our good fortune in the weather, and the superlative beauty wherever one looked was almost overwhelming. This was unspoiled, untouched nature at its most sublime.

The wildlife was scanty. A few seals on ice floes – mostly Crabeaters, but a few Weddells – some skuas and Kelp Gulls, some porpoising Gentoos and odd Adelies (and Gentoos) walking about on the ice. Round one large iceberg were three Snow Petrels, superbly immaculate in their whiteness. Down near Mt Scott – named after my father – the Lemaire Channel was covered with new sheet ice – with a covering of snow. We ploughed through the first sheet, but in the second the ship stopped, a gangway was lowered and we all went down and spread out across the ice. Actually the hard ice was only about 3 inches thick, with 2 inches of frozen snow on top and maybe a couple more of mush underneath.

Eventually hot punch came down onto the ice, someone produced a football (at my suggestion), one of the pax produced a golf club and red ball. Phil and I and Tenzing and Daku were photographed with Mt Scott in the background and with the ship in the background. The most amusing photographic gimmick was Hasse Nilsson (the Captain) standing on the ice at the ship's stem, pretending to push her backwards. 'Don't show this to the insurance company,' he quipped.

In the following year – once more in the *Lindblad Explorer* – we went to the Antarctic, my fifth visit and Philippa's fourth. This time it was a semi-circumnavigation of the continent from Ushuaia in the Beagle Channel, again via the Falklands and the Antarctic Peninsula, then on past Peter the First Island – where the ice prevented us from landing – to the Ross Sea and ultimately Port Lyttleton in New Zealand.

The Ross Sea provided us with some of the worst weather we have ever encountered.

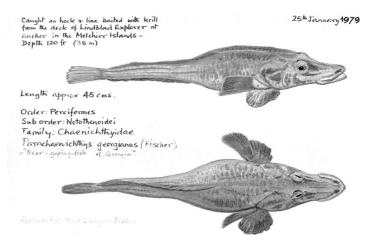

Caught on hook + line baited with krill
from the deck of Lindblad Explorer at
anchor in the Melchior Islands –
Depth 120 ft (38 m)

25th January 1979

Length approx 45 cms.

Order: Perciformes
Sub order: Notothenoidei
Family: Chaenichthyidae
Parachaenichthys georgianus (Fischer)
="Near-gaping-fish of Georgia"

Antarctic Red Dragon Fish.

At Paradise Bay on 19 January 1978 we made a SCUBA dive in wetsuits off the Gentoo rookery and several birds came 'flying' past. The visibility was not very good owing to plankton. We could only stay down for ten minutes but 3 days later at Hope Bay we dived and saw underwater Adelies and were able to stay down for 17 minutes.

WEDNESDAY 7 FEBRUARY

Barometer even lower. At 4 am it was 939.6 millibars, 27.74 inches, comfortably lower than anything ever recorded before in the Ross Sea. Previous lowest 942 (recorded by *The Bear of Oakland* in 1935), 942 millibars = 27.82 inches. Nothing else is comfortable about it. At 6 am I went to the bridge as we plug into a rising sea at 15 knots.

Antarctic Petrels (15) flew close round the bridge. It is misty and forbidding, though the wind is only about Force 5.

Barometer seems to be creeping up again now. At 6.30 it is 942.

In the course of the day the barometer continued to rise and so did the wind and sea. By 5.30 pm it was 952 mb and there was a gale force 8.

In the afternoon I was called to the radio room to talk to Scott Base. It was Baden Norris, the Scott Base naturalist, whom we are due to take back to New Zealand. He wanted to know if we should be able to pick him up at Cape Bird on the northern tip of Ross Island. The implication seemed to be that ice conditions would prevent us getting any further south. I am to talk to him about it again this evening.

The sun has appeared briefly from time to time but the wind and sea do not abate.

Wind reached storm force 10.

Blue-eyed Shag with 2 chicks.

THURSDAY 8 FEBRUARY

Still blowing force 8 but sea not so high and the sun shining fitfully. The ship has made only 35 miles in the last 12 hours. We are moving through the water at 4 knots.

At breakfast time two Minke Whales were playing like dolphins around the bows of the ship. From the starboard windows of the lounge I saw one of the whales about 5 times at intervals of a few minutes. It was quite a small animal – about 12–14 feet long – possibly 16. The paddles were all white and so was the belly, the back buffish grey with a white looping pattern curving down symmetrically from the blow-hole.

At times it lay within inches of the ship's side and was no more than 10–15 feet away from us as we watched.

Minke Whales and their 'footsteps'. There appeared to be a krill swarm from the behaviour of the whales which often came up with open mouths.

Minke Whales and their "Footsteps"

Two-banded Dotterel
Charadrius falklandicus

FRIDAY 9 FEBRUARY
Less wind and sea but the increased speed means almost as much jumping about as before. The barometer goes up, but only slowly. 975 – much higher than our 939.61 but still well below the average for the Ross Sea of 990.

SATURDAY 10 FEBRUARY
Ross Ice Shelf, Cape Crozier, Cape Bird, Cape Royds.

In mid-morning land was sighted, as we plugged into a force 8 gale, on our port bow. This was our first sighting of land except for Peter I Island since 28 January (12 days at sea).

In the early part of that expedition, before the Ross Sea storm, we had paid our third visit to the Falkland Islands, where a new conservation foundation was born on Tuesday 16 January:

Special arrangements had been made for the ship to clear customs at New Island, off West Falkland, in order to save fuel by doing the islands in reverse and coming to Stanley last. The Customs Officer was on New Island. So too, to greet the first Zodiac ashore at the settlement beach, were the 'conservation delegation' – Richard and Maisie Fitter representing the Fauna Preservation Society [now FFPS covering Fauna and Flora], Markus Stauffacher representing the anonymous Swiss donor (prepared to spend some £40,000), Michael Wright from the US Nature Conservancy (a private organisation in contrast to the governmental Nature Conservancy Council of the UK), Ian Strange as owner of the southern half of the island and Warden of the offshore islets bought by the Society for the Promotion of Nature Conservation [now the Royal Society for Nature Conservation]. The recent legal conclusion of the row between Ian Strange and Roddy Napier (joint owners of New Island) for the past few years has resulted in the partition of the island a mile or so north of the settlement, although neither of the parties have yet received the final documents.

The visit of the Conservation Delegation had been timed to coincide with the LE's arrival so that I could take part in the discussions. So here we were walking over to the Rockhopper rookery – as Phil and I had done last year, beginning the discussions.

The conservation crux of the matter is that the situation of the wild-life on the island is deteriorating due to too many sheep (and cattle) and a great increase in rabbits. There has been a considerable loss of tussock, and visible erosion since last summer. So it seems fairly urgent to establish a unified management programme to stop further degradation.

After various discussions as we stood or sat watching the penguins – including 3 nests of Macaronis – we walked back to the settlement, but detailed discussion over tea was inhibited by the presence of the Customs Officer.

Ian had made it clear that he did not need or wish to sell – even with a guaranteed tenancy for his lifetime. He was anxious to secure the future of the island beyond his lifetime. He is devoted to conservation ethics, and wants to stay on the island and paint, and become the foremost conservationist of the Falklands (which indeed he already is).

While watching penguins and walking back I put forward the idea of a Falkland Islands Conservation Foundation on the lines of the Charles Darwin Foundation for the Galápagos Islands. This seemed to have merit at two levels – first at the political level of maintaining a Continuing Scientific Presence (CSP) in an area of major wildlife importance which could secure the anonymous Swiss donation before the end of February and be in a position to rent the island (if it could not buy) and manage it as a single entity. It would also be able to achieve conservation measures in other Falkland islands, thereby broadening the conservation base at a time when tourism may very possibly become a significant industry. I am convinced that well managed tourism could be a very practical guarantee of the continued survival of the outstanding wild-life resources of the islands.

So I said to Michael Wright – whom I had first met that morning, and who is a lawyer – 'How soon could we bring a Foundation of this kind into being?' and he replied 'We could do it today'.

We repaired on board the LE for lunch during which the ship moved to Ship Harbour for the afternoon programme, and during the lunch hour Michael wrote out (in American legal phraseology) a document which could come into force with 6 signatures. As there were 6 of us present the Foundation was born as soon as the document – typed by Judy Marshall the hostess on board – had been duly signed (Ian Strange was one of the 6).

Windblown Rockhopper Penguins.

Later in the week I wrote the following memorandum to Jim Parker, then Governor of the Islands.

The Falkland Islands Conservation Foundation
It is proposed to develop a Foundation for conservation of wildlife, historic areas, buildings and wrecks in the Falkland Islands. Already an Agreement has been drawn up as a declaration of intent, and signed by the necessary number of people (6) to bring such a Foundation into existence. Many more have signed, thereby becoming Founder Members of the organisation.

The policy of the Foundation will be to promote awareness of the value of conservation of the heritage of the Falkland Islands – their history, their culture, and their wildlife. It will encourage the creation and wise management of Wildlife Conservation Areas, bearing in mind that farming, tourism and wildlife can be complementary, one to another, and all can contribute to a prosperous economy.

The Foundation will encourage research in ecology, zoology, botany, the soil sciences, marine ecosystems and archaeology. It will also monitor the environmental well-being of the Archipelago. Although it will be ready to accept ownership or tenancy of land or other property, it will depend entirely on the good-will and co-operation of the residents of the islands.

It will be set up initially with an office in the UK, and an office in Stanley, and ultimately with small field stations on appropriate islands in the Archipelago.

The Foundation will be a non-profit making charity controlled by a Council of whom the majority should be residents of the Falkland Islands.

I have been invited by the original signatories of the Articles of Agreement – which are provisional – to be Chairman for the time being.

I hope very much that the idea will commend itself to you and that you may be prepared to become one of the Founder Members.

Peter Scott

To draw up a declaration of intent and have it signed by the statutory number of people, so as to get this Foundation established, all in one day was a good beginning. But having it accepted as a charity in Britain was something different. This could not be rushed through. A constitution had to be drawn up and approved by the Board for submission to the Charity Commissioners. The process was disappointingly slow. But eventually it was done and the Falkland Islands Foundation (FIF) was away to a modest start, with a counterpart called the Falkland Islands Trust (FIT) set up in Port Stanley. Plans were laid for a fund-raising campaign, initially to give FIF a basis from which to plan its conservation work, and later to provide money for the specific projects themselves.

But on 22 March 1982 the Argentine flag was hoisted on South Georgia and on 2 April it was hoisted at Stanley. The FIF decided to 'tread water' until the end of hostilities. South Georgia was retaken on 25 April, the British bridgehead was established at Port San Carlos on 2 May and the Argentinians surrendered in Stanley on 16 June 1982. Very soon thereafter the Foundation began to swim again. It seemed probable that there were many new reasons for conservation and that the functions of FIF would be even more relevant than before. So it is proving to be.

Index

Numbers in italics refer to captions

286

287